Theatre:
A Contemporary
Introduction

Theatre:
A Contemporary Introduction

Second Edition

Jerry V. Pickering
California State University
Fullerton

West Publishing Company
St. Paul   New York   Los Angeles   San Francisco

Photo Credits

28, Photo Tech Studios; **32, 86, 168, 177,** William L. Smith; **33, 83, 127,** William Ganslen; **41,** Alfredo Valente; **45, 170,** Tom England; **58,** Greenberg, Wrayen and May, Inc.; **62, 85, 156, 163, 199, 223,** Cliff Moore; **69,** Roland Hiltscher; **70,** Robert C. Ragsdale; **73, 133, 172, 193,** Dome City Photographers, Inc.; **89, 136, 182, 188,** Gary Sweetman; **97, 164,** Gerry Kopelow; **134,** David S. Talbott; **166,** David Robbins; **169, 173,** Herbert Ascherman, Jr.; **174, 183,** Sandy Underwood; **175,** Steven Keull; **181,** Alan R. Epstein; **201,** Charles M. Rafshoon; **216, 245,** Dwaine Smith; **221,** Gordon Lemon; **241,** Charles Redmon, Jr.; **286, 291,** Jack Mitchell; **287,** Caravaglia; **289,** P. Berthelot; **293,** David and Martha Rankin.

COPYRIGHT © 1978 By WEST PUBLISHING CO.
50 West Kellogg Boulevard
P.O. Box 3526
St. Paul, Minnesota 55165

Printed in the United States of America

Library of Congress Cataloging in Publication Data

Pickering, Jerry V   1931-
  Theatre, a contemporary introduction.

  Includes bibliographical references and index.
  1. Performing arts. I. Title.
PN1584.P5   1978   792   77–27847
ISBN 0–8299–0201–5

Contents

chapter two

Tragedy   27

chapter three

Comedy · 49

chapter four

The Rise of Realism   77

chapter five

Musical Theatre   95

appendix a

Reading a Play   313

appendix b

Plot Summaries of Works Discussed in the Text   319

appendix c

Glossary of Theatre Terms   353

Index   363

Preface

The writing and preparation of a book is almost always the work of more than one person. In this case, I have been aided by a number of dedicated and selfless people, and it is a distinct pleasure to acknowledge their contributions.

I am indebted to all those professors who took time out from their busy schedules to respond to the original survey on which this book is based. It is often difficult for a writer to determine the best structure, content, and approach, but their comments helped me to prepare this text so that it would be most useful to those in the classroom.

For their reviews of and comments on the original manuscript I am indebted to Professors Robert S. Badal, Moorhead State College, Minnesota; Linda L. Conaway, Miami University, Ohio; Al Cosentine, Bronx Community College, New York; Lawrence C. Hendrick, Sacramento City College, California; Jack Holland, Orange Coast College, California; Richard M. Rose II, Broward Community College, Florida; Alan Stambusky, University of California, Davis; James Yeater, Arizona State University; and Parker Zellers, Eastern Michigan University.

For this second edition, thanks are most especially due to Professors Carl White, American River College, California; Sandra L. Luker, Columbus College, Georgia; Milo Smith, Central Washington State College; Gerard Larsen, California State University, Sacramento; S. Spring Gagliardi, Central Connecticut State College; Adam La Zarre, State University of New York, Brockport; and John Ford, Foothill College, California.

The collecting of illustrative materials for a book on theatre is an immense task. I am therefore very grateful to those colleges and professional theatres that responded to my request for photographs. There are far too many to mention here, but the producing organizations are credited beneath each production photograph.

Special thanks are due to Dr. Donald Henry for allowing me to make use of his extensive theatre library; to Mr. Richard Odle and Mr. Darrell F. Winn, who provided some of the material on scenic and lighting design; to Dr. Alvin Keller for his critical comments on the directing chapter; to Dr. Dean Hess for his critical comments on the chapters dealing with acting and musical theatre; and to Mrs. Gladys Stetler for her support of this and countless other projects through the years.

Finally, I would like most to thank my wife, Eve, for her comments and work on the manuscript, and for her support while I was writing and revising the book.

Jerry V. Pickering

Prologue

Since the earliest times peoples of the world have in some way imitated, or acted out, certain aspects of their existence. They have used drama as a living history of their tribe or community in folk drama and pageant plays; as a part of religious ritual in both folk drama and cycle plays; as their textbook on science, explaining why certain natural phenomena occur, such as summer and winter, and even seeking to control those phenomena; as their sociology, demonstrating certain forms of acceptable and unacceptable behavior; as a military tactic in guerilla theatre, street theatre, black theatre, and Chicano theatre; and, of course, as entertainment in the form of farce, musical theatre, and many highly serious plays that entertain even as they instruct. In its long history the theatre has managed to touch on every aspect of people's lives and beliefs. At times it has led to social change, as with the plays of Ibsen and his followers, and at times it has fallen behind the continuing social revolution, as the English Restoration comedies, but in every age theatre has been as relevant as human beings have made it.

And along the way, over thousands of years of dramatic activity, the theatre has often been one of humanity's chief glories. The great Theatre of Dionysus at Athens was at the very heart of Greek culture and art. Those who wrote the plays for that theatre were the greatest of the Greek poets, and the prize given to the winning playwright in the annual dramatic competition was the foremost artistic award of the time.

At the height of Athenian democracy, theatre was a community art form in the highest sense of the term, with an audience of citizens watching citizen-actors performing a play written by a fellow citizen, that provided religious, moral, and ethical guidance to the community. And the plays that those citizens saw not only were highly relevant to all playgoers during their period but have remained relevant to theatre audiences for centuries. They speak to psychological and spiritual problems that people today share with the Greeks of twenty-five hundred years ago.

You are seated in the great Theatre of Dionysus on a morning in late March of the year 429 B.C. Your seat has been cut into the side of the Acropolis and covered with flat, rock slabs, but you have brought pillows for your comfort, as well as food and drink to fortify you for the long day ahead. The theatre is crowded with people, nearly 17,000 of them, many of whom stood in line overnight just to get a ticket. They are all waiting eagerly for the play to begin, and there is a tension in the air, a feeling of suppressed excitement, in spite of the fact that the plays will be based on the traditional religious myths that everybody knows. There will be few surprises in the materials of the plays, but everybody is eager to see how the poets treat the materials, to see them acted.

Seated high in the upper rows you can just see, beyond the circular orchestra and the scene house, the top of the Temple of Dionysus gleaming marble-white in the light from the rising sun. Today is the third day of the great festival called the City Dionysia. On the first day there was a long procession in honor of Dionysus, replete with highly decorated phalli and obscene jests between the paraders and onlookers; on the second day ten long choral hymns of high seriousness were performed in honor of the god of wine and the reproductive forces of life. Today begins the production of the tragedies, which will last for three days. The silence is broken at last by the sounds of flute and drum played at a slow, insistent rhythm. The play is about to begin.

You see the people of ancient Thebes, stricken by a terrible plague, gathering to pray. Oedipus, their King, enters from the great central door of his palace (scene house) and tells them that he has already taken action to uncover the cause of the plague by sending his brother-in-law, Creon, to the oracle at

Delphi. Creon soon returns, bearing word that the affliction will be lifted as soon as Thebes seeks out and exiles the murderer of the late King, Laius. Oedipus consults with the blind seer, Tiresias, who informs him that he, Oedipus, is the man who killed the King. When Oedipus angrily protests, Tiresias also tells him that he is an unclean creature who is guilty as well of incest.

Infuriated, Oedipus accuses Creon of trying to discredit him by plotting against him with Tiresias. Oedipus' wife, Jocasta, intervenes and, when alone with her, Oedipus admits his fear that he may indeed be the murderer of Laius. He tells her that he once killed a man, and that an earlier prophecy from Delphi said that he would one day kill his father and marry his mother. Jocasta comforts him, pointing out that Laius was killed by a band of robbers, and to prove this she sends for an old herdsman who is the last survivor of the battle in which King Laius was killed. The herdsman reveals that the death of Laius was not as the survivors told it, and that Oedipus is in fact not only the murderer of his father, but the husband of his own mother. Upon hearing this, Jocasta kills herself and Oedipus puts out his own eyes. As the play ends he appears blinded before the people and begs them to cast him out in fulfillment of the curse placed on the killer of Laius.

The players exit and the play is over, but you do not get up to leave the theatre. Nobody leaves. There is loud and insistent applause and cries of praise for the poet and the actors alike, and then you all settle down to wait, for after a brief intermission the sounds of the drum and flute will signal the beginning of the next play in the trilogy.

When people disparagingly ask why theatre is worthy of intense study, they often point to some rather misleading viewer statistics indicating that the theatre is no longer a major art form. Nothing could be further from the truth. Admittedly, on any given night the number of people watching live theatre cannot even be compared to the number of people watching television drama at home or feature films in movie houses. However, in spite of numerous attempts to bury it under a flood of such statistics, theatre is very much alive. For a short period in the 1920s, following the phenomenal growth of films, theatre attendance fell off and theatre seemed to many observers to be dying—but it revived and grew. Again, in the 1950s, following the even more phenomenal growth of television, theatre audiences fell off. However, again it has revived and seems healthier than ever. Each year more and more people attend live theatre. Certainly, audiences are not as huge as when theatre was the only performing art, but on the whole they are better audiences. The curiosity seekers and the casual goers have disappeared, and today theatre has a solid audience of educated, intelligent, concerned patrons. And that is true not only of urban areas. Across the country regional theatre groups, both professional and amateur, are popping up like mushrooms after a spring rain.

And there is a reason for this development: people are discovering (or rediscovering in some cases) that theatre represents the highest level of the acting art. That has always been known within the profession, and stage training is still looked upon as the best preparation for any type of theatrical occupation, including film or television. Also, whenever actors and actresses, directors, or designers gather to discuss their art in public, for example on a television talk show, the most deference is usually shown to the stage-trained artists. In those cases where the artists have done both stage and film or television work, which often seems to be the situation, they almost invariably select stage production as being the epitome of theatrical art.

This is not intended to belittle either film or television performers (in many cases the same professionals operate successfully in all three media) in terms of their artistic capabilities, or to reject either of those two media as inartistic. In fact, both are so closely related to theatre that they have been accorded their own chapters in this text. Even so, stage acting is, finally, the ultimate test for the actor or actress. On stage there is no possibility of reshooting a badly done scene, or editing-out a performance that does not work well. That must be taken care of in rehearsals. Once a theatrical performance is underway, the director, designers, and other artists and craftsmen who put the show together must bow out. When the show at last takes the stage there are only the performers and the audience, and the well-trained, sensitive actor or actress will soon establish a relationship between the two.

This relationship between the performing artist and the audience is always a sharing one, with each responding to the other. It is a truism in theatre that an actor can rehearse forever but gives a "performance" only when before an audience. Anyone who has witnessed rehearsals, and then compared them with performances, knows how true that is. That is why so many television shows are now being filmed or taped before live audiences: to give the actors the audience "presence" to which they can respond.

And theatre is immediate because it is *live*. Anyone who can tell the difference between people and *pictures* of people will sense this during performance. Whatever is there, onstage, is real. The play may be quite unrealistic, and the actors may say and do unrealistic things, but the immediacy of the live presence of the actors, their personal reality, is always felt. That is what made Elizabethan theatre so vital, of course, along with the great plays that gave the actors something to work with. Unlike the Classical Greek theatre, seating thousands, the English Renaissance theatre was an intimate one in which the thrust stage placed the actors out in the midst of their audience—and great art was the result.

It is June, 1595, and you are outside the city of London, in the disreputable suburb of Shoreditch, standing before the main

entrance to James Burbage's theatre, known as The Theatre. You are there to see a performance of a popular new play, "Romeo and Juliet," by a rising young playwright, William Shakespeare. As you go through the main door to The Theatre into a short entry hall, you are accosted by the boxkeeper, an old man holding a box with a slot in the top. If you decide to sit in the lowest and most expensive gallery you will put three pennies in the slot and the boxkeeper will let you into a short flight of stairs that opens off the main entry hall. If you want to sit in one of the upper two galleries it will cost you one penny less because the upper seats are more removed from the action. If you desire to stand in the yard it will cost you only one penny.

The yard, a dirt space surrounding the stage, contains no seats and is open to the sky. It is the noisiest, dirtiest, and cheapest part of the theatre. The people who patronize this area are called groundlings, and they are usually the poorest of the theatre's customers, containing among them a goodly sprinkling of pickpockets, touts, and prostitutes. However, there are also some young gentlemen from the Inns of Court, a few merchants and their wives, and some prentices. The yard also holds some of the gallants who can afford the best seats, but who want to roister in the yard and, in some cases, climb up on the stage itself while the action is going on, thus making sure not only that they see, but that they are also seen.

You choose to stand in the yard because you wish to be close to the stage, and also because one penny is all you can afford. After dropping your penny in the slot, you walk straight ahead into the yard, which is already crowded with people. Keeping your hand protectively close to your purse, you edge forward through the press of groundlings toward a good viewing spot near the edge of the stage. Just as you reach your position, the Chorus—a single man dressed in a black mantle and bearing a laurel wreath—enters from stage center and speaks the Prologue. He exits and the play begins.

In Verona, you learn, dwell two illustrious and noble families, the Montagues and the Capulets, who bear an ancient grudge toward one another. Romeo, a Montague, goes in disguise to a ball given by Capulet, where he meets Capulet's daughter, Juliet. The two fall in love. In spite of the hatred that exists between their two families they hasten into a secret marriage. All seems to be going well, but then Tybalt, Juliet's hot-tempered kinsman, starts a public quarrel with the Montagues in the hope of provoking Romeo into a duel. Mercutio, Romeo's good friend, is so incensed by Tybalt's insults and Romeo's mild-mannered response to them, that he draws his sword on Tybalt. In the ensuing battle Mercutio is mortally wounded and Romeo, at last unable to contain himself, kills Tybalt.

In punishment for the unlawful duel, the Prince of Verona banishes Romeo. Juliet's father, unaware of the true situation, decides that Juliet should be hastened into marriage with Count Paris. Friar Laurence, to solve the problem, gives Juliet a death-simulating potion which she is to take on her wedding eve. After she has been sent to the family burial vault, Romeo will remove her body, she will revive, and the two lovers will flee to Mantua. Through accident, plans go awry. As a result, Romeo, believing that Juliet is really dead, poisons himself in her tomb. Juliet, upon awakening from her drugged sleep to find Romeo dead, stabs herself. The play ends with the realization by the two families that their ancient grudge was responsible for the deaths.

The play is over and the actors take their bows to clapping, shouting, and foot stamping, but nobody leaves the theatre, for now comes one of the most popular aspects of Elizabethan theatrical entertainment, the dancing. You wait with the others while the company clown comes out and dances a nimble jig, accompanied by a fiddler. The clown is eventually joined by some other members of the company and even by one of the gallants who, in his enthusiasm, leaps onto the stage to participate with the performers. When the dance comes to an end the crowd is almost as lively in its applause for the dancing as it was for the play itself. The entertainment is now over and the crowd leaves, the merchants and their wives for their homes, and the prentices and young rufflers toward London and their favorite taverns.

Just as *Oedipus Rex* in Classical Greece moved the audience to pity and fear, and instructed them in behavior pleasing to the gods and men, so that play still moves an audience today, although the gods of ancient Greece are not our gods, and certain ideals of behavior have greatly changed. So, too, the *Romeo and Juliet* that moved and delighted an Elizabethan audience, instructing them in the necessity of moral and spiritual unity, still moves and delights an audience today. Indeed, the play remains so vital that a recent motion-picture version became one of the most popular movies of the early 1970s.

The reason for this continued popularity of the great works of theatre is that, because theatre is such a humanistic art, dealing always and directly with people, it exists for all people at all times. Basically, this is true because, at its best, theatre combines within itself the finest possibilities of all the arts. The greatest poets have written for it (some successfully and some not), the greatest painters have designed and painted its sets, and the greatest composers have created its music. It is the most eclectic of all the arts, often including all of them or some combination of all of them, but always remaining essentially itself: theatre.

The great theatre of any period is indeed a universal art, and it does speak to all men of all times and places, though that was not always so. In earlier times theatre tended to be a national phenomenon. Aeschylus, Sophocles, and Euripides wrote in Greek for Greeks, and their plays gained international prominence only about two thousand years after their deaths. In their own time, Shakespeare, Jonson, and Marlowe were not widely recognized outside of England, any more than were Corneille, Racine, and Moliere outside of France. But theatre endured, and eventually its international scope was recognized and it found its proper audience.

Beginning at the end of the last century, theatre became the primary international medium. In his own lifetime, Ibsen was produced all across Europe. That was true also of George Bernard Shaw, who became a world-wide dramatic celebrity, and it would almost certainly have been true of Chekhov had he not died soon after completing *The Cherry Orchard*, perhaps his greatest play. Theatre suddenly recognized no boundaries, and a drama of middle-class existence beside the Norwegian fiords, or a dramatization of the economic and spiritual death of an aristocratic Russian family in the face of growing social change, could be played with equal success in Paris, London, and New York.

It is Monday evening, September 29, 1902, and you are standing in front of the new Belasco Theatre (the old Republic Theatre, which David Belasco has completely remodeled) on Ninety-second Street in New York. Tonight is opening night for the new theatre, and as his first offering, Mr. Belasco has chosen to revive his long-running play of the past season, "Du Barry," starring Mrs. Leslie Carter. As promised, the new, wrought-iron doors open promptly at 7:00 P.M., and the quiet, well-dressed, orderly crowd streams through into the elegant lobby, fashioned of oak panels, with carpets and drapes delicately shading from deep reds to russet browns and greens. One hour has been allowed for the patrons to inspect the new theatre, and promptly at 8:00 P.M. the curtain rises.

You immediately become caught up in the play, which purports to tell accurately of the young seamstress, Jeanette Vaubernier, who became Madame Du Barry. In the first act you see Jeanette industriously at work in the millinery shop. Here she meets the handsome guardsman, Cossé, who becomes her first and only true love. But she is tempted by an offer from Louis XV to become his mistress, an offer she accepts when a complicated misunderstanding separates her from Cossé.

Throughout the first two acts you are surprised to find the acting style of Mrs. Carter quite restrained; not at all the wild,

emotional frenzy you had been led to expect. At first you tend to be distracted by the spectacular richness and beauty which Belasco has created to depict the palace at Versailles, but as you watch Act 3 progress you gradually become more involved, for it is building to the emotional explosion for which Mrs. Carter is so well-known.

Jeanette's young guardsman, weak and wounded, is trapped in her bedroom. To save him from execution by the King she knocks him unconscious and hides him in her bed. Finally she betrays him to the King in return for Louis' promise to spare his life. By this time Mrs. Carter has pulled out all the stops. She weeps, rants, raves, and tears her hair in the most emotion-freighted performance you have ever seen.

Just as you feel a faint hope that Louis' promise will end the horrors that Du Barry has undergone, the French Revolution intervenes with the storming of the palace at Versailles. The imprisoned Cossé is freed by the mob, which is sympathetic to any enemy of the King, and then Du Barry, the beautiful mistress of Louis, after a tearful scene with her true love, is dragged through the streets of Paris to her date with the guillotine.

The play is over and the curtain calls seem endless; almost, in fact, an anticlimax. You wait until the applause dies out and then rise to leave. When at last you exit from the spectacular reality of the theatre you experience a profound sense of shock that another world exists outside of the theatrical one, and then you merge into the crowds and humidity and bustle of night-time New York.

If theatre were nothing more than entertainment—a category that unfortunately includes a large portion of television drama and somewhat less (though still far too much) of contemporary film—then it would be difficult to defend as a serious, relevant art form. This is not to say that theatre does not entertain; it does, and such entertainment is an important part of its function. More than ninety percent of the time, however, it does far more than entertain: it explores the mystery of humankind's existence; it looks at the humanity and efficacy of humankind's institutions; it examines peoples' relationships with their gods and their fellow human beings; it explores the depths of humanity's spiritual and emotional being; and it provides a screen onto which people can project their most secret fears, desires, and beliefs.

The experience of attending a play has obviously differed at various times throughout theatrical history. Audiences have changed from the homogeneous groups made up of the citizens of fifth-century Athens, the burghers of Medieval York, the motley crowds of Elizabethan England; or the monied aristocrats of early twentieth-century New York society.

The classless group that attends theatre today in the United States is different in economic, religious, ethnic, and racial backgrounds but united in a generally high level of education and a devotion to the artistic presentation of the human race in all its aspects. Even so, the similarities of the performances far outweigh such differences. The most important of these similarities, at the heart of any production at any time, is the combination of actor and audience. As far as can be seen, this relationship has not varied in over twenty-five hundred years. Theatre, at all times and in all places, begins and ends with the live actor and the audience.

It is 1958 and you are at the Royal Court Theatre in London to attend the world premiere of what has been reported to be a strange and unusual and exciting new play by that Irish expatriot to France, Samuel Beckett. This play is titled "Endgame," and it is Beckett's second play. You saw his first play, "Waiting for Godot," and were delighted, puzzled, amused, and frightened. This play promises much in that vein, in part because this London premiere will be acted in French. The Royal Court is not a particularly large theatre, and you are fortunate to have gotten good seats.

The play is set in a claustrophobic, sunken room, probably a cellar. Outside, you discover, are lifeless lands and motionless, probably equally lifeless water. As the play opens you meet Hamm, the master, and Clov, the servant. Hamm is seated at stage center in a wheelchair. He is paralyzed and cannot stand. Clov, the servant, never sits. In two ashcans by the wall are Hamm's legless parents, Nagg and Nell.

Clov, you discover, hates Hamm and wants to leave him, but he cannot do so, for if he does he will die since Hamm possesses the world's only food supply. Also, if Clov leaves, Hamm too will die, unable to feed himself. Hamm fancies himself as a teller of tales, and each day he adds a new bit to an epic work he is creating that may tell how the disaster happened that destroyed the world.

Hamm's parents in their ashcans are sentimental, romantic fools. They lost their legs in the most romantic way possible, while bicycling through the Ardennes on their bicycle built for two. They reminisce about such romantic idylls as the time they went rowing on Lake Como, in April, and Nagg retells a funny story that made Nell, his bride, laugh, and that he has repeated a thousand times since.

Hamm hates his parents, who treated him with an absurd neglect and cruelty when he was a child, and Nell, his mother, secretly urges Clov to leave Hamm, knowing that Hamm must then die. Finally, as the end of the play approaches, Clov looks out of one of the high windows with his telescope and announces that he has seen a small boy. Hamm tells Clov that it is the end and he does not need him anymore, though he clearly does, at least on a practical level. While Hamm is indulging in a last, self-pitying monologue, Clov appears dressed to leave. He is wearing a costume that looks like something out of vaudeville. But when the curtain drops he is still standing there.

The play is accompanied by a pantomime called "Act Without Words," but when the final curtain falls the audience response to the play is based on "Endgame" itself. The applause is long and loud, though in the lobby and on the street afterward people are saying to each other, "But what does it mean . . . ?"

one

The Dramatic Experience

Exactly what is the *dramatic experience*? This seems, on the whole, to be a reasonably straightforward question, and one that any introductory work on theatre might well be expected to deal with quickly and easily. It is not all that simple, however, for the dramatic experience is the very essence of theatre, involving the playscript, the performer, and the audience in a variety of relations that cannot easily be sorted out. It includes what might be called the *purposeful* function of theatre, along with a number of lesser functions that adhere to it, making the whole of the dramatic experience more of an accretion, a composition of many minor elements, than a single major aspect or item or issue. Also, while it may involve a number of production elements, the dramatic experience is still primarily an audience-related phenomenon; that is, it is something that *happens* to people viewing a theatrical event. This makes it doubly difficult to define, because people represent an infinite variety of attitudes and beliefs; what happens to each member of the audience at a play is personal and subjective, and, therefore, slightly different in both type and degree. For these reasons, the dramatic experience does not depend on any specific dramatic form, or any particular style of acting, or any individual scenic design. Rather, the dramatic experience must be defined in terms of what theatre does; that is, how it affects its audience.

Theatre of Purpose

In its earliest periods, even before the outpouring of great drama that took place in Classical Greece, the theatrical event was always purposeful, with a specific function to fulfill within the primitive society, and the form and content of the event was inseparable from its function. Into those early dramatic events, as much a ritual as a theatrical performance, the folk poured their knowledge and beliefs. The little playlets served as receptacles for the accumulated wisdom of the primitive folk. The playlets functioned as applications of their science by providing a method for controlling the natural forces that surrounded the tribe, and, later, functioned as a record of their history by telling of the great heroes and their deeds.

For those folk, controlling nature was of utmost urgency, related directly to the immediate necessity of growing and gathering food. If the seed did not germinate and sprout properly, a poor harvest would bring starvation in the following winter. The rain and sun must not fail them; the growing seedlings must not wither and die. Natural phenomena, such as sunshine and (especially) rainfall, have never been certainties. Even the rising and setting of the sun and the changing of the seasons had to be viewed by primitive folk with a certain unease. Always before, the sun rose and set with regularity, and summer always followed winter, but that was no guarantee for the future. And so they created their gods and their myths to explain the natural events on which they depended, and the methods, the petitioning of their gods, through which they hoped to influence these natural phenomena were usually dramatic.

Thus, dramatic rite and ritual developed, and in those early forms it usually included dramatic activity or impersonation, music, and dance. On one level this activity was dramatized prayer; that is, it was a dramatic enactment of that which was being asked of the gods. If rain was needed for the crops, an action was performed in which water was sprinkled on the earth, or in which a member of the tribe was dipped into a nearby lake or stream. When, in late winter, it became necessary to ask the gods to let spring and summer begin, a dramatic ritual would be performed in which a dead man, representing the seasons, was brought back to life, thus graphically reminding the gods that dead winter could be ended by causing fertile summer to be revived. If meat supplies were running low, and a successful hunt was therefore necessary, a dramatic action was performed in which a hunter successfully slew an animal (one of the tribe dressed in animal skins) to demonstrate graphically the favor that the people were asking of their god or gods. If a human enemy threatened, a war dance or ritual was performed that would visually demonstrate the desire for success in battle.

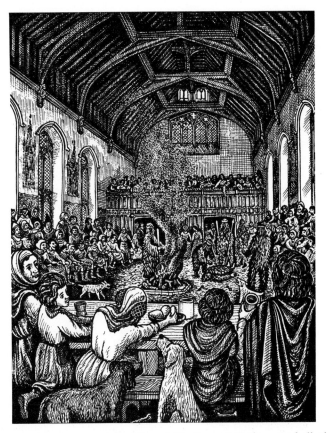

The Christmas mummers present the Play of St. George *in the great hall of a Medieval castle. Note the "leaf-covered" figure at the center of the woodcut. This costume is traditional for mummers and indicates how these plays originated as part of the spring vegetation ceremonies.*

Besides being dramatized prayer, those rituals also served to create a kind of sympathetic magic by way of which certain events could be influenced in a desired manner. The principal concept behind this form of primitive magic was that something could be caused to happen in reality by first making it happen mimetically. Thus, the symbolic sprinkling of water on the earth would make a magic which would cause rain to fall, or the symbolic slaying of a beast would ensure success in the next day's hunt.

In any case, whether as prayer or magic, primitive drama was always purposeful. This is not to say that it did not also fulfill the function of entertainment. It is hard to imagine the tribespeople not being entertained by the colorful, rhythmic ritual in which fellow members of the tribe impersonated the elements of nature, or gods, or beasts; but entertainment was certainly secondary to the primary function of control of nature in some manner. Those rituals later changed, becoming full-fledged little dramas with only tatters of the original symbolic meanings clinging to them, as with the English St. George plays and the Robin Hood plays. Just how that came about is uncertain. Indeed, the eventual appearance of an artistic drama is not fully explained by those earlier, ritualistic dramas, and perhaps may be explained as much by Aristotle's contention that drama exists because humans are by nature imitative, or mimetic, creatures, taking pleasure both from mimicking persons and the actions of persons, and also from witnessing such imitations.

The dramatic experience created by the earliest form of theatre (that is, what happened to the audience involved in the ritual-theatrical situation) is incalculable. Certain audience reactions, however, can be deduced from the material and the purposes to which it was put. On the first level, the audience went to those performances as both a social and a religious obligation. As such, their reaction had to be one of prayerful awe, for the performance had the purpose of assuring the continued and prosperous existence of the tribe, and, thus, the existence of each individual viewing the performance. The audience must also have felt, in varying degrees, security as the necessary ritual was successfully completed, admiration for the deeds of the gods and heroes which the theatrical rituals recounted, and pleasure as they were caught up in the rhythms of the music and dance. Later, of course, as the tribe became more sophisticated, the pleasurable, entertaining elements became increasingly important, and by the time we meet the remnants of those ritual plays in Europe at the end of the Medieval period, the symbolic actions that earlier were so important have become relatively meaningless and the entertainment aspects of the play have become paramount.

When Western theatre, as we know it, appeared in Greece in the sixth century B.C., it was still purposeful in nature. Just as the earlier primitive drama grew out of religious ritual performed to influence the tribal gods and goddesses, so the Greek theatre grew out of religious ritual designed to do honor to Dionysus, the youngest of the pantheon of Hellenic gods. The legend of this god's death and rebirth follows the pattern of the earlier primitive drama, which demonstrates the end of winter death and the rebirth of summer fertility, but with some new and quite important aspects added to the pattern. Those plays not only promoted tribal well-being by pleasing the god of wine and fertility and vegetation, but also fulfilled certain other functions by promoting the city-state religion and by exercising a profound psychological influence on the audience.

As Greek theatre progressed, becoming steadily more sophisticated in content and steadily less of a religious art, its purpose changed. No longer was there a belief that those plays could in any way control natural phenomena, or even that they were meaningful religious observances. Even so, they did remain purposeful. In some cases they clarified and praised principles of justice and civil law, as in Aeschylus' play *The Eumenides*, which comments on the values of religious unity, promotes the observance of civil law, and glorifies the jury system of dispensing justice. Aeschylus and, to a lesser degree, Sophocles were the last of the Greek writers who still seemed to feel that the drama was a legitimate religious observance. Later plays tended to depart from religious conventions, with the gods becoming merely contrivances introduced by the playwrights to resolve difficult problems. And in Greek comedy the gods played no serious part at all. In Aristophanes' *Lysistrata*, for example, the comic emphasis of the play is on resolving the Athenian war situation (the Peloponnesian War had been dragging on for nearly twenty years, Athens had just suffered a disastrous defeat in Sicily, and the city was on the verge of revolt), and the gods play no part at all in this resolution.

In its later periods, from fifth-century Greece onward, theatre continued to provide audiences with purposeful materials; during this time, however, theatre was designed to affect the audience members themselves and not the gods and nature. In addition, theatre of entertainment took its place beside (and in many cases onstage with) theatre of purpose. In Medieval Europe, alongside the cycle plays, which recounted for the audience's spiritual edification the religious history of Christian man from Creation to Judgment, were farces and other entertainments played in inns, innyards, and village squares, and most of these productions had no other purpose than entertainment. In a very few cases, such as the French masterpiece *The Farce of Master Pierre Pathelin*, the farce was also purposeful, designed, in this play, to correct legal abuses through laughter. Also, some of the religious plays, such as *The Second Shepherd's Play* from the Wakefield cycle, contained almost as much comic entertainment as they did serious religious material. The late Medieval period also saw the appearance of the morality play, a dramatic form originally designed to teach

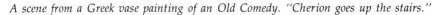

A scene from a Greek vase painting of an Old Comedy. "Cherion goes up the stairs."

people the pathway to eternal salvation, and later adapted to teach in such diverse areas as politics and education.

From the plays of Shakespeare, which illustrated the Elizabethan ideals, to those plays of Bertolt Brecht which promote Marxian communism, most theatre has always had purpose: to change humankind in some way by controlling nature, appeasing the gods, or correcting people themselves by holding up the mirror of truth to certain undesirable aspects of life. The corrective agent may be the laughter evoked by comedy, or the

An etching of the Coventry Miracle Play, with Jesus standing before Pilate. (From Thomas Sharp's "A Dissertation on the Pageants or Dramatic Mysteries Anciently Performed at Coventry," Coventry, England, 1825.)

Titania demonstrates her love for the enchanted Bottom in this scene from Shakespeare's A Midsummer Night's Dream. *California State University, Sacramento. Directed by Carl Thomas.*

pity and fear that is the result of tragedy, or the spiritual-emotional involvement that is a product of realism. But, in most cases, theatre has purpose, and purpose must be at the heart of the dramatic experience.

Perhaps on this basis the dramatic experience can be defined as a discovery by an audience of some profound truth about humanity's existence; that is, a truth discovered by perceiving it in terms of theatrical action rather than by sifting scientific facts or thinking through the history of humankind's political-social-economic situation.

In nearly all plays of all times, at least those to which we have access, the illusion of experience is at the heart of the matter. That is not to say that an audience must somehow lose itself in the implied reality of theatre (some forms of theatre rather obviously have made no pretense at objective reality) or that the audience must in some way identify with an Oedipus or a Hamlet or a Willy Loman. Instead, the audience becomes a willing participant in an artistic event in which he is at all times aware of the theatrical world and of the world of reality, and he believes in and learns from both worlds.

Within the confines of the dramatic experience, the relationship of audience member to theatrical event is a complex one. Samuel Taylor Coleridge tried to explain the relationship by postulating that the theatre spectator somehow chooses to believe in the theatrical event to the point where he makes it a part of his real world. This "willing suspension of disbelief," as Coleridge phrased it, while accurate in the sense that the audience is willing to accept the theatrical conventions of the time, does not fully explain the relationship between the audience and the play, which goes far beyond a willingness on the part of the audience not to "not-believe." As Alan S. Downer has so carefully pointed out, "it takes an effort of will to disbelieve, while in the playhouse; or rather, belief and disbelief are not involved, except insofar as the playgoer accepts certain conventions, and these in themselves are temporary and change from time to time and from culture to culture."[1]

Largely because of this audience belief during the course of the play, this illusion of reality created by even the most unrealistic of plays or theatrical styles, Aristotle and a number of later philosopher-critics have been lavish in their praise of the theatrical art. Of all the arts, Aristotle has pointed out, theatre is the closest imitation of life. By this he means that theatre always exists in the present, happening fresh before the eyes of the audience, and it can be seen and heard *objectively*, as opposed to the *subjective* way in which we see and hear novels or poetry. Achieving this reality, however, rests on audience acceptance of the dramatic illusion.

Dramatic Illusion

The dramatic illusion—that is, the illusion of reality that even the most unrealistic of plays can somehow create in an audience—is what gives theatre its enormous impact. Largely this is because even in the most unrealistic of situations, with essentially unrealistic dialogue, theatre has onstage the ultimate reality: the live human being. It is the presence of the live actor acting and reacting, fleshing out the skeletal dialogue, moving, talking, touching that enlarges the written play from literature to experience. The way this difference affects an audience is difficult to define, but it exists and can be felt and observed.

A recent college production of Edward Albee's *Who's Afraid of Virginia Woolf?* was followed by a question-and-answer session to give the audience

[1]Alan S. Downer, *The Art of the Play* (New York, 1955), p. 5.

an opportunity to communicate directly with the players, the director, and the scenic and costume designers. One young woman, more by way of wondering comment than direct question, pointed out that she had been required to read the play as an assignment for an introductory drama class. While reading the play, she said, she had not laughed once. When confronted with the play onstage, however, in the theatrical situation, she had laughed her way through the first half of the play and at least intermittently through the second half. "Why?" she asked. Nobody could answer satisfactorily, probably because it raises some very complex issues.

A play's effect on a reader, as opposed to an audience member, is caused partly by the fact that the playwright works primarily with dialogue, and therefore most of what the reader gets from the play must come from the external and highly personal points of view of the various characters. This dialogue is not, in most cases, even supported by simple narrative descriptions of set or characters. The novelist, on the other hand, gets inside his characters, which makes it possible for him to tell the readers not only what the characters say but also how they think and what

Edward Albee's Who's Afraid of Virginia Woolf? *at the Pasadena Playhouse. Directed by Alvin Keller; scenic design by Jim Cavan.*

they feel. Additionally, the novelist provides narrative material that pictures the characters physically and describes the various settings. In theatre the actors provide the living equivalent to the omniscient and the narrative material that the novelist makes available for his readers. Thus, for the young woman watching *Woolf*, the actors provided the reactions, the nuances, and the characterizations that allowed the humor (often black) of the play to come through.

Also, and perhaps even more significant in terms of dramatic illusion, theatre provides the audience with a form of reality based on the presence of the live actor. This reality helps make the illusion more complete, and, in addition, allows and even provokes the audience into that instant sympathy, reaction, and response that is the common result when one human being faces another in a highly charged, dramatic situation. It is an intensely personal response, not merely a result of seeing the action and hearing the dialogue—film or video tape could provide these. Rather it is a recognition of a mutually shared humanity, a seemingly inherent necessity for differentiating, at least on the subconscious level, between people and *pictures* of people.

And yet, no matter how strong the dramatic illusion, theatre is not truly reality, or even a near perfect re-creation of reality. Because the intent of theatre is to communicate productively with an audience, there are certain built-in limitations as to how closely theatre can reproduce reality. The theatre building itself is a limitation in that it not only limits the space in which the actor can perform and the materials, the sets and props, available for the performance but also, in most cases, limits the relationship between the actor and the audience by restricting each to a specified part of the house. The running time of the show is also a limiting factor, requiring that the playwright use only the most important dialogue, in most cases dispensing with the trivial chatter that characterizes human relations. The running time also holds the actor to a limited time in the creation of a real human being. Perhaps the greatest restriction of all in terms of theatrical reality is the necessity for actors to externalize the internal state of being, thereby forcing actions and speech patterns and styles that almost never exist outside the theatrical situation. Thus, theatre has developed a number of devices by way of which an audience can be induced to accept the play as reality for the duration of its limited passage onstage, and these devices are generally known as conventions.

Theatrical Convention

Convention, as traditionally used in theatre, means essentially that a contract is entered into by both the players and the audience that, while the play is onstage, certain departures from reality, such as actions or situations or technical devices that are obviously unreal, will be accepted as reality in order to make possible the necessary theatrical communication.

Certain of these theatrical conventions are so common, so instantly understandable and obviously necessary, that even a first-time playgoer will tend to accept them without question. For example, when the actors project their voices there must be an immediate recognition on the part of the audience that nobody regularly carries on conversations this loudly in the offstage reality. However, everyone in the audience also knows without being told that unless the actors speak in this manner they will not be heard throughout the auditorium, and, thus, the play would be ended as a significant artistic event. The same is true of blocking or composition; that is, the manner in which a director positions his actors on the stage. No matter how talented the director and actors, and no matter how aesthetically pleasing the stage positioning may be, the audience easily recognizes the fact that people in real life never position themselves in such a way that they at all times face *essentially* toward the audience. This tends to be especially true in the proscenium stage situation, where the audience is permanently positioned at one edge of the set and therefore actors must deliver the largest share of their lines in the audience's direction, or at least with very few lines delivered away from the audience. Arena stages, where the audience surrounds the action, allow more realistic blocking in one sense, but require that players keep shifting positions so that all areas of the audience are treated to their fair share of each actor's front view. Another obviously practical convention is that actors must "wait out" laughs without appearing to or even seeming to notice that they are being overheard and reacted to.

Beyond these easily accepted, obvious, and understood conventions, the theatre in its various periods has developed a number of less obvious methods for creating the theatrical illusion, methods far more demanding on audience willingness to believe. A number of these conventions are no longer used much in contemporary drama, but it is worth taking the time to understand the conventions of other ages in order to enter fully into the contract and thus feel the full impact of the great dramas of the past.

ASIDES may be simply defined as speeches given by one character that are understood by the audience not to be heard by the other characters who are onstage at the time. Essentially there are three types of asides. The first is a passage that clearly represents the character's thoughts or feelings. It is an expression of the internal and is understood to be such.

The second type of aside, however, and the one most difficult for an audience to understand or accept, has a character speaking in a conspiratorial manner to one or more characters on stage but not overheard by other characters who may physically be very close to the speaker. Such a passage can be seen in Shakespeare's *Love's Labor's Lost*, in a passage between Boyet and Dumain. Don Adriano de Armado, "a fantastical Spaniard," has just finished telling the Princess of France that "I do adore thy sweet Grace's slipper."

BOYET: (*Aside to Dumain*) Loves her by the foot.

DUMAIN: (*Aside to Boyet*) He may not by the yard.

A third and reasonably uncommon type of aside is one in which a character onstage makes a guarded but pointed comment on some aspect of the action. This comment is half-heard by another character, and then the one making the original comment is forced to revise it in some manner that makes it seem innocent. This device is often used for comic purposes, but may equally expose the dark and devious aspects of tragedy. In Shakespeare's *Richard III*, Gloucester's eventual murder of the two young princes is foreshadowed by the following, partially heard aside. Then because it is partially overheard, it is rephrased even more meaningfully:

PRINCE: But say, my lord, it were not registered,
               Methinks the truth should live from age to age
               As 'twere retailed to all posterity,
               Even to the general all-ending day.

GLOUCESTER: (*Aside*) So wise so young, they say, do never live long.

PRINCE: What say you, Uncle?

GLOUCESTER: I say, without characters, fame lives long.
               (*Aside*) Thus, like the formal vice Iniquity,
               I moralize two meanings in one word.

THE CHORUS, a particularly important device in early Greek drama, lasted through the English Renaissance as a major dramatic convention. It is still operative as a minor convention even in contemporary drama. Because the Greek drama was a direct descendant of the choral group that sang hymns, *dithyrambs*, in honor of the god Dionysus, early Greek tragedy and comedy were dominated by the Chorus. In comedy the importance of the Chorus diminished quickly and steadily, totally disappearing by the time of the Roman writers Plautus and Terence. In tragedy, however, the Chorus never quite disappeared, though it diminished in size and function. In the early Greek tragedy the Chorus was always in character; that is, the Chorus of Theban Elders in *Oedipus Rex*, for example, delivers lines that are appropriate for the old men, the Elders, of the city. Later, as the size and importance of the Chorus diminished, they stepped out of character to become commentators on and observers of the action. By the time of the English Renaissance the size of the Chorus had generally diminished to one character, who might be incorporated in the action, as the character Horatio in *Hamlet*, or excluded from the action of the play, as the Chorus in *Romeo and Juliet*. In some later cases the Chorus has been made an integral part of contemporary drama, but such cases have become rare indeed, with the great emphasis on realism in the last one hundred years.

The Dramatic Experience

EXPOSITION, as a theatre convention, is the setting forth or explaining of the particular background information that the audience needs to know to follow the present action of the play. In some cases this is done in a subtle, sophisticated manner, so that the dialogue for the present stage action is cunningly freighted with the past history of the situation. This manner is particularly evident in such plays as Henrik Ibsen's *Ghosts*, where the conversations between the major characters not only enhance their characterizations but provide the necessary insights into past action to make the present meaningful. In other cases the exposition is handled in a bit more straightforward fashion, as if the author is determined to get the past action out of the way as soon as possible, so that he can begin concentrating on the action of the present. Such an approach can be seen in Moliere's *Tartuffe*, where all of Act 1 and a large part of Act 2 is spent in setting up the situation and the characterization.

THE MONOLOGUE is a convention that today is usually used for comic purposes, but that in the Elizabethan period also existed in tragic (or at least noncomic) drama. In most cases the character delivering the monologue is alone onstage, and the thing that clearly differentiates the monologue from the soliloquy is that the material spoken is obviously external material and is delivered to the audience directly. Thus, in Shakespeare's *Two Gentlemen of Verona*, the comic servant, Launce, in describing the scene when he departed from his family, says:

> *Nay, I'll show you the manner of it. This shoe is my father. No, this left shoe is my father. No, no, this left shoe is my mother. Nay, that cannot be so, neither. Yes, it is so, it is so, it hath the worser sole.*

The "you" to whom the actor is speaking, to whom he is going to show "the manner of it," is clearly the audience, and it is to them that he delivers his monologue.

THE NARRATOR, like the actor in the monologue, speaks directly to the audience, either setting the scene, outlining the action, establishing the mood, presenting the argument of the play, providing necessary background information, or some combination of all of these. The name by which the narrator is known may vary, from Prologue or Chorus (especially in Elizabethan plays) to such later characters as the Stage Manager in Thornton Wilder's *Our Town*. In most cases, especially with Elizabethan through eighteenth-century drama, the narrator delivers the prologue or epilogue, begging the audience's indulgence, explaining the author's point of view, and even urging the audience to enjoy the play and applaud.

THE SOLILOQUY is probably the best known of theatrical conventions, perhaps because of the beautiful, highly poetic material that so often forms the core of the soliloquy, or perhaps because Shakespeare's best known play (possibly the world's best known play), *Hamlet*, contains several

Monte Markham as Hamlet delivers the "gravedigger" speech in the California State University, Fullerton, production of Hamlet. *Directed by Kirk Mee.*

beautiful examples. In any case, the soliloquy is a speech delivered by an actor who is alone onstage. Unlike the monologue, it is not delivered directly to the audience. Rather, it is a vocalization of the character's innermost thoughts. When we hear a soliloquy we do not merely hear a person *speaking*; we hear a person *thinking*, vocalizing those internal materials. When Hamlet begins his famous "To be, or not to be" soliloquy we are not supposed to believe that he is speaking these lines to any purpose other than to allow the audience to hear his thoughts regarding the steadily mounting pressure on him to avenge his father's murder, and the horrors this revenge has caused. The convention of the soliloquy has not been much with us of late, until the recent movement toward nonrealistic drama, for the demands of realism cannot be fulfilled by a scene in which a character vocally expresses purely internal material. However, the necessity is in a sense still there if a play is to create a complete experience for the audience.

VERSE, as a dramatic convention, has been a major aspect of theatre from the Classical Greek period until the development of dramatic realism. Obviously verse is not a normal or natural way of speaking, and verse drama imposes a highly difficult demand on the audience: to accept it as reality while the play is onstage. Elizabethan blank verse, basically un-rhymed iambic pentameter, with its run-on sentences and occasional vari-

The Winter's Tale, *Shakespeare's fairy-tale romance, at the Guthrie Theatre, Minneapolis-St. Paul. Ken Ruta plays the vengeful King Leontes, and Helen Carey is his gentle, wronged wife, Hermione. Richard Gray plays their son, Prince Mamillus. Directed by Michael Langham; designed by Desmond Heeley.*

ations to break up the pounding iambic rhythm, comes closer than most in approximating nature. Certainly it sounds less unnatural to the ear than, for example, the rhymed couplets of such works as *The Farce of Master Pierre Pathelin*, but by no stretch of the imagination could verse dialogue be considered realistic. For this reason, and also because there are no more true poets writing for theatre, verse has been nearly abandoned as a dramatic convention. Exceptions are some of the plays of Maxwell Anderson, T. S. Eliot, and Christopher Fry. In a very major way this state of affairs is unfortunate. Those who have managed to complete the contract of dramatic convention, and thus have experienced the theatre of Shakespeare, can testify regarding the degree to which great verse can increase the intensity of the dramatic presentation.

Finally, the dramatic experience in all of its complexity can be found only in the ultimate theatrical situation. In the auditorium, as the end result of the collaboration between audience, actors, directors, designers, and technicians, theatre is created and the dramatic experience can happen. Theatre, on the other hand, does not just happen. Beauty can happen (sunsets happen, for example), but theatre is *art*, which is to say that it is a conscious creation by a number of artists working together toward a common goal. When the work of these artists is presented before an audience, the dramatic illusion is created and the audience responds in an infinite variety of ways. Each audience member selects out of this experience, this movable feast, that which he needs, that which is meaningful and relevant and nourishing to him personally.

This impact on the audience, then, is the special value and virtue of theatre, which is restricted in time and place, but infinite in its possibilities. It is valuable to each audience member in terms of that member's own special demands and needs. And when the play is over and the audience has departed, each viewer carries with him into the street the result of the dramatic experience.

two

Tragedy

Tragedy has loomed larger in our lives since 1949, when Arthur Miller's *Death of a Salesman* took the stage and went on to win not only the Pulitzer Prize but also a full collection of other prestigious awards. Tragedy as an important dramatic form, perhaps the most important, thereby impressed itself anew on the theatregoing public and (by the way of the attendant publicity and the later television production) even on those who never set foot in theatre. The disagreement of scholars and critics over whether Miller's play is truly tragic or merely pathetic is not the issue here. What is in point is that tragedy takes on a new significance as an art form at a time when even young adults have lived through the assassinations of a beloved president, a popular senator, and an admired Black civil rights leader, a time when we found ourselves as a nation playing out our own purgative version of Greek tragedy for the three days preceding the funeral of President Kennedy.

In the last thirty-seven years we have fought in a world war, a major police action in Korea, and an unpopular war in Vietnam. We have wit-

Arthur Miller's Death of a Salesman *at the Studio Arena Theatre in Buffalo, New York. Pat Hingle stars as Willy Loman, with Joan Lorring as Linda. Directed by Warren Enters.*

nessed a continuing conflict in the Middle East and Africa, more than twenty years of political infighting, pressure, repression, and cold war in Europe, and innumerable brushfire conflicts around the world. We find ourselves constantly at the edge of disaster, facing situations which have made "brinksmanship" a household word. All too often, human misery, failure, and death have seemed the only constants in our world. What else but tragedy could be the primary art form of our time?

And yet, despite its immediate importance to us, tragedy generally succeeds in raising a number of questions. Is it, as some scholars seem to believe, something that can be represented only by that small collection of Classic Greek plays by Aeschylus, Sophocles, and Euripides? Can the genre include as well works by William Shakespeare and Christopher Marlowe, who certainly cast aside the rules deduced by Aristotle from the great Greek originals? Can the standard concept of tragedy include plays by Pierre Corneille, Jean Racine, Eugene O'Neill, and Arthur Miller? Such seemingly simple and obviously rhetorical questions have been puzzling scholars and critics for centuries and are likely never to be answered to everyone's satisfaction. However, one highly productive way of approaching an answer is to examine tragedy from two seemingly separate points of view, looking first at the *tragic spirit*, which does not depend on a specific dramatic form but upon a point of view toward those aspects of life that man has traditionally termed tragic and which have remained essentially unchanged from the fifth century B.C. to our own time. Second, because form and content (that is, spirit) are fundamentally inseparable, it is necessary to look at the *tragic form*, examining the various ways in which the tragic spirit has been captured and cast for dramatic production.

The Tragic Spirit

"The tragic writer in all ages has always been chiefly concerned with man's fate, and a man's fate is that he is ultimately doomed to defeat because he is born to die."[1] Out of that perception of humanity's fate the tragic spirit is born. And yet the tragic spirit is surely far more than a recognition of human mortality, for simple recognition and acceptance of that fact would imply a passive acceptance of that which the human race cannot accept. And the tragic hero is never passive. Thus, in tragedy we find the tragic hero recognizing his ultimate defeat, but struggling against it and continuing to struggle until the bitter end. It is because of the tragic hero's continuing battle to assert his humanity in the face of inevitable defeat that philosophers, scholars, and artists throughout the ages have found tragedy to be ennobling rather than pessimistic. The heart of the tragic spirit is therefore what the struggle is all about, and why it is necessary.

Arthur Miller has defined the struggle of the tragic hero against his inevitable fate as "the consequence of a man's compulsion to evaluate himself justly."[2] Obviously, Miller is attempting to set up a model for tragedy that will allow common men like his own Willy Loman in *Death of a Salesman* to serve as tragic heroes in place of the distinguished personages prescribed by tradition, by way of Aristotle. In setting up this rather self-serving model, however, Miller has struck very close to the truth of the human necessity to engage in the tragic struggle. In almost every case great tragic heroes such as Oedipus, Lear, and Faustus struggle to exceed the limitations that are inherent in being human. In some cases the struggle becomes a prideful pursuit of an earth-related goal, as becomes evident in Sophocles' *Oedipus the King* when Oedipus opens the play by describing himself as "I, Oedipus, whom all men call great." In other cases the

---

[1]Robert W. Corrigan, ed., "Introduction" to *Tragedy: A Critical Anthology* (Boston, 1971), p. ix.
[2]Arthur Miller, "Tragedy and the Common Man," *New York Times* (February 27, 1949), II, pp. 1, 3.

A scene from Oedipus the King *by Sophocles. Directed by Gerard A. Larson at California State University, Sacramento.*

struggle may become a presumptuous effort to equal or exceed the gods themselves, which can be seen when Marlowe's Dr. Faustus takes up the study of magic, urging himself to "try thy brains to [become] a deity."

This insight, then, explains the basic paradox that seems to be at the very heart of tragedy. Why, if tragedy always results in the fall (usually to death) of the tragic hero, do we find that audiences are exalted rather than crushed by the dramatic experience? The answer is found in the struggle against insurmountable odds. Recognizing the inevitability of his fate, the tragic hero still cries out against it and seeks to defeat that fate, thus exceeding the limitations imposed on the human condition. By so doing, by going down fighting in its own lost cause, humanity triumphs spiritually over its own limitations, even though it does not triumph physically.

The tragic spirit manages to remain triumphant to the degree that it puts its stress on the mystery of existence rather than the known end. That is to say, it finds life to be greater than the sum of its objective parts, an unknown though not unknowable mystery, and it pushes the perimeter of understanding to its utmost limits in an attempt to understand ever more of the mystery. In Shakespeare's *King Lear*, for example, an elderly king resigns his throne in order to divide his country among his three daughters. To justify giving the best portion of the kingdom to his favorite, Cordelia, Lear asks each daughter to express how much she loves him. The two designing daughters respond in excessive terms, describing a grand love that they in no way feel. Cordelia, on the other hand, responds honestly that she loves Lear as a child should love a parent, and that she also expects to love the man she marries. Lear blazes up wrathfully, disinheriting Cordelia and dividing the country between the two pretending daughters. Tragedy is the result.

If we, as audience, fail to rise above the commonplace and utilitarian, we will find ourselves playing a wishing game or an "if only" game; if only Lear had not given up his crown, if only he had understood Cordelia's honesty and the dishonesty of the other two daughters, if only . . . if only . . . if only. . . . By playing this game, by finding Lear to be little more than a senile old man who has no intuitive understanding, we miss the grave significance that follows when Lear probes the tragic cause and effect of his own misery. If we insist on seeing only utilitarian patterns in our drama, we will miss the tragic spirit entirely, miss the intuition of the mystery, by becoming bogged down in insignificant facts and personal desires.

The mystery that is stressed and probed, then, is one that is unique to humankind: the order of justice. It brings us back to Arthur Miller's contention that tragedy is a result of man's attempt "to evaluate himself justly." A rat may solve the problems of a maze to get a lump of sugar as a reward, but in no way will the rat then question whether it is right for him to have, or accept, the sugar. Such a consideration is presumably beyond the rat's capacity. A human being, however, who is usually considered to be a knowledgeable, ethical creature, cannot escape asking such questions.[3]

Knowledge, then, is a necessity if the tragic spirit is to exist. This tragic knowledge is, essentially, a recognition of the patterns of justice that exist in life. The tragic hero does not go whimpering to his doom, vainly protesting that the tragic action is not really his fault. In the greatest of

---

[3]The above is based in part on insights gained from Richmond Y. Hathorn's *Tragedy, Myth, and Mystery* (Bloomington, Indiana, 1962), p. 220ff.

Richard Kneeland plays the mad King Lear at the Trinity Square Repertory Company, Providence, Rhode Island.

tragedies, such as *Oedipus the King* or *Hamlet*, the tragic hero recognizes the pattern and the part he has played in establishing it. So, having fought against it to the bitter end, he accepts it even to the degree that it involves his own destruction. In spite of this acceptance, the tragic hero is not truly passive, or the tragedy would degenerate into something close to melodrama. Instead, the hero accepts his fall positively and, indeed, actively as a method of expiation. Justice in the world of tragedy will be purchased at the expense of the hero's suffering. Some of the lesser tragic heroes never really approach this degree of tragic knowledge; Agamemnon, for example, in Aeschylus' play *Agamemnon* seems totally unaware of the pattern. However, Aeschylus himself was highly aware of the ways in which justice manifests itself, and he wove this perception very carefully into the fabric of his play, so that the spiritual blindness of the hero is balanced by audience awareness.

Finally, contrary to what seems to be a general misconception that tragedy is made up of the pessimistic and spirit-quenching and dour, the tragic spirit is eager, questing, optimistic, and, most of all, healing. Heal-

The innocent Desdemona (Deborah May) is dead at the hands of her anguished husband, Othello (John Hancock), in the American Conservatory Theatre of San Francisco's production of Shakespeare's Othello. *Directed by Allen Fletcher.*

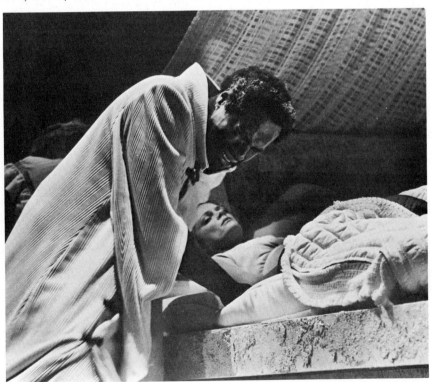

ing a wounded or sick world has been the function of tragedy from the very beginning. The physical and spiritual suffering of Oedipus heals Thebes by ending the blight that has fallen on the city, and the deaths of Romeo and Juliet heal the unnatural division of the state created by the feud between their families. Such tragedies are paeans to humanity's struggle for justice, or at least that which is just, in the face of overwhelming odds. That is why the audience at a tragedy is not simply downcast at the fall of the tragic hero, but is also enlightened and optimistic for the future of the human race. Humankind's willingness to do battle and to suffer can make the world whole. That is why, over the centuries, the great tragedies are the plays that remain most alive and vivid and meaningful, and why we return to them time after time and cherish them above all other plays.

The Tragic Form

It has long been a generally accepted critical opinion that form and content are, ultimately, inseparable. That is to say, somehow the form in which a work of art is cast has as much to do with its emotional, or subjective, and intellectual, or objective "meaning" as any other aspect of the work. In drama the particular form in which a play is molded or formed can be as important as any specific character or device within the play, and perhaps far more important. Down through the ages, tragedy has existed in a number of quite different dramatic forms, each contributing its own possibilities to the tragic effect. Understanding those forms and how they work not only can contribute greatly to an appreciation of tragedy in all of its various periods but can also help us in defining a tragic form that is viable for a modern audience.

Classical Greece

The tragic drama in Greece, like the prehistoric folk drama, grew out of ritual religious observance. However, differing from the folk drama that preceded it, tragedy no longer fulfilled such basic folk-myth-ritual demands as death and revival, summer-winter combat, or the water charm. In part, that is because Classical Greek tragedy, unlike the earlier drama, was not the end result of a gradual accumulation of ritual actions, but a conscious, craftsmanlike attempt to create a meaningful art form. Because it was performed in honor of Dionysus, the god of wine, vegetation, and fertility (a dying and reviving god, similar to those in the folk drama), Greek tragedy is certainly related to the earliest ritual forms, and although a god, or any other character, may not die and be revived onstage, winter death and summer revival had to be present in the minds of the audience. This concentration on the myth was reinforced during the play by the presence, in the center of the orchestra, of an altar, the *thymele*, on which was a bust or statue of the god in whose honor the play was being per-

A production of Anthony Burgess' translation and adaptation of Oedipus the King *at the Guthrie Theatre, Minneapolis-St. Paul. Directed by Michael Langham; designed by Desmond Heeley.*

formed. In some cases the theatre itself served as a kind of temple. The great Theatre of Dionysus in Athens stood on ground consecrated to the god, and until the stage house grew large enough to hide it, his temple was visible almost directly behind the playing area.

Because this was a religious rite as well as a carefully crafted drama, Greek tragedy had, apparently from beginning to end, a highly formalized ritual structure. Of the original Greek tragedies very few have survived, so we have only a small collection of texts to examine. A large part of our understanding of the genre must, therefore, depend on *The Poetics* of Aristotle. The age of the great tragic writers was already long past when Aristotle first came to Athens in 367 B.C. Aristotle himself pointed out that tragedy had already reached its highest development in the works of Sophocles and Euripides. Therefore, when he set out to examine the genre of tragedy—to construct a philosophical model for perfect tragedy—he was working with plays that had already passed into history. Essentially, the model that Aristotle constructed was based on carefully selected examples and primarily on *Oedipus the King* (c. 430-429) by Sophocles. He refers to Euripides as "the most tragic of poets," but gives his work short shrift and pays even less attention to Aeschylus, the first of the great tragic dramatists. Because Aristotle's work was the first such critical examination of tragedy, and because it is still the most influential work on the subject, a brief examination is necessary of the most important aspects of his model.

For Aristotle, tragedy is an imitation of a serious action that is complete in itself. This imitation is attained by employing rhythm, language, and melody, which is to say that it is poetic drama using alternate sections of dialogue and choral odes. The action is direct in that the audience sees and hears it, and there is no narrative because that would merely tell audiences about the action rather than showing it to them. The purpose of all this is to arouse pity (what we feel when someone suffers more than he deserves for his faults or mistakes) and fear (what we feel when suffering happens to someone like ourselves), and to cause a pleasurable purging, a *catharsis*, of these two emotions. Plato had rejected tragedy on the ground that it aroused pity and fear, thereby making men emotionally weak. Aristotle, on the contrary, believed that tragedy purges those emotions, thereby making men stronger.

A tragedy must be a complete whole, with a beginning, a middle, and an end, and within this whole the events must be ordered in a necessary and probable sequence, where each event grows logically out of the preceding event and leads logically to the event that follows. It must be neither too short nor too long, so that the audience can grasp both the separate parts and the unity of the whole within a single memory span. The natural limit in size is that the play must provide a change in the hero's fortunes, and this change must be the result of proper dramatic causation.

The unified plot that Aristotle insists upon cannot consist of disconnected events, even events dealing with the fortunes of the same hero. Rather, the events must be causally connected and unified by one central theme.

For Aristotle, the poet-dramatist is not a historian but a creative artist, which means that he imitates not what actually *happens* in life, but what is *probable* and *meaningful*. He arranges events not necessarily in the order of their occurrence but in an order that is likely, believable, and, above all, inevitable. The poet who follows this pattern imitates ideal truth, the universal which grows out of the specific. For Aristotle, this makes drama of greater import than history, which deals only in objective facts.

In terms of specific form, the tragic plot must contain *reversal*, results opposite to those intended; *discovery*, which means within the play itself the change from love to hate, or from ignorance to knowledge, with consequent arousal of pity and fear (there is also some justification for defining discovery as transference of knowledge from the protagonist to the audience); and *suffering*, from murder, torture, or injury of the hero, also arousing pity and fear. This ideal plot is complex and involves a hero who passes from happiness to misery. He will not be perfectly virtuous and just, since, if he were, the tragic happening would be unfair; and he will not be evil or base, since the tragic event would then be only poetic justice. Instead he will be a basically good person of distinguished standing, so that his fall will be the greater, and his downfall will come about because of a flaw in his character. This flaw may be an excess of some virtue.

The Aristotelian statement outlined above is certainly not a final or completely accurate depiction of Greek tragedy; of the plays that we have, it fits completely only *Oedipus the King*. It does provide a model, however, a pattern against which we can measure the existing plays, and a reasonably clear statement of exactly what the Greeks got from their tragedies.

Rome and the Middle Ages

For several hundred years after the Greek Golden Age there was little tragedy of note. It received little attention as a dramatic form until the Roman critic Horace wrote his *Art of Poetry* in the ninth century B.C. The Romans, who produced two great comic playwrights in Plautus and Terence, seemed to have no real genius for tragedy—at least no great tragic manuscripts have survived. They became interested in the tragic genre, its grandeur, its sweep, and its sense of ever-impending doom, when the Greek slave Livius Andronicus produced a Greek play in translation in 240 B.C. However, the few tragic playwrights the Romans produced have not stood the test of time, and of their plays only nine manuscripts by the dramatist-philosopher Seneca have survived, along with one play by an unknown author, probably preserved because it was once attributed to Seneca. Whether the plays of Seneca were ever staged, or whether they

Seneca's Oedipus *as produced by the Oxford Playhouse, Hollywood, California, in the American premiere production. Adapted by Ted Hughes.*

were written and produced as recitations or readers theatre, has long been debated. In any case, they seem to have been of minimal theatrical importance during Seneca's own lifetime, although in their later revival during the English Renaissance they proved to be among the most influential plays of all time.

No significant tragedy was written in the Medieval period, which began for theatre in the sixth century when the Emperor Justinian closed the theatres because of the violence and sexuality of the performances. The miracle, mystery, and morality plays of the Medieval period certainly have tragic themes in abundance, but they concentrate primarily on illustrating scripture, presenting inspirational glimpses of saints and martyrs, and providing theological cautionary tales in order to demonstrate to humankind the proper pathway to redemption. The plays sometimes suggest the tragic consequences of an arbitrary fate, but the emphasis is always on the necessity of avoiding the temptation to amass worldly goods or seek worldly success. Even the illustrious princes who fall from their high position are treated less as tragic heroes than as examples of the evils attendant on coveting riches or power, and as a dramatic reminder of man's primal fall.

A scene from The Son of Getron, *a Medieval miracle play, anonymous, Fleury mss. Directed by Alan Stambusky at the University of California, Davis.*

English Renaissance

English tragedy began in 1562, when Thomas Sackville and Thomas Norton wrote *Gorboduc* in what they conceived to be the Senecan style. The Elizabethan writers were never really dependent on Aristotelian terms or definitions. Instead, they developed their own freewheeling form that totally disregards such Aristotelian dictums as unity of time and place, and at least partially ignores unity of action. In Elizabethan drama, tragic action was usually explosive, diverse, and extensive in time and place. The tragic action was freely mixed with the comic. Serious players shared the stage with the low comics.

The Renaissance was, in all of Western Europe as well as England, based primarily on a revival of Classical learning, which in turn led to a revolutionary questioning of the stable Medieval environment, a perfect situation for the rebirth of tragedy. The unity of the Christian faith was beginning to fall apart, and Renaissance man, like the ancient Greeks before him, was beginning to question and probe matters that had long been inviolate. He was becoming "human-centered," deciding that bettering his lot in this world was not a sin but a virtue. Thus, tragic heroes like

The *"Seven Deadly Sins"* appear before Faustus in a production of Marlowe's The Tragical History *of Dr. Faustus at California State University, Fullerton. Directed by Robert Rence.*

Faustus, relentless challengers of everything that diminishes humankind, that makes humans less than divine, were the embodiment of the Renaissance ideal.

In constructing their tragedies, the Elizabethan playwrights went first to Seneca, whose plays had been revived and were being read and admired at the universities. They used many of the techniques that Seneca had exploited, such as plots based on revenge, and plays that contained ghosts, netherworld beings, disguisings, etc., along with many of the standard Classical Greek devices, such as recognitions, reversals, and discoveries, to write tragedies emphasizing contemporary tensions resulting from the conflicts between the earlier Age of Faith and the skeptical Renaissance.

In addition to these more standard devices, many of the Renaissance dramatists, especially Shakespeare, made brilliant use of the comic subplot. This device, perhaps discovered and developed independently and perhaps a legacy from Terence, the only Classical writer to maintain his popularity throughout the Medieval period, mixed the comic and tragic in a way that would later be unthinkable to the strict neoclassicists. It worked, however. Artistic unity was not destroyed and, surprisingly, was actually

The National Theatre of Great Britain players depict a scene from Shakespeare's pastoral comedy As You Like It. *The all-male cast offered contemporary audiences a new dimension of the comedy by playing it as it would have been presented in Shakespeare's time when women were not permitted on the stage. At the Greek Theatre in Los Angeles.*

Bobby Clark made a merry romp out of Moliere's The Would-Be Gentlemen *when it played at the Booth Theatre in New York. With him is June Knight.*

augmented by allowing the audience to see the action twice, in its serious vein and then with its potential comic overtones.

French Classical Period

Medieval drama ended in France by 1548, but it was not until 1636 (or January, 1637, as later scholarship would have it), more than twenty years after the death of Shakespeare, that the French theatre acquired *Le Cid*, one of its most enduring masterpieces. In part, the fact that French theatre took so long to develop may be due to the early development of a French National Academy devoted to the protection and preservation of the French language and the promotion of Classical rules for artistic creation. Those rules were, at least in terms of theatre, largely derived from Aristotle, or at least from the early seventeenth-century understanding of Aristotle, and they were enforced with a rigidity that, for some writers, was so constricting that the very life was squeezed out of their art.

The most repressive aspect of these rules was the severity of their enforcement in terms of the unities of time, place, and action. A strict adherence to these unities is not *necessarily* conducive to artificiality. Other playwrights than the French, at other times, have worked well within these very strictures. Indeed, Jean Racine, probably the greatest tragic writer that France has produced, had a background in Classical studies and the kind of balanced temperament and outlook on life that made the restrictions of neoclassicism seem no more than an extension of his own natural style.

In terms of the specifics of form, these French tragedies usually reverse the standard pattern of Classical Greek drama, which tends to build in a pattern of ever-ascending crises to the tragic action or turning point, which occurs close to the end of the play. In French Classical tragedy, in contrast, the tragic action usually happens rather early in the script, with the rest of the action largely a lament over the consequences.

The strictures of neoclassicism led most French tragic writers to adopt a generally formalistic style of dialogue. That is true not only of the style of phrasing but also of the subjects the characters talk about and the words they choose in so doing. The characters in these plays tend toward the elegant, usually observing the proprieties of refined society, and they spend a great deal of time talking gravely and philosophically in the midst of pressing crises and fateful circumstances. And all this is done in rhymed hexameter couplets.

Eighteenth and Nineteenth Centuries

After Shakespeare, Jonson, and Marlowe, in England, and Corneille and Racine, in France, the writing of significant tragedy fell off for more than two hundred years. When the Stuart monarchy was restored to the English throne by way of that rollicking rakehell Charles II, one of his first official acts as king was to reopen the theatres. He gave exclusive production rights to two acting companies, and the drama that grew out of this situation, with the hedonistic courtiers on one hand and the sternly disapproving Puritans on the other, was primarily a limited and narrow comedy aimed at the court group, with almost no leavening of tragedy.

The few tragedies the playwrights produced were of the genre usually referred to as *heroic tragedy*, which is to say plays that were long, poetic, and usually highly melodramatic. In those works, as in some of the earlier French works that partially fostered them, an idealistic young hero and heroine are faced with the traditional conflict between love and honor. In some cases the conflict is resolved and a happy ending is appended; in other cases the problem goes unresolved ending in tragedy (actually melodrama). In those plays the background of the play is usually martial, and the tragic acts are followed by extensive handwringing. As the heroic drama declined in popularity, it was replaced by neoclassic blank-verse tragedy, which was an improvement over the earlier genre, though not a great one. The few acceptable tragedies that were created in this neoclassic form tended to be weak neoclassical versions of works by earlier and greater writers. In some cases, such as John Dryden's 1677 play, *All For Love* (a retelling of *Antony and Cleopatra* designed to fit the sensibilities of a Restoration audience), it was merely Shakespeare rewritten.

In 1685, Charles II was succeeded by his brother James II. James lasted only three years, however, before the Glorious Revolution removed him and put William and Mary on the English throne. William was a reserved and rather sour man, highly suspicious of England and the English, who was far happier fighting the French than attending the theatre. The change in court attitude resulting from this shift of monarchs, plus a rapidly growing merchant middle class, put an end to both heroic tragedy and neoclassic blank-verse tragedy. In its place came a form of tragedy that is sometimes described as sentimental, sometimes as domestic, and sometimes as a bourgeoisie. Under whatever description, this new tragedy was less tragic than pathetic. Each play contained certain predictable nontragic ingredients, such as unrecognized virtue, accidental separation, and many mix-ups resulting from misunderstood conversations overheard out of context and from misplaced prop items such as jewels or fans. These unlikely situations were designed to wring tears from the audience and make them susceptible to the overbearing moralizing that became a standard of the age.

A scene from William Wycherly's The Country Wife *at the University of Illinois at Urbana-Champaign. Directed by Clara Behringer; set design by Bernhard Works; costumes by Michael Cesario.*

The most notable play of this genre, and one of the earliest, was George Lillo's *The London Merchant* (1731). The importance of the growing merchant class as a potential theatre audience is seen in the play's title. Within the play itself the "thoroughly good" patriarchal character of the merchant, Mr. Thorowgood, makes the philosophical position of the work quite plain. Thorowgood lectures his apprentice, Trueman, on how trade "is founded in the reason and nature of things . . . promotes humanity . . . keeps up intercourse between nations . . . and diffuses mutual love from pole to pole." The action of the play is highly melodramatic, with the honest young hero-apprentice, George Barnwell, being led astray by a prostitute and ending on the gallows in spite of his abject repentance.

The dramatic styles and concepts that were new and exciting in 1731, however, began to pall by the end of the eighteenth century, and by the advent of the romantic period, the Western tragic drama had reached a very low point indeed. Romantic tragedy tended to be overblown, and revivals of the great dramas of the Renaissance emphasized all too often the romantic elements and the bombast of those earlier plays. Percy Bysshe Shelley, in his closet drama *The Cenci*, tried to develop a theory and style of

Vanbrugh's The Relapse *at the Guthrie Theatre, Minneapolis-St. Paul. Directed by Michael Langham; sets by John Jensen; costumes by Carl Toms; music by Henry Molicone; choreography by Jeff Henry.*

tragedy that would be viable for the romantic audience, and the idea behind it seems ever more important although the play has been no more than an attractive (at least to literature students) failure as a stage vehicle for nearly one hundred and fifty years. As Shelley indicated in a dedication to his friend the poet Leigh Hunt, and in a letter to Edward Trelawney, tragedy for the romantic age had little to do with the fall of princes through internal and (in a sense) humanizing flaws. Shelley's tragedy would concentrate on the destruction (that is, brutalization or corruption) of the pure human spirit by forces that surround us over which we can exercise no real control. In spite of the worth of Shelley's ideas, romantic tragedy left only a few landmarks to dramatic activity.

Modern Tragedy

What is *modern drama*? Does this term refer to the period that stretches from Henrik Ibsen to right now, some one hundred years, or does it mean only the last twenty years or so? One hundred years ago may seem like ancient times to some of us, but modern drama did, in a sense, begin with Ibsen, and modern tragedy may very well have begun with his play *The Master Builder* (1892). That was not his first play with a tragic theme; *Ghosts, Hedda Gabler*, and several other of his plays have tragic aspects, but *The Master Builder*, based in part on Ibsen's study of Classical Greek tragedy, totally escapes the *problem-play* tag that is hung so often on his earlier social

The Goodman Theatre Center produced Eugene O'Neill's Long Day's Journey Into Night *with Drew Snyder as James Tyrone, Jr.; Edward Binns as James Tyrone; Frances Hyland as Mary Tyrone; and John V. Shea as Edmund Tyrone. Directed by George Keathley.*

dramas. In the problem plays Ibsen was interested in exploring and commenting on specific flaws in his society. In *The Master Builder*, by considering such timeless problems as the battle between youth and age and the conflict between pure art and materialism, and by *observing* rather than *passing judgment* on the human condition, he approached real tragedy.

After Ibsen, the tragic gauntlet was picked up by Eugene O'Neill, also a student of the great Greek tragedies. In *Desire Under the Elms* (1924) he transported to a stony New England farm the fateful Greek triangle of Theseus, Hippolytus, and Phaedra. Theseus becomes, in O'Neill's version, an aged but still lusty and powerful farmer; Hippolytus becomes the farmer's mother-fixated son who is jealous of his new stepmother; and Phaedra becomes a sensual former housekeeper who has married the elderly farmer to attain economic security. *Desire Under the Elms* certainly lacks the elevation of character that Aristotle deemed necessary for tragedy, but it possesses the requisite strength and never falls into the kind of melodrama that marks other O'Neill attempts at tragedy, such as his three-part retelling of the Orestes myth, *Mourning Becomes Electra* (1931).

During the last twenty-five years Arthur Miller's *Death of a Salesman* has been held up by some critics as an example of modern tragedy, by other critics as a modern play which comes as close to tragedy as it is possible to come given the contemporary social situation, and by still other critics as a modern play that never succeeds even in approaching the tragic

A scene from John Steinbeck's Of Mice and Men *by the Guthrie Theatre Company, Minneapolis-St. Paul. Directed by Len Cariou; sets and costumes by John Jensen.*

but strongly evokes the pathetic response. Which group of critics is the closest to right cannot be resolved here (or perhaps anywhere). To object to the play as tragedy on purely Aristotelian grounds seems senseless, however, for each age must devise its own tragic structure for itself. If one looks at tragedy as a result, as an emotional understanding generated in the audience, then *Death of a Salesman* does indeed fall somewhat short of the mark. The primary function of tragedy, of the search for justice that results in the tragic action, is healing, and when Willy Loman dies a suicide at the end of the play the world is not changed, not healed, not made whole.

And yet the feeling of the audience at the play's end, of an essentially good man destroyed not only by a world he never made but by a tragic flaw in his own nature, strikes very close to the proper tragic reaction.

Tragedy considers the human being in terms of internal, spiritual (or, if you will, psychological) drives and needs. It observes humans as they strive against the unknown, in the face of insurmountable odds, to seek a universal justice. It watches as the human being goes down fighting, paying the ultimate price for humanity and daring. Very few modern plays fully achieve this quality, but, as with tragedy itself, the possibility of victory is always there.

three

Comedy

Comedy is probably the more difficult to define of the two dramatic types, perhaps because it has had such a complex theatrical history, passing through so many forms and styles, or perhaps because the *comic spirit*, as it exists within the individual human being, is itself so complex as to resist definition. Adding to the difficulties faced by anyone trying to define comedy is the temptation to explore such side issues as the psychological and even the physiological basis of laughter, thereby becoming bogged down in what are essentially peripheral considerations. Therefore, perhaps the best place to begin an examination of dramatic comedy is not with the specifics of the type, but with the general, with the comic spirit.

Unlike the tragic spirit, which recognizes humankind's eventual doom and celebrates its determination to carry on the battle for justice in spite of insuperable odds, the comic spirit concentrates on humanity's insistence on, and apparent need for, carrying on its foibles and pretensions, even in the face of ultimate doom. Tragedy portrays humanity's moral triumph and illustrates the healing process that comes about through the hero's willingness to suffer; comedy concentrates instead on humanity's many little defeats, on the tribulations and trials faced in getting through each day. In tragedy humanity struggles nobly onward; in comedy humanity muddles through.

It is tempting, when placed in the position of having to define comedy, to resort to the most common and simplistic of all such definitions: "comedy is what makes us laugh." And basically this is quite accurate, for laughter is the yardstick by which we usually measure comic success. For audiences and critics alike, the most successful comedies are those that get the most laughs. However, laughter is not restricted to comedy but is also an end product of various emotions and physical situations that have little or nothing to do with dramatic, artistically created comedy. Laughter may be the result of certain types of physical stimulation, such as tickling, or of too many martinis, or of hysteria, or of an attempt to cover up either embarrassment or an excessive emotional reaction. In many cases, people choose to laugh because they are too ashamed or embarrassed to cry. Thus, laughter does not necessarily define comedy as such. Even so, selecting some of the most common causes of laughter may give insight into the comic spirit.

The first necessity in provoking comic laughter is to establish or at least agree upon a code of seriousness. This is necessary before even the

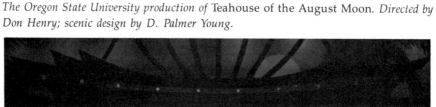

The Oregon State University production of Teahouse of the August Moon. *Directed by Don Henry; scenic design by D. Palmer Young.*

A scene from the perverse comedy What the Butler Saw, *by A Contemporary Theatre, Seattle. Directed by Gregory Falls; scenic design by S. Todd Muffatti.*

most basic comic ploy can be successful, for the truth can be clearly seen to be the truth only when both sides of a situation are made clear. In this sense, comedy is the other side of tragedy, and the two must stand side by side if the whole truth is to be seen. As one of our most perceptive drama critics, Walter Kerr, has pointed out, "The occasion could not be entirely representative if one part of its truth were to be altogether suppressed."[1] Comedy reveals that which tragedy ignores, and provides a complete whole. As Christopher Fry has stated, "In tragedy every moment is eternity; in comedy eternity is a moment."[2] And eternity is composed of moments.

At the heart of the comic spirit is an emphasis on life as it is in fact lived, day by day and even hour by hour, and this basic concept is the point where tragedy and comedy take quite different paths. Tragedy ignores the everyday mundane concerns of comedy and concentrates instead on humanity's attempts to perfect itself. Christopher Fry explains this difference when he writes:

> *The difference between tragedy and comedy is the difference between experience and intuition. In the experience we strive against every condition of our animal*

[1]Walter Kerr, *Tragedy and Comedy* (New York, 1968), p. 26.

[2]Christopher Fry, "Comedy," in *Comedy: Meaning and Form*, Robert W. Corrigan, ed. (San Francisco, 1965), p. 15.

A 1960 production of Mister Roberts *by Oregon State University. Directed by Don Henry; set design by E. S. Cortright.*

life: against death, against the frustration of ambition, against the instability of human love. In the intuition we trust the arduous eccentricities we're born to, and see the oddness of the creature who has never got acclimatized to being created. [3]

Perhaps because of this emphasis on looking at life as it is lived, the comic spirit is every bit as affirmative as is the tragic spirit. Tragedy ennobles humanity by concentrating on its willingness to suffer and do battle for just ends. Comedy confirms humanity's worth by exhibiting a persistent faith in its determination to survive. No matter how many times humanity is knocked down it will drag itself up again, painfully aware of its limitations, but ready to soldier onward.

As a consequence of this concentration on life's many defeats, large and small, comedy imitates pain, but it can exist only in the absence of pain. In the fifth chapter of *The Poetics*, Aristotle undertook a brief but perceptive definition of comedy, and one that still makes sense in terms of today's understanding. Comedy, Aristotle pointed out, consists of an imitation of ordinary persons who are not completely base but who are the embodiment of that part of the ugly in life which excites laughter. The part of the ugly which excites laughter is that flaw "which causes neither pain nor harm, as an ugly, distorted mask immediately brings laughter but causes no pain."[4] Pain destroys the joy in life that is so important to the comic spirit. Pain is serious, and as such it is in the province of tragedy. Comedy concentrates on the merriment of life that is bypassed by the tragic situation. When we go to the movies and watch the cartoon we see

[3]Fry, *Ibid.*, p. 16.

[4]Aristotle, *The Poetics of Aristotle*, trans. by Preston H. Epps (Chapel Hill, North Carolina, 1970), pp. 8-9.

the mouse give the cat an exploding cigar, but we remain comfortable. The cigar explodes in a great red flash, and as the smoke clears we see the cat, facial fur charred, eyes reddened and veined, teeth crumbling like crockery, and yet we can laugh because we know that within the next few frames the eyes and fur will be back to their original condition, and the teeth will have been reassembled. This absence of pain must always be evident to the audience. The cat may leap about and howl in an exaggerated pain reaction, but it must clearly be a put-on, and the audience must be included in the joke.

Finally, the comic spirit may very well be humanity's intuition of the comic aspects that underlie even the most serious situations. Laughter provides a release from the constant tensions of everyday life. Spectators at a comedy see people undergoing the same problems they themselves face outside the theatre, but in a comic manner because no pain is attached to the comedy. This situation allows them to laugh away their own fears and tensions and provides them with a recognition of kinship not only with the actors but with all their fellow human beings.

Comic Techniques

To achieve the comic effect, certain techniques have been developed over the centuries that seem to be common to all comedy. *Incongruity*, *surprise*, *exaggeration*, *repetition*, and the *wisecrack* are among the most important of

San Diego City College presented Harvey *by Mary Chase. Directed by Lyman Saville; set by Robert Green; costumes by Carol Riordan and Gloria Kendall.*

these techniques, and rhythm and language are the vehicles of their communication to the audience.

Incongruity

All comedy depends, to a greater or lesser degree, on acceptance of a norm. Comic incongruities, then, occur whenever a serious situation is based on a ludicrous departure from the norm. For example, a person may speak to a horse, but within our normal expectations we do not expect the horse to comprehend and reply. Such behavior is incongruous because it defeats our expectations based on the norm. In recent years a television comedy show, *Mr. Ed*, was based on this specific incongruity, and it was a popular if not a critical success. Outside of television, in the area of legitimate drama, Murray Schisgal used such incongruity in his play, *Luv*, which reversed the traditional expectations of what happens when a man covets his neighbor's wife. In this play a married man persuades his best friend to woo his, the married man's, wife, and the results are hilarious. In *The Odd Couple*, playwright Neil Simon also departs from the norm to humorous effect. When a married man arrives home late to dinner, his wife's anger is not necessarily comic. On the other hand, when Oscar Madison, in *The Odd Couple*, arrives home late to find his male roommate, Felix Unger, reacting as would an angry wife, sidesplitting comedy is the result.

Every kind of comedy is based at least in part on incongruity. There have been many different theories of comedy, expounded by such men as Pierre Charles Baudelaire, George Meredith, and Henri Bergson, and all agree that the comic consists of a departure from the norm. In Bergson's theory, that which is ludicrous and thus comic grows out of humanity's recognition that many of its actions are mechanical or nonhuman. Whenever a force outside the body controls the body's actions and movements, these become laughable because the body has taken on the image of the machine.[5] Suzanne Langer, on the other hand, comes to a similar conclusion but from a different point of view. She feels that laughter is caused by a sudden surge of vital feeling or love for life. When the audience views the mechanization of the human being, it brings life in all its real freedom into focus, and laughter results when this difference is realized and the audience rejoices that life is not nonhuman or mechanical in nature.[6]

Alan Thompson's book *The Anatomy of Drama* sums up the reasons that human beings respond to incongruous and ludicrous situations that are shadowed with potentially tragic consequences. Comedy, he states, is possible only when people responding with laughter see no threat from the object of their laughter. In this moment of enjoyment the individual is

[5]Henri Bergson, "Laughter: An Essay on the Meaning of the Comic," in *Comedy*, ed. by Wylie Sypher (New York, 1956), pp. 61ff.

[6]Suzanne Langer, "The Comic Rhythm," in *Comedy: Meaning and Form*, ed. by Robert Corrigan (San Francisco, 1965), pp. 120-121.

The kidney transplant is a triumphant success in The National Health *at the Guthrie Theatre, Minneapolis-St. Paul. Directed by Peter Nichols; artistic direction by Michael Langham; sets and costumes by Sam Kirkpatrick; lighting design by Duane Schuler.*

the superior being, the being who realizes that the situation as it exists is neither hopeless nor dangerous. Therefore, laughter occurs. "We cry because the disparity is unthinkable, and we laugh because there is no other thing we can do about it."[7]

[7]Alan Reynolds Thompson, *The Anatomy of Drama* (Berkeley, California, 1964), p. 209.

Incongruity may also be accomplished in the drama by setting up in the audience an internal expectation, which is to say a false or theatrical norm. For example, four performers are hidden behind some kind of object. Three of them pop up into view in timed succession—one, two, three—thereby setting up an expectation in the audience. Therefore, when the fourth appears out of sequence, after a pause, and does not exactly pop up but slowly elevates his head just to that point where he can see over the object, the audience expectation prepared by the scene is defeated; the norm established by the first three is broken, and laughter is the result.

And such false norms can also be used for comic purposes. When a horse answers back, it defeats a justified expectation and moves the work into the realm of comic fantasy. However, when a beautiful woman speaks up, and her voice is high and squeaky or a deep rasping bass, incongruity is the result because her voice does not conform to our expectations based on her physical appearance, even though there is no existing norm to indicate that all beautiful women have beautiful voices. The same result could be achieved by having a handsome, well-muscled, masculine-appearing man speak in a high, effeminate voice. Again, as in a recent television commercial, when a well-dressed, obviously sophisticated woman attending a concert of chamber music looks up and informs everyone within hearing that her "girdle is killing her," incongruity—and thus comedy—is the result.

Surprise

The comic element of surprise is closely related to incongruity. Incongruity is based on inappropriate occurrences; surprise is the next step beyond those occurrences. That is to say, the outcome of the incongruous situation surprises us, and laughter is the result. In *Tragedy and Comedy*, Walter Kerr tells of a situation from a recent cartoon. Two men, starved and bearded, sit in chains at the base of a towering room. Thirty feet above them is a barred window that is too small for either man to pass through. There is nothing else in the chamber. One of the gaunt men is saying to the other, "Now here's my plan. . . ."[8] The men have hope and faith, even though it is evident that they cannot escape, and the cartoon ridicules that hope. The incongruity of the situation, and thus its humor, is the attitude of the men in view of the norm or reality established by their situation. It is incongruous that they could even think about escape. The element of surprise would occur if the men actually did escape. Surprise, therefore, is accomplished when the audience's legitimate expectations are defeated and the incongruous is accomplished.

In a sense, surprise is always a spin-off of incongruity. The beautiful woman who speaks in the high squeaky voice is incongruous. If, now, the lines she speaks are something like a Shakespearean sonnet we have added the element of surprise. We expected something beautiful from her,

[8]Kerr, *Op.cit.*, p. 145.

The Mayor seeks to bribe the "Inspector's" servant in this production of Gogol's The Inspector General. *California State University, Fullerton. Directed by Edwin Duerr.*

corresponding to her physical appearance, and then we hear the incongruous voice. We are then surprised because in the lines she speaks we get the beauty that we expected in the first place but no longer expect.

Surprise is an integral part of the structure of a comic play, which is generally built on incongruous situations. These situations cause the character involved to make attempts to overcome the complications. Surprise is the outcome of the incongruous situation which defeats the expectation and accomplishes the unexpected.

Exaggeration

As a comic device, exaggeration, like incongruity, depends on a norm from which to depart. That is to say, people generally have a common concept of proportion in life. Thus, exaggeration occurs whenever this generally accepted norm is broken, when some aspect of life is enlarged beyond the boundaries of the norm. Using the technique of exaggeration, comedy enlarges humanity's follies, its inconsistencies, its capitulation to its desires, and its foolishness, thus allowing the audience to bring these flaws

A modern-dress version of Scapino!, *featuring John Christopher Jones in the lead role. Adapted by Frank Dunlop and Jim Dale from Moliere's comedy* Les Fourberies de Scapin. *At the Studio Arena Theatre, Buffalo, New York. Directed by Grover Dale; scenery and costumes by Frank J. Boros; lighting design by David Zierk.*

into focus, to concentrate on them and examine them. As Lane Cooper has pointed out, "Take us to witness a comic drama where universal inequalities of wealth and poverty, the accidents of distribution, are still further exaggerated on the stage, and become ludicrous to all. As the play advances, we begin to see the law of proportion in a clearer light."[9]

This technique forms a large part of the basis for the comedy of all ages and types. In Moliere's comedies, for example, certain aspects of behavior are exaggerated to achieve comic results. Thus, in his *Tartuffe* (1664) we see Orgon's extreme credulity and naivete in accepting the protestations of the conniving Tartuffe, who, while professing an extreme dedication to Christian ideals, is in fact the ultimate confidence man seeking to cheat Orgon

[9]Lane Cooper, *An Aristotelian Theory of Comedy* (New York, 1922), p. 68.

out of his money, his house, and even his wife. Many contemporary plays also use exaggeration as a primary comic device. In Neil Simon's *The Odd Couple*, for example, the fussy tidiness of Felix and the sloppiness of Oscar are carried to exaggerated lengths to achieve comic result.

Repetition

Repetition, as a comic device, works both physically and verbally. In the physical sense, the repetition of a comic, perhaps incongruous incident can be highly effective. For example, imagine the first act of a comedy in which, during the height of the action, a small man carrying a potted palm appears and silently walks across the stage. This is comic because it is incongruous; it has no relationship to what is happening in the scene being played. A bit later he appears again, carrying a slightly larger potted palm, and again walks across the stage, through the scene, without a word. Later he appears again, and each time he appears the palm has grown larger. Finally, at the end of the play, he staggers across the stage once more, this time barely managing to carry what appears to be a full-grown but still

The Great Magician, *a play in the* commedia dell'arte *tradition, at Carnegie Mellon University. Directed by Lawrence Carra; set design by S. Todd Muffatti.*

potted palm tree. The effect of these repeated appearances, in conjunction with the incongruity of the growing palm tree, is hilarious.

A verbal equivalent of the potted palm occurred on the old Jack Benny radio show, when the word "cinnamon" was mispronounced as "cimmaron," with "cimmaron rolls" the result. This slip of the tongue got a laugh from the studio audience, and Benny, the master comic, playing with this and managing to reinsert the words "cimmaron rolls" into the text of the comedy, built up a repetitive sequence that got more comic as it went along. Thus, a minor slip of the tongue that was only mildly funny became highly comic through repetition, providing Benny with laughs for months after the original slip.

Wisecrack

Much of the verbal humor in twentieth-century American plays, such as the plays of George S. Kaufman, is a special kind often referred to as wisecracking. Joseph Wood Krutch has pointed out that the wisecrack has certain things in common with cynicism. Thus, a wisecrack is

> cynical, it is knowing, it is elliptical, and it is, very often, ironic—a sort of shorthand reference to facts or attitudes calculated to abash or annihilate the victim who stands convicted of a sentimental disregard for what every intelligent person knows. [10]

Although the wisecrack is cynical, knowing, elliptical, and ironic, it encompasses all of these elements in a special way. First of all, the wisecrack is based on the circumstances of the moment, not necessarily on any experience from the past. Secondly, the wisecrack manifests, through vocabulary and syntax, the true character of the user. A wisecrack could be defined as the rewording of a standard retort in order to magnify the meaning and intent of a normal reply. More often than not, the character delivering such a retort collects all of his defiance and spews it out in one gushing phrase "which takes its point from a suggested analogy or metaphor." [11]

The wisecrack, then, is the character's verbal ammunition, and it is fired quickly at its target. The target, the recipient of the verbal injury, must be unable to effectively rebut the annihilating remark, and so his impotent reaction to the wisecrack provides the comedy. Though frivolous in tone, the wisecrack may speak volumes and has been known to issue from the lips of saints. Mahatma Ghandi was asked, "How do you feel about Western civilization?," and innocently exclaimed, "What an excellent idea!"

---

[10]Joseph Wood Krutch, *The American Drama Since 1918* (New York, 1967), pp. 142-44.
[11]*Ibid.*, p. 145.

The Center Theatre Group presented The Importance of Being Earnest *at the Mark Taper Forum, Los Angeles. Featuring Nicholas Hammond and Jean Marsh.*

A Brief History of the Comic Art

Dr. Samuel Johnson, himself one of the great definers, once pointed out that "comedy has been particularly unpropitious to definers." Indeed, not only is comedy difficult to define, the attempt to do so can be dangerous in an aesthetic sense. At the end of Plato's *Symposium* we find Socrates, with an audience including the tragic poet Agathon and the great comic drama-

A scene from The Royal Family *by George S. Kaufman and Edna Ferber. Produced by the McCarter Theatre Company, with Mary Layne, Rosemary Harris, Sam Levene, Eva LeGallienne, Joseph Maher, George Grizzard, and Mary Louise Wilson. Directed by Ellis Rabb.*

tist Aristophanes, attempting to define comedy by insisting that the technique of writing comedy is the same as that used in writing tragedy. The response of both those creative artists to the philosopher's definition is to go promptly to sleep. The image of the great philosopher putting the great comic artist to sleep by trying to define his art is one that should give pause to all subsequent definers.

Comedy

Traditionally, the basic comic form and type is supposed to have been created approximately around 480 B.C. by Epicharmus of Syracuse. It is likely, however, that the basic elements of comedy derive from the phallic choruses and processions that took place at the planting and harvest rituals, and later during the festivals of Dionysus. Comedy means, literally, "song of revelry," and those drunken revels in honor of the god of fertility early impressed on comedy a sexual frankness and a savage ridicule of contemporary characters who were considered to be either absurd or offensive. The plays, generally referred to as Old Comedy, tended to be loose, broad farce, including a great deal of buffoonery and obscenity. The plots were usually satires on important contemporary issues in Athens. In terms of plot and play structure, the most important aspect of Old Comedy was the development of a plot construct that could be called *the happy idea*. The happy idea is conceived by the leading character—usually a character on a somewhat lower order than the leading characters of tragedy—early in the play. The comedy then grows out of the attempts of that character to put the happy idea into effect. The importance of this concept can be understood by looking at such classic contemporary film comedies as *The Man in the White Suit*, where the little man with the big idea attempts to put his idea for indestructible cloth into practice. This concept is the essence of such comedies as Aristophanes' *The Birds*, where two down-at-the-heels gentlemen adventurers conceive the idea of establishing a utopia in the land of the birds, thus precipitating a series of comic adventures.

Old Comedy gradually died out, and by the time of the formation of the Hellenistic states, following the death of Alexander the Great and the disintegration of his empire, New Comedy had succeeded the transitional form known as Middle Comedy and had made itself the primary dramatic form. Essentially, New Comedy was designed to entertain an educated leisure-class audience, and thus it became a comedy of manners with emphasis on the private affairs of Greek citizens of the class that attended the plays. There was a growing realism in terms of both plot and dialogue, and certain stock characters, such as the courtesan, parasite, bold adventurer, loyal slave, conniving slave, boor, foundling, twins, and miser, became quite common. Generally the plots were based on the problems of two young lovers, and there was always a reversal and a recognition scene, ending the play happily—a definition that also quite accurately fits today's situation comedy.

Roman comedy took most of the conventions of Greek New Comedy, added subplots and broad farce, and came up with Rome's greatest contribution to drama. The finest Roman comic writers were Plautus (c. 254-184 B.C.) and Terence (c. 195-159 B.C.). Plautus' plays were mostly free adaptations of Greek New Comedies, with generous elements of broad farce, song and dance, and dramatic irony. The plays of Terence stayed close to their Greek originals, and were more subtle and polished than those of Plautus. Terence contributed the double plot, integration of plot and character, and a graceful, urbane style.

Medieval comedy tended to be of one type, farce, growing out of two

Aristophanes' The Birds *was presented as "theatre for children" at California State University, Northridge. Directed by John Biroc; costumes by Van Thanh Do.*

sources: folk ritual and the church. Folk ritual provided a rough and tumble farcical diet for its audience, with the comic combats of St. George or Robin Hood and the boisterous activities of the hobby horse, which went capering through the crowd, pinching girls and indulging in various forms of amorous horseplay. That such antics originally had a serious

A drawing of a bas relief depicting a scene from Roman comedy. (From Dorpfeld, Griechische Theatre, 1896.)

meaning is undoubted. In the beginning the combat, with its resultant death and resurrection, was almost certainly a method of urging the end of dead winter and the beginning of fruitful summer; and the sexual play of the hobby horse was designed to implement fertility for the cattle, the newly planted crops, and also for the women of the tribe or village. However, such meanings were essentially prehistoric, and by the time such plays were produced during the Middle Ages, the remnants of ritual meaning still clinging to them were few indeed. The folk staged and attended those productions to be entertained by the purely farcical elements.

The other kind of Medieval farce originated in the church, either in the ritual or in some of the attendant ceremonies, such as the Feast of Fools. In the drama that grew out of the liturgy we can find no better example than *The Second Shepherd's Play*, where the sheep-stealing Mak and his equally guilty wife, Gill, share the stage with the representation of the Christ Child. Growing out of the attendant ceremonies are such dramas as *The Farce of Master Pierre Pathelin*, created by students of the lawyers guild to mock the legal profession in the same way that the Feast of Fools mocked the clergy.

The Renaissance inherited the classic mode of Roman comedy, and also developed something that was especially its own. In Italy the *commedia dell'arte*, an improvisational theatre that performed extemporaneously from brief scenarios, had its birth in the streets and became so popular that within one hundred years it was the most popular type of theatre in all Europe, and *commedia* troupes were playing not only in the streets and villages but also in the palaces and great halls of the nobility. The *commedia* specialized in stock characters, many of them growing out of the stock

Theatre: A Contemporary Introduction

The shrewd peasant stands before the "bar of justice" in The Farce of Master Pierre Pathelin. *Translated and directed by Jerry V. Pickering at California State University, Fullerton.*

characters of New Comedy, and the influence of characters such as Arlecchino and Pulcinella can be seen in the fact that their descendants, Harlequin and Punch, are still with us.

In England the great playwright Ben Jonson developed a kind of academic comedy based on the concept of *humor characters*. That concept assumed that in every human body there were four humors that controlled behavior: blood, phlegm, black bile, and yellow bile. When they were in balance, behavior was normal, but when they were out of balance, when a man's body contained an excess of one or another of those humors, then the man would behave oddly or excessively and thus become a fit subject for comedy. While Jonson created this theory, at least as a dramatic device, the plays of most of the great Renaissance dramatists, including Shakespeare, are filled with humor types of characters whose oddities of behavior are exaggerated to the grotesque.

In England during the Renaissance, comedy and tragedy were so generally mixed that some of the traditional distinctions became blurred and the result was the genre called *tragicomedy*. The plays that fully fit within that genre are few, including works by Beaumont and Fletcher, and by

James Shirley. Some works of Shakespeare also exemplify aspects of tragicomedy. The character of Lear is both tragic and comic, and the play itself, though generally referred to as tragedy, has a happy ending, though certainly not a comic one. Lear is punished for his folly—in his grief and destitution he is struck by madness—but out of his madness grows spiritual regeneration and understanding, and it is this understanding that keeps *Lear* closer to Aristotle than most of Shakespeare's tragedies. Sir John Falstaff in *Henry IV* (Parts 1 and 2) is the essence of the tragicomic character. He is "humorous" but is every bit as complex as the traditional tragic hero. He elicits laughter, love, contempt, and even sympathy when, in Part 2, he is deserted and scorned by Hal.

In the same period the French, in contrast, never combined their genres in the way the English did. Racine writes tragedy and Moliere

Jacques Callot's sketch of commedia dell'arte *performers. The simple, outdoor stage of the* commedia *can be seen in the background.*

Theatre: A Contemporary Introduction

Sir John Falstaff (Victor Buono) gives some questionable words of wisdom to Prince Hal (Kristoffer Tabori) in the Center Theatre Group's production of Shakespeare's Henry IV, Part 1, *at the Mark Taper Forum, Los Angeles. Directed by Gordon Davidson.*

writes comedy, and the twain never meet. Moliere's comedy is an interesting combination of *commedia* style, social satire, and comedy of manners. Moliere's earliest training was with a French *commedia* troupe, touring the provinces, and stylistically that early training shows up in all of his plays. Internally, however, Moliere's plays are in most cases intellectual comedies of manners, examining that which is fraudulent or pretentious in society.

In England the comedy of manners developed from the exiled court's exposure to French court drama; and it was also the result of a social situation in which the select court audience, removed from any contact with the real world outside the court, created its own artificial world, reflected in the drama. The English comedy of manners, however, was so delicate and fragile and perfect in its own limited way, that it defined the form for all time. Essentially, the Restoration comedy of manners dealt with the relations of ladies and gentlemen living in a highly sophisticated society where work is nonexistent, money is available (if not always plentiful by their own standards), and the time can be devoted to playing social games. The comedy, then, grows out of violations of the rules governing those games, and out of the witty and polished dialogue. In most cases the games are sexually oriented: attempts of the men to obtain or get rid of a mistress; attempts of the women to obtain or get rid of a lover; attempts of husbands and wives to deceive each other. The period that those dramas spanned in England was short indeed, beginning in the early 1660s and ending soon after the turn of the century. Only a handful of truly distinguished plays were produced.

A reaction against the licentiousness, the immoral situations and generally indecent dialogue, of Restoration comedy set in even before the beginning of the eighteenth century. The result was the birth of sentimental comedy. Drama emphasizing sentiment then dominated the Western theatre for nearly one hundred years, insisting on presenting middle-class heroes and heroines who are totally noble and self-sacrificing, who suffer monumental tribulations, who mouth unimpeachable sentiments, and who evoke tears from the audience rather than smiles or laughter.

Following the takeover of theatre by the purveyors of sentiment, comedy went underground, surfacing only sporadically and briefly. In the last part of the eighteenth century the comedy of manners made a brief reappearance in Oliver Goldsmith's *She Stoops to Conquer* (1773), Richard

Tartuffe attempts to seduce Orgon's wife while her husband hides underneath the table. From Moliere's Tartuffe *at California State University, Fullerton. Directed by Frank Rossi.*

A scene from The Way of the World *at the Stratford Festival, Stratford, Ontario, Canada. Featuring Maggie Smith as Mrs. Millamant and Jeremy Brett as Mr. Mirabell. Directed by Robin Phillips; designed by Daphne Dare; lighting by Gil Wechsler.*

Brinsley Sheridan's *The Rivals* (1775), and *The School for Scandal* (1777). By the end of the nineteenth century, comedy did reappear in the theatres.

In England, whenever the drama forgets how to laugh, one or two Irishmen always seem to turn up to reinstruct the country in the art of dramatic comedy. That applies to Congreve, who was Irish-educated, and Goldsmith and Sheridan, who were Irish-born. At the end of the nineteenth century Oscar Wilde and George Bernard Shaw, both Irish-born, showed up to revitalize comedy. Wilde's contribution was a revival of the comedy of manners, and at least one of his plays, *The Importance of Being Earnest* (1895), has managed to wear well, being constantly revived and twice reworked as a musical. Shaw, on the other hand, was influenced by Ibsen and Chekhov and concentrated primarily on creating an intellectual comedy of ideas. Disregarding the popular conventions of the well-made

A scene from The School for Scandal *produced at the Hilberry Theatre, Wayne State University. Directed by Robert T. Hazzard; scenery by Russell Paquette; costumes by Daniel Thomas Field; lighting by Gary M. Witt.*

Anita Gillette and David Dukes in a scene from Tom Stoppard's Travesties *at the Mark Taper Forum, Los Angeles.*

play, he set out to appeal to the intellect rather than the emotions. He put on the public stage subjects that had in the past been the province of the legal profession, the church, or politics. He wrote of slums, prostitution, munitions manufacturers, landlords, religion, health, and phonics. Ideas rather than actions were the mainsprings of his drama, but they were ideas well seasoned by wit and eloquence, and he had a career of popular and critical successes. In all, including both one-acts and full-length plays, he turned out fifty-three plays in a career spanning nearly fifty-eight years of playwriting. Most of the plays are either comedies or have strong comic aspects.

The turn of the century saw the revival of comedy in all areas of drama and entertainment. Vaudeville and burlesque became major aspects of entertainment, reviving the spirit of farce and opera bouffe. Shaw and Wilde were followed by the philosophical comedy of Luigi Pirandello and the mannered comedy of Noel Coward. Even Eugene O'Neill, a playwright committed to serious drama, wrote the sentimental comedy *Ah, Wilderness!* (1933). The 1930s produced the influential wisecracking comedy of George S. Kaufman and the inimitable antics, on both stage and screen, of the Marx Brothers. The 1930s also saw a continuation of the brilliant screen work of the 1920s by Charlie Chaplin, W. C. Fields, Harold Lloyd, Laurel and Hardy, and Buster Keaton.

Beginning as a major form in the 1930s, and becoming ever more popular following World War II, was the comic genre sometimes called *black* and sometimes *sick*, earlier called *gallows humor* and even, sometimes, tragicomedy or comitragedy. It was hardly a new comic form. *King Lear* has

A scene from Eugene O'Neill's comedy, Ah, Wilderness, *at the Alley Theatre, Houston, Texas. Featuring Harry Townes and Timothy Wayne-Brown. Directed by Beth Sanford; sets and costumes by John Kenny.*

elements of it, and it existed in such other primarily literary forms as the essay, of which Jonathan Swift's "Modest Proposal" is a good example, and the novel, such as Henry Fielding's *Jonathan Wild*. For our time, however, it seemed a new, exciting, and particularly appropriate form, and it has managed to level out the differences between comedy and

A recent theatrical phenomenon has been the one-man show in which a lone actor, usually with a minimum of makeup and props, becomes a character of literary or historic significance. One of the most outstanding of such shows is William Windom's Thurber.

tragedy, so that the two often become either one or indistinguishable. Excellent examples of this genre are such works as Paul Green's *Johnny Johnson* (1936) with music by Kurt Weill and, to turn to film and television, M.A.S.H., which explores the horrors of the Korean conflict.

In addition to what may be termed the mainstream of comic drama, in recent years we have been treated to such special forms as the Theatre of the Absurd, so named by Martin Esslin and consisting of works by such playwrights as Samuel Beckett and Eugène Ionesco. Essentially those works seem existential in nature, akin to Søren Kierkegaard's earlier religious absurdism, and are serious in intent in that they break the boundaries of conventional theatre to deal with such topics as the contemporary failure of communication and the inability of traditional institutions to deal with problems of the modern world.

The knowing purgative laughter that greeted Aristophanic satire is gone, as is the hearty, bawdy laughter at the farcical aspects of life that characterized the Middle Ages. The "toxic mood of cheerfulness" that Sigmund Freud attributed to comedy seems, at least for the time, to be a thing of the past. But the comic spirit is not dead, and comedy, no matter how black, remains with us, a guard against our ego and our pretensions, showing ourselves to us as we really are. In that sense, comedy is one of the most valuable treasures that we possess, and we must cherish and use it, if only so that we can depend on it in times of tribulation to show us what we are not.

four

The
Rise
of
Realism

Tragedy and comedy are the two major types or forms of drama. Realism—
and to a limited degree its derivative, naturalism—is not a type or form,
but rather a mode or style; which is to say that realism may be either comic
or tragic in nature. In recent years, realism has somewhat diminished in
importance, beset by such competing modes as absurdism, Living Theatre,
Open Theatre, and even street and guerrilla theatre. In spite of such
inroads, realism still remains the dominant Western theatrical form. So
realism must be placed in its proper perspective.

Aspects of Realism in Classical Drama

We must look far back for the beginning of what we usually think of as
realism; that is, characters moving about onstage in a realistic manner,
speaking in dialogue that sounds much like ordinary speech, and partici-
pating in situations that are believable in terms of everyday experience.

There were realistic moments in even the Classical Greek drama, a highly stylized theatrical mode. In *The Libation Bearers* of Aeschylus, for example, the old nurse Cilissa, has a long passage in which she natters away about her master, Orestes, when he was a baby. Her musings on babies' bladders and wet diapers are totally realistic, even by today's terms. We must assume, however, that the movements and delivery of the actor playing the role did not match the reality of the lines—they could not, given the costume of the Greek tragic actor. The fact that the Greeks even used what is essentially realistic dialogue becomes important, however, for later periods when the cumbersome Greek costumes disappeared. And Aeschylus was not the only playwright to use such dialogue. Much of the conversation in Euripides, though poetic in basic format, has the ring of realism.

This painting, done about 1506 by an unknown artist in Lower Saxony, depicts a scene from a passion play being performed in a market place. It shows the mocking of Christ, who stands between two characters in oriental costumes. (Altar piece from Braunschweig Cathedral.)

The Middle Ages

The Roman drama—the plays of Plautus, Terence, and Seneca—showed little talent for theatrical realism, or even interest in it, but the Medieval period managed to expand the constricted perimeter of realism a bit. A prime example of continuing realism in England is *The Second Shepherd's Play*, one of the plays from the Wakefield cycle. The first part of the play is a farcical version of the birth of Christ, with a real lamb, stolen from the three shepherds, concealed in a crib in the house of the sheep stealer, Mak, while his wife pretends to be in labor. The second part of the play, however, is an awe-inspiring, reverent re-creation of the real birth of Christ. The first part of the play may be rough farce, but the opening passages in which the three shepherds comment on humanity's earthly woes not only is revolutionary in content but is couched in the language of common experience.

In fifteenth-century France the greatest of all Medieval farces, *The Farce of Master Pierre Pathelin*, uses all the physical buffoonery of farce and combines it with a realistic style of language that manages to come through even though it is written in rhymed couplets. This rare combination manages to create what is probably the sharpest, most devastating satire on the legal profession ever staged.

The English Renaissance

The English Renaissance continued to expand the concept of dramatic realism, especially in the play *Arden of Feversham* (1592), uncertainly attributed to Thomas Kyd. This play deals in a basically realistic manner with the effects of illicit passion and greed on a middle-class English family. In fact, an epilogue to the earliest printed edition insists that the events within the play are an accurate portrayal of an incident in the town of Kent, where a man was "most wickedlye murdered by the meanese of his disloyall and wanton wife." *Arden of Feversham* influenced a number of subsequent plays, such as Thomas Heywood's *A Woman Killed with Kindness* (1603). Capitalizing on the popularity of *Arden's* basic plot, Heywood's play tells of a woman who, because of an affair, is on the verge of murdering her husband. She repents and confesses, and her husband treats her with such kindness that she dies of her guilt feelings. This hardly strikes us as realistic today, but it was an early attempt to deal realistically with a serious domestic problem.

Domestic Tragedy

The popularity and basic content of such plays as *Arden of Feversham* and *A Woman Killed with Kindness* led directly, in 1731, to George Lillo's *The London Merchant, or the History of George Barnwell*. The play was a great

Richard Chamberlain appears as the towering and tortured King in Shakespeare's Richard
II *in the Center Theatre Group's production at the Ahmanson Theatre, Los Angeles.
Directed by Jonathan Miller.*

popular success and spawned a whole generation of imitations, generally
referred to as *domestic tragedy*. While Lillo's play was too high-flown in
language to be called realistic by today's standards, and while the plot was
melodramatic in the extreme, the play dealt with the problems of the rising
new merchant class in a manner that seemed the very height of realism to
early eighteenth-century playgoers who were weaned on a diet of heroic
verse drama and Restoration comedy.

The German Classical Period

Across the channel, following Lillo's lead in domestic tragedy, was Gotthold Ephraim Lessing, one of Germany's leading playwrights and philosophers of the theatre. Lessing's first popular dramatic success was a
German version of the kind of material turned out by the English novelist
Samuel Richardson who wrote *Pamela: Or Virtue Rewarded*. In this vein of

realistic domestic tragedy, Lessing went on to create several more major plays, including *Emilia Galotti* (1772), the plot of which illustrates the melodramatic aspects of what passed for realism in the eighteenth century. A young girl, abducted by a prince while she is on the way to her wedding, feels pangs of lust for the prince. Ashamed of this betrayal by the flesh, when she is finally rescued she asks her father to kill her, to save her honor.

Eighteenth-Century France

At the same time that Lessing was writing in Germany, a new disciple of realism arose in France: Denis Diderot, philosopher and encyclopaedist. Diderot's own realistic play, which he described as a lexicon of family rela-

Beaumarchais' The Marriage of Figaro was a popular and controversial play in its time. In recent years it has most often been staged as the basis of Mozart's opera of the same title. In this production at the University of Montana the setting was designed by William Raoul; costumes by Abigail Arnt.

tionships ("fortune, birth, education, the duties of fathers toward their children, of chidren toward their parents"), was a public failure. Nevertheless it influenced Pierre Augustin Beaumarchais to write a play of the same type. This was Beaumarchais' dramatic debut, and it failed although he stoutly defended the realistic form of drama. In later plays, probably as a result of this early failure, Beaumarchais turned to the creation of farcical satires.

Realism in the Romantic Period

The romantic period of the late eighteenth and early nineteenth centuries made a strong and immediate impression on the stage, though the great plays of the period are now remembered more for their historical importance than as living theatre. In England such great romantic poets as Byron and Shelley wrote plays, though none have stood the test of time and very few were successful even in their own period. In Germany the leading romantic dramatists were Friedrich von Schiller and Johann Wolfgang von Goethe, whose *Faust* is perhaps the monumental romantic work. In France, Victor Hugo led the romantic rebellion, beginning the battle against neo-classicism with his "Preface to *Cromwell*" (1827), and completing his victory

Goethe's Faust, *Part 1, was produced by the University of Illinois at Urbana-Champaign. Directed by Clara Behringer; set design by Don Llewellyn; costumes by Michael Cesario.*

The American Conservatory Theatre's production of Edmund Rostand's Cyrano de Bergerac, *featured J. Steven White and Peter Donat in the title role. Directed by William Ball.*

with the production of *Hernani* (1830), which provoked riots between the supporters and opponents of romanticism when it opened at the *Comédie Française.*

Romantic theatre was hardly realistic by any definition, but it was a necessary explosion that burst the strictures of neoclassicism, thereby allowing the theatre to change, freeing it from the stern rules which had constricted it for so long. Indeed, though romanticism cleared the stage of certain restrictions, it had such a built-in propensity for abuse, for excess, that its history as a *pure* dramatic form is a short one. During its reign it promoted Rousseau's "natural man," who was good because he was a child of nature rather than of civilization and all of its attendant evils. It concentrated on the faraway, the unknown, and the exotic as a method of underlining and embodying the everchanging mystery of life. It celebrated the alienated hero, isolated from humankind, who was good because he stood outside the bounds of society. And all this was done in a high-flown colorful language intended as a verbal equivalent to the subject matter.

By the mid-nineteenth century, theatre had become moribund. It had lost its neoclassical guidelines, and romanticism had provided no new ones of artistic merit. Eugene Scribe and Victorien Sardou had developed the *well-made play* as far as it could go. Basically, this was a standardized drama dealing in stereotyped characters, containing certain predictable situations and dramatic devices, and always ending with the hero victorious and the villain suitably punished.

The romantic period did succeed in putting new types such as peasants, laborers, and prostitutes not simply onstage, for theatre had always included such characters, but stage center, a position they had not previously occupied. Alexandre Dumas *fils*, in his *Camille* (1852), written as a rejection of the artificial standards of the well-made play, made his heroine a courtesan. When the play reached the stage, and the consumptive lady of the evening, Marguerite Gautier, coughed away her life and was reunited at the moment of her death with her only true love, Armand, a whole generation of playgoers wept and a new stereotype character became popular. The prostitute with the "heart of gold" was born, and her daughters are still a staple of realistic drama.

Realism and the Scientific Revolution

The beginning of the scientific revolution and the first strong stirrings of technology and industrialism had a profound effect on the theatre. Emile Zola, the great French naturalistic writer of the late nineteenth century, turned to the burgeoning science as a foundation for art. In the works of Charles Darwin he found evidence that life is a never-ending struggle with the environment. In the experiments of Dr. Claude Bernard on the structure of the nervous system, Zola found justification for his belief that scientific investigation offered the best hope for eventually understanding humankind.

Zola's philosophy, however well expressed, seemed not to work for him, at least in the medium of theatre. In such novels as *Nana* (1880) he was able to capture the spirit of naturalism and to move the novel toward a new form. In playwriting, however, his genius failed him in terms of creating a new or significant theatre piece. *Thérèse Raquin* (1873), his major play, did not establish a new drama. In subject it was close to the traditional domestic tragedy established by *Arden of Feversham*, dealing with an unfaithful wife and her lover, who together kill her husband. Then, like the wife in *A Woman Killed with Kindness*, they are overcome by their guilt and commit suicide. In form, *Thérèse Raquin* also fell short of establishing a new dramatic mode, following traditional structure in telling its traditional story. Zola did manage to avoid the clichés and stereotypes of the well-made play, against which he was reacting, and the dialogue is, indeed, realistic in terms of previous works, but Zola's concept of the primacy of instinct and emotional compulsion fails to show through.

The Development of Naturalism

Though Zola failed in personally creating a new drama, his influence in all areas of the arts promoted the philosophy of naturalism. Though it grew out of realism, and always remained very close to its parent mode, naturalism did take a slightly different course. In a sense it became realism with a philosophical ax to grind, and for this reason it is particularly appropriate to define naturalism before moving on.

Essentially, there are two definitions of naturalism. The first and the simplest is primarily a theatrical definition, a director's definition, that characterizes naturalism as being "heightened" realism. This is a useful rule of thumb for the director in determining how to identify and begin the process of directing a naturalistic play; it provides a way of separating the naturalistic play from the realistic play and it indicates a method for translating those differences to the stage. Such a definition is, however, too simplistic to be of more than minimal value.

The second definition of naturalism is far more complex. Basically it holds that naturalism is a product of social Darwinism. That is to say,

In the 1930s such naturalistic plays as Clifford Odets' Awake and Sing *seemed to speak directly to the problems of the Depression. This photo shows a scene from the McCarter Theatre Company's production featuring Morris Carnovsky. Directed by Kenneth Frankel.*

Darwin's principle of natural selection was applied to the human situation and taken as proof that people, just like the lower animals, are purely a product of their environment. Such beliefs were part of the growing faith in the new and rapidly expanding scientific establishment. People in all areas of endeavor, looking at the experiments of the physiological researchers, decided that science and not art represented the best hope of understanding and thus defining humankind. The mysticism of romanticism, the concept that internally and spiritually the human race was unknowable, disappeared in a welter of scientific discovery.

Differences and Similarities between Realism and Naturalism

Having committed themselves to social Darwinism, the naturalists soon found that they were severely limited in terms of subject matter. Realism, by definition, could deal with people as they in fact existed at any given level of income, education, or sophistication. It is possible to deal realistically with the problems faced by the head of the board of a major corporation, and it is equally possible to deal realistically with the problems of the janitor who cleans out the corporation offices. Both exist in reality, facing real problems that are often quite different but sometimes remarkably similar, and some semblance of either reality can be transferred to the stage.

David C. Jones, William Damkoehler, and Norman Smith in the Trinity Square Repertory Company's production of John Steinbeck's Of Mice and Men. *Directed by Adrian Hall.*

The naturalists, on the other hand, discovered that their philosophy tended to restrict them to one particular group: those in the lower economic orders. If a person were to be shown onstage being molded and shaped by environment, and selected out if proven unable to cope with it, squeezed and pinched and denied freedom of choice by the surrounding social and economic forces at work, then to be believable that person must come from the lower economic orders. Presidents of boards of large corporations, the naturalists believed, had proved that they could cope, and even control their environment. They could make free choices, and were likely to have alternatives, even when caught up in tight situations. Common people, however, people without the necessary economic clout, were denied the possibility of such choices and alternatives.

This, then, is the primary difference between naturalism and realism. In realistic plays the emphasis is placed on all aspects of reality; in naturalistic plays the emphasis is on the molding and shaping effect of the environment. In realistic plays men and women are shown to have at least some freedom of choice; in naturalistic plays choice is nonexistent and all change grows out of the pressure exerted by the environment. In realistic plays the emphasis is first on individuals as they exist, and only secondarily on the environment; in naturalistic plays the emphasis is on the environment and its effect on the individual.

Ibsen, the Father of Modern Realism

Following Zola, and to a degree influenced by his preoccupation with the advancing science, came Henrik Ibsen, the great Norwegian playwright and father of modern realism. Ibsen penetrated the traditional façade on which most previous drama had concentrated, exploring instead the vulgarities, compromises, and deceits that often exist under the cover of middle-class respectability. Unlike Zola, however, Ibsen could not accept the proposition that man is at the mercy of heredity and environment. His characters in every case make choices, often based on misunderstandings, fear, and outmoded social conventions, that impel the tragic consequences. In *Ghosts* (1881), for example, we see Osvald Alving destroyed by hereditary syphilis. The point of *Ghosts*, however, is not Osvald's inability to conquer his own heredity, or even his father's philandering, but rather the destruction of Osvald's mother, Mrs. Alving, because of the choices that she has made throughout her life.

Strindberg Advances Naturalism

At the same time that Ibsen was writing his greatest plays, the Swedish dramatist August Strindberg had embarked on the journey that would take him from the naturalism of *The Father* (1887) to the early expressionism of *A Dream Play* (1901 or 1902), staged in 1907. *The Father*, which deals

A contemporary sketch of Andre Antoine's Théâtre Libre *production of Ibsen's* The Wild Duck. *(From Rudolphe Darzen's* Le Théâtre-Libre Illustré, *Paris, 1890.)*

with the strife that grows out of the marital relationship and the resulting family relationships between children and parents, was written when Strindberg was totally cynical about women, doubtful that he was the father of his own children, and unable to cope with his own metaphysical yearnings. As a result the characters of the play are largely deprived of choices, operating instead on some kind of blind instinct. The play was hailed by the French naturalists, and immediately upon completion it was accepted for production by André Antoine's *Théâtre Libre* in France. The play was, in spite of this, first produced in Denmark, then Sweden, and then Germany, but the French never lost their enthusiasm and Zola himself wrote the preface to the French edition.

Modern Realism Begins

Following Strindberg, just at the turn of the century, a triumvirate of dramatists established modes of realism upon which almost all later work has been based. In England, George Bernard Shaw began his career under the influence of Ibsen, progressed to Chekhovianism, and along the way developed a drama that in a witty and ironic way presents in parable, as Shaw has pointed out, the details of the conflict between human will and environment. While Shaw was creating his parables for modern times, two

Captain Shotover (Max Gulack) and his daughter Lady Utterwood (Barbara Reid McIntyre) in Heartbreak House *by George Bernard Shaw. Asolo State Theatre, Sarasota, Florida.*

Russians, Anton Chekhov and Maxim Gorky, were developing their own distinctive approaches to realistic theatre. The approach taken by Gorky (a pseudonym meaning "bitter") is best exemplified by his play *The Lower Depths* (1902), which portrays with an almost horrifying reality the lives of a few of the characters who haunt Moscow's underworld, huddled together in a damp cellar. The dialogue is realistic but the play comes very close to naturalism in the sense that the characters seem to have arrived at their unfortunate state as a result not of their own ill-advised decisions but of the terrible social conditions of the late Czarist society. While Gorky was investigating the horrors faced by the economically disadvantaged outcasts of society, Anton Chekhov was examining the attrition and waste in the lives of upper-middle-class Russian society, caught between the romantic ideals with which they had been imbued and the numbing realities of life as part of a dying society. His last play, *The Cherry Orchard* (1904), best exemplifies Chekhov's approach to dramatic reality. The dialogue is realistic, the characters represent all aspects of upper-middle-class and aristocratic society, and the situation, in which the decadent descendants of a once vital family lose their ancestral property because they are no longer able to operate on a realistic basis, exemplifies conditions in Russia just one year before the revolution of 1905. The family is brilliantly symbolized by the cherry orchard of the title, which is beautiful when in bloom but no longer serves any practical purpose because the formula for preserving the cherries has been forgotten by the family. Thus, when the sound of a woodsman's ax echoes across the stage at the end of the play, chopping down the orchard, the audience realizes with absolute certainty that an era has come to its end.

Expressionism

Realism, along with naturalism, has remained the dominant theatrical mode of the twentieth century, even in an age of experimentation that has included the Theatre of Cruelty and the Theatre of the Absurd. One other mode that is closely allied to realism should be discussed: expressionism.

As usually applied to drama, expressionism is a movement that began in Germany shortly after the turn of the century and ended as a significant movement in the middle of the 1920s. Its ancestral mentors were such highly subjective dramatists as August Strindberg, whose *Dream Play* set patterns for portraying the subjective internal realities to which the later dramatists would return time after time, and Frank Wedekind, whose plays explored subjects, such as the family and family relationships, that the expressionists would investigate.

The philosophical basis of expressionism, like the basis of naturalism, was found in the scientific revolution. The naturalists, however, went to social Darwinism for their concepts, whereas, the expressionists went to

The Rise of Realism

Sketch of a stage design by Cesar Klein for Georg Kaiser's expressionistic 1923 drama, From Morn to Midnight.

popular Freudianism. The social condition in Germany before World War I was one that seemed stifling and narrow, particularly to young artists. It was a patriarchal society that promoted a repressive, puritanistic lifestyle, with an emphasis on authority that began with the patriarch and ended with the political leaders. Rebelling against this situation, the young playwrights began looking for a method of displaying the seething inner passions that their society repressed, and they found it in popular Freudianism.

Freud had promoted the idea that the internal, subconscious desires of people come to the surface in the dream, and the artists accepted this. Thus, they decided to use the dream form or *dream vision* as a method of concretizing their own internal desires, and the result was to give a special dramatic form to expressionism. Expressionism, the playwrights felt, should deal with internal rather than external reality and should, in fact, be considered realism. Also, just as Freud found the sexual drive to be the primary motivating force for the human animal, and just as Wedekind had concentrated on the hypocrisy of human sexual relationships, so the expressionists concentrated on the sexual aspects of human existence.

After the middle of the 1920s, expressionism came to a dead end. It had produced little drama of lasting value but had contributed ideas and techniques to the traditional theatre that would be used by playwrights on both sides of the Atlantic. Eugene O'Neill experimented with expression-

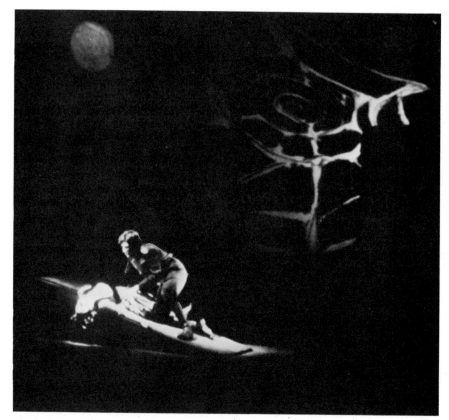

Georg Buchner is often considered one of the fathers of expressionism. The expressionistic elements in his drama Woyzeck *are apparent in this photo of a production presented by California State University, San Francisco. Directed by Ken Margolis; stage design by Larry Cross and Jerry Sutherland; lighting by Darrell F. Winn.*

istic techniques in such dramas as *The Emperor Jones* (1920), but they never became a major aspect of his dramatic style. The same is true of Elmer Rice, whose *The Adding Machine* (1923) is often held up as an example of expressionistic drama.

Finally, the importance of realism as a dramatic mode can be misunderstood and even undervalued if it is looked at merely as an attempt to translate photographic reality to the stage. Naturalism ceases to be important if it is viewed merely as heightened realism or realism that promotes a special philosophical point of view. Instead, realism must be viewed against the mainstream of drama, as a mode that has existed since the days of the Classical Greek playwrights. A mythology for contemporary life, and heroes aplenty, are available for modern audiences of realistic drama, much as they were for the Greeks, the Elizabethans, the neoclassicists, or the romantics. And there will be more to come, for realistic theatre is far from dead.

five

Musical
Theatre

The combination of music and theatre is hardly new; most primitive drama contained music and dance, as did the theatre of Classical Greece. Some of Shakespeare's great plays contain numerous songs, and eighteenth-century French drama made significant use of music. Such forms as opera, operetta, and ballad opera are all combinations of music and theatre, though in opera the music is usually so dominant that to think of it as a truly theatrical form is difficult.

However, in spite of the long history of combined musical and theatrical forms, when we say "musical," or "musical comedy," or more accurately "musical theatre," most of us think of a purely American form of theatre that has been, for at least the last quarter of a century, the most popular theatrical form with general audiences. This has been especially true in the years since 1960. Nine musicals have had original runs of more than a thousand performances, while only three nonmusical plays have achieved this plateau. [1] And the great popularity of stage musicals is further

[1]For much of the information in this chapter I am indebted to David Ewen's *New Complete Book of the American Musical Theatre* (New York, 1970).

Theatre: A Contemporary Introduction

attested to by their success as multimillion dollar film extravaganzas, such as *The Sound of Music* and *My Fair Lady*; and major television productions, such as *Brigadoon* and *Annie Get Your Gun*.

But in spite of this great popularity the musical has regularly suffered from disinterest and even abuse from theatre critics. In most cases this attitude stems from a critical belief that the musical is artistically below the average of most drama. Like opera, this belief goes, musicals make use of the most simple, melodramatic stories merely as excuses for their songs; thus, musicals are, dramatically speaking, mediocre at best. And these songs, the belief goes on, are only slightly above the average of general popular music and, indeed, one or two of the best songs from most musicals usually prove this by becoming brief popular favorites. Even the dance one sees in musicals, according to this concept, is little more than movement designed to be splashy and colorful and popular—certainly not serious as in such artistic forms as modern dance and ballet. Finally, as this line of thought would have it, if you take below-average drama and then combine it with undistinguished music and unartistic dance, the result is pure mediocrity. If all these basic critical assumptions were true, this might be the case, but in many instances one or more of these assumptions is false, and often, even when they are true, the sum is greater than the total of the parts.

To lay such assumptions forever to rest, it must be pointed out that ever since *Showboat* (1927), based on the novel of the same title by Edna Ferber, many musicals have been dramatically sound and sometimes even

A scene from South Pacific *by Rodgers and Hammerstein II. Produced by Central Washington University, Ellensburg, Washington. Directed by Milo L. Smith; musical direction by A. Bert Christianson; sets designed by E. Dee Torrey; costumes by Milo L. Smith.*

A minor musical, but one that has proved to be extremely durable, is Dames at Sea *by George Haimsohn and Robin Miller. This production, by the Manitoba Theatre Centre, Winnipeg, Manitoba, Canada, featured Edda Gburek as Joan and Michael Ricardo as Lucky. Directed by Voigt Kempson; sets and costumes by Robert Doyle; lighting by Bill Williams.*

outstanding. *Showboat* dealt seriously with what was then an almost unheard of theatrical topic: miscegenation. Subsequent shows have dealt with such serious themes as racial prejudice and the eternal battle of good and evil, as *West Side Story* (1957) and *Man of La Mancha* (1965), respectively. In addition, extremely distinguished composers have written for the musical stage. Kurt Weill composed music for *Knickerbocker Holiday* (1938), and Leonard Bernstein composed for *On the Town* (1944). Musical dance, like that choreographed for *Oklahoma* (1943) by the outstanding artist, Agnes De Mille, has also achieved sophisticated artistry.

But ultimately it is not really the excellence of its artists to whom musical theatre owes its immense popularity. Rather, its popularity springs from an indefinable quality imparted by its drama, music, and dance. To understand how this process works we must look at where musical theatre came from, and how it developed.

A Brief History of Musical Theatre

The first musical production in America took place in 1735 in Charleston, South Carolina, when an English-style *ballad opera* entitled *Flora* was performed in a courtroom. While grand opera failed to achieve any real popular success in this country until the late nineteenth century, the ballad opera proved to be a popular, enduring vehicle. Essentially, ballad opera as it developed in England and as it was reproduced in America, consisted of a popular and often topical play, with spoken dialogue and a large number of songs that featured new lyrics set to existing popular tunes. While ballad opera was a far cry from the American musical theatre that would eventually develop, it was one of its ancestors.

Along with ballad opera, another early form of musical theatrical entertainment was *burlesque*. This form, which became popular in the early nineteenth century, was in no way similar to the burlesque that developed during the twentieth century. It contained no women taking off their clothes or comics concentrating on the lewd or vulgar. Instead, early burlesque consisted primarily of musical parodies or satires of well-known plays or entertainments, the most famous of which was probably *La Mosquita* (1838), William Mitchell's satire of the famous Viennese dancer, Fanny Elssler. The great popularity of such burlesques lasted throughout the century and, to a limited degree, lasted into this century, as the caricature and satire of *Hellzapoppin* (1938) proves. Again, this early burlesque was not itself yet musical theatre, but contributed to it.

A third ancestor of musical theatre was the minstrel show, which became popular in mid-nineteenth-century America in the years immediately preceding the Civil War. Essentially, the minstrel show was an entertainment that developed out of the black *patter songs* popularized by a white entertainer, T. D. Rice (1808-1860), who performed in blackface makeup. T. D. Rice was also known as Jim Crow.

At first most minstrel shows were performed by white men with blackened faces, but eventually black performers began to put on their own shows. The format most such shows followed was placing the performers in a semicircle on the stage, along with their banjos, tambourines, one-string fiddles, bones, and spoons. They sang songs, danced, and provided some comic interplay by way of the "end men," Mr. Interlocutor and Mr. Bones, often placed at each end of the semicircle. Between 1840 and 1880, the minstrel show was probably the most popular entertainment form in America, and it lasted well into this century. No longer performed because so many consider it demeaning to blacks, the minstrel show was nevertheless an ancestor of musical theatre.

The combination of elements from these three quite distinct varieties of musical entertainment began just before and after the Civil War when European troupes introduced the *extravaganza*. The first extravaganza was produced in New York in 1857 by a European ballet troupe, the Rozani Company. This particular production was not a rousing success, but the idea of the extravaganza caught on and American versions were soon popular, resulting in the work that is often considered the first example of American musical theatre: *The Black Crook* (1866). In spite of attempts to place *The Black Crook* as America's first musical, it was far more in the tradition of the extravaganza. It did, however, contain such elements as dancing girls in tights, large dance numbers, and spectacular stage effects that would significantly influence such later showmen as Florenz Ziegfeld in his *Follies* and George White in his *Scandals*.

A final influence on American musical theatre was the importation, in the late nineteenth century, of the European *operetta* and *opéras bouffes*. Americans were delighted with the flowery make-believe of mythical Ruritania, created by such composers as Johann Strauss II and Gilbert and Sullivan. The most popular expression of this took place at the Boston Museum, in 1878, when *H.M.S. Pinafore* was presented to enthusiastic crowds.

The uniting of all these various influences into something uniquely American began early in the twentieth century with the works of George M. Cohan (1878-1942), whose musicals were bright, breezy, and full of energy. Cohan had two failures and then, in 1904, his *Little Johnny Jones* ran for fifty-two performances on Broadway before embarking on a successful road trip. Cohan followed this triumph with *Forty-Five Minutes from Broadway* (1906), and the American musical was on its way. Alongside Cohan's musicals were the revues of the early part of the century, including Ziegfeld's *Follies*, White's *Scandals*, and Irving Berlin's *Music Box Revues*.

For several years the revue and musical theatre proceeded to develop along separate lines. The revue remained plush, spectacular, and extravagant. It concentrated on stage effects, costuming, the inclusion of beautiful women, and the presenting of skits, dances, and comedy routines. By the 1920s, however, the *intimate revue* became more and more popular. Without well-known stars or elaborate stage effects, these intimate revues provided caustic wit, satire, and sophistication.

The stage musical took a bit longer than the revue to develop into a serious form, and it was not until the late 1920s and early 1930s that imaginative writers and directors began to create a musical theatre dealing with serious subjects, peopled by real characters, and containing music that was fully integrated into the structure. Also, the satire and sophistication that had come to characterize so many revues were incorporated into the musical, often with exciting results. Leading the way in this movement to turn the musical into a serious art form were Richard Rodgers and Lorenz Hart, Jerome Kern, George and Ira Gershwin, and Oscar Hammerstein.

Any attempt to summarize all the musical productions of the last fifty years, since *Showboat* changed the popular conception of the musical as a light, frivolous entertainment, would be both impossible and excessive. However, certain of these shows deserve mention, not only because they have had great popularity, but also because they have contributed to the development of the musical as a serious, significant, and ever-popular American theatrical form.

In 1931, the wit, the sophistication, and the satire that had been initiated by the intimate revues all coalesced in *Of Thee I Sing*, with book by Morrie Ryskind and George S. Kaufman, lyrics by Ira Gershwin, and music by George Gershwin. This was a musical satire that avoided the conventional romanticism of previous musicals, concentrating its devastating wit on the political situation in Washington, D.C., during the second year of the Depression. Both audiences and critics laughed—but it was also taken seriously and *Of Thee I Sing* made theatrical history by becoming the first musical to win the Pulitzer Prize for drama.

In 1935, *Porgy and Bess* brought new dimension to musical theatre. The work was based on the play *Porgy*, by Dorothy and Dubose Heyward, with lyrics by Dubose Heyward and Ira Gershwin, and music by George Gershwin. Though *Porgy* is clearly an opera, and was so considered by Gershwin and Heyward, it opened on Broadway and not in an opera house. Also, its creators were thoroughly grounded in Broadway musicals and much of *Porgy's* humor, pacing, and style can be traced to popular musical theatre. Always well-liked, *Porgy and Bess* is regularly revived, most recently and successfully in Houston, winning for its producers a 1977 Tony Award.

In the Labor Stage Theatre an amateur political revue was put on by the International Ladies Garment Workers' Union in 1937. Titled *Pins and Needles*, it went on to run for over a thousand performances. The book was by Arthur Arent, Marc Blitzstein, Emanuel Eisenberg, and others, with lyrics and music by Harold Rome. Indebted largely to earlier intimate revues and to the political satire popularized in *Of Thee I Sing*, *Pins and Needles* looked with a "progressive" eye at labor problems, Washington politics, and a steadily worsening international situation. During its long run the show was continually updated with material from current events, and its great success sparked a number of other popular though less significant revues.

By 1938, with the idea that musicals could (and perhaps should) deal with current political affairs, the playwright Maxwell Anderson and composer Kurt Weill collaborated on *Knickerbocker Holiday*. Based loosely on Washington Irving's *Knickerbocker's History of New York*, Anderson attempted to draw a parallel between conditions at the time the play takes place and conditions in 1938. The musical's book is so single-minded in its political propaganda that recent revivals have been successful only because of Weill's score, containing the now famous "September Song."

Musical theatre attained complete maturity with the 1940 production of *Pal Joey*. Written by John O'Hara, and based on his *New Yorker* stories, *Pal Joey* had lyrics by Lorenz Hart and music by Richard Rodgers. The shady character of Joey was new to musical theatre, and the seedy, dishonest characters with which O'Hara surrounded him were rare even for nonmusical plays. The plot, which concerns the rise and fall of a heel named Joey Evans, is relentless in its exposure of life's less attractive aspects, including adultery, blackmail, and a generous portion of lying, cheating, and hypocrisy.

By 1943, the Depression was over and the United States had been in the throes of World War II for two years, which meant that political satire and self-criticism were no longer popular. Perhaps as a result of this change, musical theatre took a new and important direction with the production of *Oklahoma*. Based on Lynn Riggs' folk play, *Green Grow the Lilacs*, with book and lyrics by Oscar Hammerstein II and music by Richard Rodgers, the production broke nearly all the old rules for musicals. There was no attempt to fill the stage with chorus girls and dancers, the music was written with a simple folk flavor, and the traditional dance production numbers were replaced, by Agnes De Mille, with what amounted to folk ballet. The show was the greatest hit, to that time, in the history of the Broadway stage, and given its five-year run, its long road tours, and its numerous revivals, it may well be the single most important musical in the history of the genre.

In December, 1944, with the end of World War II at last in sight, a musical about three sailors on a twenty-four hour shore leave in search of girls made musical theatre history by introducing Leonard Bernstein to Broadway. The musical was *On the Town*, based on the ballet *Fancy Free*, with book and lyrics by Betty Comden and Adolph Green and music, of course, by Bernstein. Perhaps as a result of nearly four years of wartime depression, *On the Town* returned to the purely romantic style of musical theatre, but such music as "New York, New York," and some outstanding choreography by Jerome Robbins won this musical the Page One Award from the Newspaper Guild of New York.

The years after World War II saw many highly successful musicals, most in the romantic tradition that the agonies of war seemed to revive. In 1946, there was *Annie Get Your Gun*, and in 1947 both *Brigadoon* and *Finian's Rainbow* won public acclaim. Then, in 1948, *Kiss Me, Kate* became one of the outstanding successes of musical theatre. The book, by Bella and Samuel Spewack, was not so much based on Shakespeare's *The Taming of the Shrew*; instead, it made use of Shakespeare's play, integrating parts of it, in a "play-within-a-play" technique, into what is essentially a play about modern times. The music, by Cole Porter, contributed three offstage popular hits, and deservedly became Porter's greatest success.

Guys and Dolls (1950) managed to combined the revived romantic tradition with a Runyonesque picture of the special world of Broadway. The book by Jo Swerling and Abe Burrows was based on stories and characters created by Damon Runyon; lyrics and music were provided by Frank Loesser. *Guys and Dolls* has been described by many reputable critics as the perfect musical: no excess scenes and no unnecessary reprising of songs. It received the Tony, the New York Drama Critics Circle, the Donaldson, and the Outer Circle Awards for best musical of the year.

A musical that failed to achieve more than a thousand performances (the bench mark of success after the run of *Oklahoma*) but that managed to make a major mark on the industry, was *Kismet* (1953). First, and most important, *Kismet* re-established the musical spectacular, dead since the 1930s, as a viable box office attraction. Billed as a "musical Arabian night," it was lush, colorful, and extravagant. Secondly, with the book by Charles Lederer and Luther Davis, based on the play of the same name by Edward Knoblock, and with the music adapted by Robert Wright and George

Forrest from the works of Alexander Borodin, *Kismet* proved that two existing works could profitably be combined and popularized. It was a technique that had paid off earlier in *Song of Norway* (1944).

The year 1956 yielded a new musical, *My Fair Lady*, with book and lyrics by Allan Jay Lerner based on George Bernard Shaw's play *Pygmalion*, and music by Frederick Loewe. *My Fair Lady* won almost unprecedented acclaim from audiences and critics alike. It won the Tony, the New York Drama Critics Circle, and the Outer Circle Awards for best musical of the year, and then went on to run for nearly three thousand performances. *My Fair Lady* did little to reshape the musical, but its restrained romance, brilliant, witty dialogue, beautiful music perfectly conceived to fit the continental spirit of 1912, and beautiful costumes and sets, seemed to combine the very best of every aspect of musical theatre.

Flower Drum Song (1958), with its book by Oscar Hammerstein II and Joseph Fields, based on a novel by C. Y. Lee, and music by Richard Rodgers, somewhat failed to live up to the talents of its creators. It was a popular success, running for six hundred performances, and it has a pleasant story dealing with the generation gap between the older Chinese determined to carry on Old World Chinese traditions, and the younger

A nightclub scene from a production of Guys and Dolls *by Bowling Green State University. Directed by Lee Miesle; sets by Briant Hamor Lee; costumes by Mildred D. Lintner.*

Arena style musical theatre has become a popular summer entertainment. This photo depicts a scene from Song of Norway, *produced by the Sacramento Light Opera Association (Music Circus), featuring Alan Stambusky as Maestro Pisone.*

Americanized Chinese trying to assimilate into the culture of their new country. What *Flower Drum Song* did manage to do is take the audience into a world totally foreign to most. American musicals had dealt with strange worlds of myth and fantasy, but Chinatown, a very real world, was both new and strange and in a sense would lead, in only a few years, to the equally strange and unknown world of Tevye in *Fiddler on the Roof*.

Fiddler opened on Broadway at the Imperial Theatre, in 1964, a musical based on stories by Sholom Aleichem, with book by Joseph Stein, lyrics by Sheldon Harnick, and music by Jerry Bock. In its out-of-town tryouts *Fiddler* had given no indication of being more than a modest success, but on Broadway it became, in the jargon of the trade, a blockbuster. Critics and audiences alike loved it, and the play was awarded the Tony and the New York Drama Critics Circle Award for best musical of the year. In a way *Fiddler* followed in the pattern set by *Flower Drum Song* in that it took as its subject what was, for Americans, a strange, unknown, and almost exotic society, set in the midst of an essentially hostile world, and then showed the destruction of this society. In this case the society was that of the Eastern European Jew, and the ultimate destruction of this society, not by assimilation as in *Flower Drum Song*, but through the hos-

Theatre: A Contemporary Introduction

One of the most exciting events in the history of musical theatre was Richard Kiley's performance as Cervantes-Don Quixote in Man of La Mancha.

tility of the surrounding Christian community, gave this musical a textual significance greater than any of its ancestors.

Fiddler was followed, in 1965, by a musical every bit as significant thematically, as popular, and as brilliantly conceived: *Man of La Mancha*. Like *Fiddler*, in its out-of-town tryout *Man of La Mancha* gave indications that it would achieve only a modest success at best. The book, written by Dale Wasserman, was based in part on the novel *Don Quixote* and in part on the life of the novel's author, Miguel Cervantes. This was not the first attempt to stage *Don Quixote*, and even the play-within-the-play format adopted by Wasserman, in which the tale of Don Quixote is recounted by Cervantes, who then takes on the character of Quixote, attracted little interest for its ingenuity. The lyrics by Joe Darion and the music by Mitch Leigh garnered even less attention, as both were relative unknowns in terms of major Broadway productions. However, the rave reviews after the Broadway opening proclaimed the show a masterpiece, and it went on to earn the Tony Award and the New York Drama Critics Award for best musical of the year. It cannot be pretended that *Man of La Mancha* contributed anything new to musical theatre, beyond its individual excellence. However, its affecting story of the mad, gallant knight, and of the eternal conflict between good and evil, makes it truly a musical for all time.

Cabaret, in 1966, finished three successive years of outstanding musical theatre. The book by Joe Masteroff was based on John van Druten's successful play, *I Am A Camera*, which in turn was based on the Berlin stories of Christopher Isherwood. Lyrics were created by Fred Ebb, and the music was composed by John Kander. In its re-creation of the social, moral, and political climate in Germany just before the rise of Hitler, *Cabaret* harkened back not only to the politically oriented drama of the 1930s, but also to Bertolt Brecht's 1928 masterpiece, *The Three-Penny Opera*, which had also satirized this identical period in Germany. *Cabaret* is excellent musical theatre. It is bitter, bittersweet, and candid in its view of the decaying morality that led Germany into the grasp of goose-stepping Nazism. *Cabaret* received the Tony Award and the New York Drama Critics Award for best musical of the year.

After an almost incredible outpouring of great musical theatre in 1964, 1965, and 1966, the output of significant material fell off sharply. However, in 1968, the "American Tribal Love-Rock Musical" titled *Hair* managed to encompass nearly all the splenetic movements of the 1960s. The book and lyrics by Gerome Ragni and James Rado featured no plot, no over-riding theme, and no sequential ordering of events. Instead, *Hair* merely exploded onstage, protesting everything from war to patriotism, racism to American morality, the draft to personal cleanliness. The music by Galt MacDermot was as formless as the plot, placing strong ballads alongside acid rock and several intermediate forms. *Hair* was the only truly successful musical to represent the revolution of the 1960s, and its brash, formless style has so far failed to make a significant impression on its successors.

In 1970, a serious sociological commentary on the married and single states, titled *Company*, won the Drama Critics Award for best musical of the year. The book by George Furth and the lyrics and music by Stephen Sondheim both manage to capture a spirit that is totally urban, upper-middle-class, affluent, and sophisticated, and that is also in a way spiritless, materialistic, and impersonal. It is a musical without the basically romantic costuming and sets that had made such a comeback after World War II. Musically speaking, *Company* was not only unusual but seems to be the first in a pattern that has affected musical theatre from 1970 to the present; that is, it is the first totally successful musical that failed to

Whitney Rydbeck appears as the Emcee in Cabaret. *Directed by Don Henry at California State University, Fullerton.*

produce at least one song that made the popular record charts. Sondheim's score, while musically sophisticated and thus appealing to the musically educated, seems to lack the general popular appeal which, up to this time, had been a hallmark of successful musical theatre.

In this vein, Broadway's 1975 blockbuster, *A Chorus Line*, is one more of a series of musicals with scores lacking hit songs. Conceived, choreographed, and directed by Michael Bennett, with lyrics by Edward Kleban,

Donna McKechnie and Robert LuPone in a scene from A Chorus Line, *the Broadway musical hit created by Michael Bennett. The show won nine Tony Awards and a Pulitzer Prize.*

book by James Kirkwood and Nicholas Dante, and music by Marvin Hamlish, *Chorus Line* is a dancer's musical. Held together by the concept of a choreographer-director auditioning a group of dancers to select eight performers to dance in his new show, the main theme of the show is the relationship of each dancer-artist's personal life to his art. The music, as might be expected from a composer with the talent of Hamlish, is tuneful, gay,

Close to musical theatre is Jesus Christ Superstar, *a rock opera by Andrew Lloyd Webber and Tim Rice. This production was staged at California State University, Northridge. Directed by William Schlosser; sets by Katherine Keleher; costumes by John S. Furman.*

and a perfect medium for the dancers. It is not, however, at all in the popular tradition of pre-1970 musicals.

From the mid-1920s to today the American musical theatre has provided the most popular productions on the stage. It has undergone a number of changes, especially in terms of subject matter and staging, but in most respects it has remained the same; that is, bright, light, tuneful, and full of color and excitement. At the present time, however, musical theatre seems to be entering a new phase, at least in terms of its score. Perhaps this new direction is due to the current division in popular music, with the under thirty group devoted to rock and the older group still fond of the more traditional styles. Or it may merely reflect a growing musical sophistication on the part of the composers currently creating musical scores. In any case, whatever happens there is every reason to believe that musical theatre will continue to be one of the most interesting and exciting dramatic forms.

six

Movements
in
Contemporary
Theatre

Since the end of World War II the theatre has been in a state of constant disorder in both the United States and Europe. Movements, styles, and modes have come and gone with a rapidity that is not only surprising but also a bit frightening. In the United States a world war, the Korean police action, the House Un-American Activities Committee, the Vietnam War, and the civil rights movement have helped create a revolutionary theatre, a theatre of protest, that, while it has not displaced the theatre of tradition, has manged to change the face of traditional theatre in myriad ways, leading to more fluidity of design, greater freedom of expression, and a deep seriousness of subject matter.

Much theatrical fare, particularly in the 1960s, tended to shock or frighten people. Theatre was taking off its clothes, screaming obscenities, questioning traditional wisdom, promoting revolution, and complaining bitterly about bondage to the written word. As a result of such dissatisfactions it became, at least for a period, a highly physical, colorful, action-oriented, visual theatre. In fact, it was an art form in flux, preparing itself

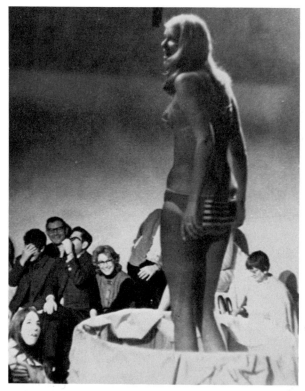

An experimental theatre production of Mary Fornes' Promenade. *The room in which the production took place was arranged in a number of levels. There was no defined seating for the audience, and all the action occurred among the spectators. The acting areas changed nightly, depending on how each night's audience defined the spatial relationships among themselves.*

to receive new information by casting off the remaining shackles of an earlier Victorianism. The theatre, in this orgiastic upheaval, did manage to free itself in the sense that now, in the 1970s, nothing much is prohibited and all aspects of life are available for theatrical investigation.

But the results of this freedom seem, at least presently and in part, to be negative. Instead of moving forward, or even sideways the theatre, carried on a wave of nostalgia, has begun to look backward, toward a time when we appear to have been cleaner and simpler. Perhaps this investigation of our own roots will be positive. In some ways that seems to be the case, with a developing emphasis on the "word" as the primary theatrical source.

The search is far from over, however, and for this reason any discussion of contemporary theatre movements tends to bog down in generalities and vague speculations on the unknown and, to a large degree, the unknowable. For this reason, the best way to become acquainted with the ever-changing world of contemporary theatre is to look closely at several of the specific movements, groups, and people who have so much influenced its current erratic course.

The Theatre of the Absurd

The Theatre of the Absurd is not truly a dramatic movement, or even a style or type—it is far too eclectic. Instead, it exists as a broadly based concept that stands as a point of departure for all the various movements and groups and "isms" that have become so much a part of the contempo-

A scene from Harold Pinter's The Homecoming, *with Judson Earney as Max and Keith Mills as Sam. Directed by Jerry V. Pickering.*

rary theatrical scene. For this reason a brief discussion of Theatre of the Absurd, or absurdism, is necessary, and must, as is so often the case, begin with one man. In this case the man is Martin Esslin, who first recognized the relationships that existed between the developing theatrical patterns.[1]

In 1938, Esslin was at the point of beginning his theatrical career as a director in Vienna, Austria. He had majored in English and philosophy at the University of Vienna and had attended the Reinhardt (theatrical) Seminar. But, in 1938, the Nazis moved into Vienna, and Esslin departed for England. After a one-year stop in Brussels along the way, he became a script writer and producer for the British Broadcasting Corporation (B.B.C.), writing a large number of radio features on political, social, and literary topics.

Esslin's book *The Theatre of the Absurd* introduced the term "absurd" into the world's theatrical vocabulary and, subsequently, the term became a catch phrase. Esslin believes that theatre, in spite of what some consider to be its eclipse under the shadow of the mass media, has a continuing and growing significance. Theatre is an art form that is more broadly based than, for example, poetry or abstract painting. It is the one art that presents to a mass audience the deeper trends of changing thought, long before such trends reach the public through film, television, or any other of the plastic, creative, or performing arts. Because of his abiding belief in this idea, Esslin has made an attempt to define the theatrical mode called Theatre of the Absurd, in order to present the work of some major playwrights whose plays fall within the general definition of absurdism, and to provide an analysis and explication of their most important works. He has also introduced a number of lesser-known writers who work or in recent times have worked in the same or similar conventions. He presents the absurd trend as a continuation of ancient and highly respectable modes of literature and theatre, combined with new understandings and techniques. His final aim, and probably the most important aspect of Esslin's work, is to explain the significance of absurdism as a legitimate theatrical expression of the present situation of the Western world.

As a dramatic mode, the Theatre of the Absurd is important and significant in that it has produced some of the finest theatrical achievements of our time. That is not to say that the modern theatre *is* Theatre of the Absurd, but rather that Theatre of the Absurd is a very important *aspect* of the modern theatrical scene. Clearly, the rise of this valuable dramatic mode does not wipe out all that has gone before, or invalidate the work of important dramatists past, present, and still to come, who operate through some other means of theatricalism. However, such diverse dramatists as Eugène Ionesco, Harold Pinter, and the Nobel Prize winner Samuel Beckett, all working somewhere within the bounds of this mode, testify to its immediate importance and to the probability of its continuing significance.

[1]Martin Esslin, *The Theatre of the Absurd* (Garden City, New York, 1961).

Gerard A. Larson wrote and directed Jekyll-Hyde 69 *at California State University, Sacramento. Original productions of scripts based on famous gothic novels have become popular during recent years.*

"Absurd" originally meant "out of harmony" in a musical context. In its dictionary definition it is an adjective that means, essentially, "ridiculous, senseless, and untrue, contrary to all reason and common sense." This last is an excellent definition of the word as it is commonly used, but it is not what is meant when we speak of Theatre of the Absurd. Eugène Ionesco's definition of absurdity, from an essay on Kafka, is quoted here because, in a theatrical sense, it appears to be the best one written so far: "Absurd is that which is devoid of purpose—Cut off from his religious, metaphysical, and transcendental roots, man is lost; all his actions become senseless, absurd, useless."[2]

The senseless anguish, the meaninglessness, the essential absurdity of the human condition provides the theme of plays by such absurdist writers as Beckett, Adamov, Ionesco, and Genêt. It is not merely the subject matter, however, that determines a work's essential absurdity. The works of such men as Giradoux, Anouilh, Salacrou, Sartre, and Camus all display a similar recognition of the senselessness of life, with an accompanying loss of humanity, individuality, and purpose, and yet those men are not basically absurdists. Also, the Theatre of the Absurd has never debated or even explicity promoted the view that the human condition is absurd; it merely *presents* the senselessness in terms of verbal and physical theatrical images. This manner, in a sense, illutrates the difference between the philosopher and the poet.

[2]Eugène Ionesco, "Dans les Armes de la Ville," *Cahiers de la Compagnie Madeleine Renaud-Jean-Louis Barrault* (Paris, 1957).

In spite of the similarities they all have in common, the writers of absurdist plays are a singularly diverse lot, and their common concern with the basic absurdity of humankind's estate has led them in often dissimilar directions, to explore quite different themes and aspects of existence. One of the most important of these writers is Samuel Beckett, an Irish expatriate to France whose absurdist plays are among the earliest and best of the genre. In many ways, all of Beckett's works, including his novels, can be seen as an attempt to penetrate what he considers to be the façade of reason that has for so long enslaved Western thought. In one of his novels the character Watt lies in a ditch, trying to determine how many weeks there are in a year, and keeps coming up with the useless and repetitive answer of 52.142857142857142857 etc., illustrating the futility of traditional scientific reasoning. Beckett has also devalued language as a means of communicating ultimate truths, but he is a master of language as an artistic medium. In *Endgame*, a play that exists without traditional characters or plot and is composed of what seems to be, at least on the surface, disconnected dialogue, Beckett shows how it is possible for man to bypass rationality altogether, just as an abstract painting bypasses the surface image of natural objects.

Arthur Adamov, on the other hand, rarely seems concerned with Western rationalism or even with the failures of language as a medium of communication. Instead, he concentrates on finding identity in an irrational world. This places him in close conjunction with the recent existentialists, who have come a long way since Kierkegaard and whose general concerns often seem to be with self-knowledge in an indifferent universe. Thus, Adamov's plays are brilliant statements on the metaphysical anguish that forms the basis of existentialist literature and also are near the heart of Theatre of the Absurd, with the alienated hero, separated from society as ruthlessly as he was separated from his mother at the moment of birth, crying out for self-knowledge.

Eugène Ionesco, perhaps the best known of the absurdists and certainly one of the most popular, sees himself not as the bearer of a new theatrical standard, but as part of a tradition that includes Sophocles, Aeschylus, Shakespeare, von Kleist, and Buchner, because those people have all concerned themselves with the human condition in all of its brutal absurdity. Indeed, Ionesco insists that the *avant-garde* absurdist theatre is not new but merely the rediscovery of submerged parts of the main dramatic tradition.

Jean Genêt, whose works are primarily plays of social protest, sparked by the wrongs, real and imagined, that Genêt himself has suffered, has a strong affinity with the Theatre of the Absurd. In Genêt's plays the traditional ideas of characterization are abandoned in order to produce characters who are symbols of isolation and discontent. Similarly, these characters are not motivated in traditional ways; instead, they operate on a mystical-spiritual basis that has little relationship to logical reality. Also in Genêt's plays, as in the plays of the absurdists, language fails as a means of

From Mark Rose's Victory, Come Out of the Sandpile, *produced by California State University, Sacramento. Directed by Robert Smart.*

communication; scientific facts or logic can be communicated, but when communication is reduced to human emotions and metaphysical concepts, Genêt's characters are unable to reach each other. His plays are also within the absurdist camp in the sense that they are not products of an Aristotelian linear development, with a clear beginning, middle, and end. Instead they display their characters' state of mind or examine the human condition by way of those characters. Finally, Genêt refuses to lecture; the playgoer is simply confronted with the harshness and cruelty of the world and with his own isolation from society.

Finally most students of the field number among the absurdists such outstanding playwrights as Max Frisch, Harold Pinter, and even Edward Albee. In 1961, when Esslin published the work that identified Theatre of the Absurd as a specific dramatic mode, he explained that one of the reasons for a dearth of examples of Theatre of the Absurd in the United States is that the convention of the absurd "springs from a feeling of deep

A scene from Edward Albee's Tiny Alice, *produced by A Contemporary Theatre of Seattle. Note the model house onstage. Directed by Gregory Falls; set design by S. Todd Muffatti.*

disillusionment, the draining away of the sense of meaning and purpose in life, which has been characteristic of countries like France and Britain in the years after the Second World War,"[3] whereas in the United States there had been no corresponding loss of meaning and purpose. Change in the United States since World War II has, however, been vast, a fact that Esslin recognized in a later edition of his book. The events of the 1960s especially have destroyed much of the traditional optimism and self-confidence, and as a result, during the past few years there has been a tremendous surge of literary materials in the absurdist mode.

Assessing the contribution of absurdism to theatre is difficult if only because for nearly two decades it has been a major dramatic movement and has included in some way many of the finest playwrights. It has contributed much to what might be called the mainstream of traditional theatre. Technically it has broken down the barriers imposed by a tradition of insistence on realistic sets and stage effects. Thematically it has helped do away with the absolute adherence to the Aristotelian ideal of plot structure that Western theatre has accepted with few exceptions for more than two thousand years. Finally, however, its greatest contribution has been philosophical in that it has attempted to display dramatically the moral and ethical hole looming at the center of the contemporary universe.

In all of its greatest periods, theatre has had a society united on at least one level. No matter how much individuals might differ, there was always one area of agreement at the center of life that helped create a sense of community; that is to say, there was an accepted theological or metaphysical core at the heart of society which provided certain ultimate answers to humanity's largest problems. Today, with the fragmenting and, indeed, even the discarding of the old metaphysical systems that gave ultimate meaning to life, humankind finds itself bereft and searching for some cosmic truth or concept. In a very real way, absurdism is the expression of this search, and its impetus. It shows human beings as futile, lost, and groping for final truths in a universe that concedes nothing.

The Living Theatre of Julian Beck and Judith Malina

More, perhaps, than any other theatre group in recent times, the group that called itself the Living Theatre has influenced existing theatrical presentation; that is, it has explored new pathways, returned to poetic drama, and made possible new (or in some ways, old) language.[4] In part that is because of the wide-ranging interests and the deep commitment to theatre of its founders, Julian Beck and Judith Malina. Also in part it is because of the energy and determination of the company to survive as an immediate viable theatrical entity. Founded in the late 1940s, the Living Theatre lasted

---

[3]Esslin, *Op. cit.*, p. 225.
[4]The information in this section is based largely on material contained in "Storming the Barricades," a preface by Julian Beck to Kenneth H. Brown's *The Brig* (New York, 1963), pp. 3-35.

Dale Helward in Arthur Kopit's Indians *at the Alley Theatre in Houston, Texas. Directed by Beth Sanford; produced by Nina Vance; set design by William Trotman; costumes by Barbara C. Cox.*

until 1969 as a specific unit, and in a sense it still exists in the activities of the cells into which it has divided.

The Living Theatre became possible when Judith Malina, daughter of an orthodox rabbi who had fled Kiel in 1928, met Julian Beck, son of a middle-class New York Jewish distributor of Volkswagen parts. This meeting in 1943, did not lead to action until 1946, when these two projected a temple for the nurturing of "real" (that is, artistic as opposed to popular) music, poetic dance, painting, and a meaningful theatre that would com-

Movements in Contemporary Theatre

bine all those arts. The founders even composed that requisite of all revolutionary theatre, a manifesto, in which they defined their theatre as a method of encouraging poets to write plays by giving them a stage where such plays could be produced. This emphasis on poetic drama became a constant of the Living Theatre, from its actual birth, in 1946, when they rented a basement which was called the Wooster Stage, until they split up in 1969. The background of this project included the experiences of these two people in the Depression of the 1930s, World War II and the concentration camps, the growing revolutionary movement, and a total commitment to art generally and to theatre as a holy of holies.

The Wooster Stage did not last long. The company was barely into the rehearsal of some Pound-Fenellosa versions of Noh plays when it was closed by the police, who were convinced that it was a front for a brothel. When they wrote Ezra Pound about their closure and the reason given, he responded by wondering how else a serious theatre could manage to

Marat/Sade *by Peter Weiss seemed to combine nearly all the avant garde theatre movements of the 1960s. This scene is from the production by Columbus College. Directed by Dennis Ciesil; designed by Sandra Luker.*

Two minor characters from Hamlet *suddenly find themselves center stage in a play of their own: Tom Stoppard's* Rosencrantz and Guildenstern Are Dead, *at the Guthrie Theatre. Jeff Chandler as Rosencrantz; Mark Lamos as Guildenstern; Susan Dafoe as Gertrude; Christopher Pennock as Hamlet. Directed by Stephen Kanee; designed by John Conklin; lighting by Duane Schuler.*

support itself in New York. From 1948 to 1951, the Living Theatre stage was in the Beck-Malina apartment, where they tried to do poetic drama in a rather structured manner. They eventually did Lorca, Goodman, Rexroth, Stein, Eliot, Auden, and William Carlos Williams, but the internal structure of the poetry itself, perhaps, denied the fluidity of staging that the Living Theatre was to accomplish later.

In 1951, they leased the Cherry Lane Theatre, and their first presentation was a series of short plays by Gertrude Stein, Paul Goodman, Bertolt Brecht, and Garcia Lorca. The first full-length production was another play by Stein. This interest in Stein grew largely out of an early commitment to form. Stein's work attracted Beck-Malina because it was revolutionary in terms of the word; it was part of a revolution that tried to revivify language and, along with this, to purify the basic structure and form of literature by getting rid of the platitudes and clichés and expanding the boundaries of meaning. Stein's plays and librettos try, often painfully, to dredge up metaphysical knowledge in the form of emotional and psychological associations, and in so doing she left almost totally to the director the physical actions that would fit the rhythms of her work.

Technically, during its early period the Living Theatre tried a wide variety of stage effects. For a play by Kenneth Rexroth, they used many types of artifice, such as masks, dances to express inexpressible climaxes, plain costumes all black or white or gold, and sets consisting of large squares of cloth supported by ropes. Another time they tried a symbolic set featuring hearts, livers, and other organs, and achieved a startling scenic effect when the architectural façade representing the civilization of Rome disappeared, leaving the stage bare of all trappings at the moment when one of the play's characters speaks to the audience, reproaching them for not stepping in to halt the bloody action of the play.

In terms of acting, they spoke Rexroth's ponderous ornamented verse in a romantic, musical manner, and Goodman's spare verse in a manner that was strong, hard, and bold. They rehearsed a play by the poet W. H. Auden for over a year, trying through verbal technique and variation to break down the barriers created by the multiple meanings of the verse, searching for a style that would be clear and simple and yet preserve the several levels of the poetry. Racine's *Phèdre* was staged so formally in terms of movement that it was compared to a Japanese ballet, and for other plays they combined various acting styles, from the formal style of a Corneille production to a realistic contemporary style.

Technically it was a period of broad experimentation that never satisfactorily resolved the basic problems inherent in handling verse drama. Ultimately, however, it led directly to the clean, simple, fluid style that characterized so much of the Living Theatre's later work.

Cherry Lane was closed by the fire department, and the company moved into a loft on One Hundredth Street, opening in 1954. After nine major productions, spanning more than five years, the loft was closed by the building department. On July 15, 1959, the company opened the Fourteenth Street Theatre. This theatre lasted until 1963, when they were evicted by the landlord, and the building was occupied by the Internal Revenue Service.

Beck himself has pointed out that the work of the Living Theatre breaks up into three neat periods (to which should be added a fourth) that relate directly to the theatres occupied by the company. At the Cherry Lane they were making their initial statements and experimenting with their direction; at One Hundredth Street they were exploring techniques and learning their craft; at Fourteenth Street they were using what they had learned to break through the traditional limitations of theatre, moving from their early, formalistic notions toward something fluid and adaptable. In 1963, the Fourteenth Street Theatre closed, the Becks were tried for their tax debt and jailed for contempt of court, after which the company set off for the first of several tours of Europe, returning to the United States only to tour. It was on tour in Europe that the fourth phase of their work took form. In such creations as *Antigone*, *Mysteries*, and *Frankenstein* they developed a unitized, flowing style that, in much the same manner as the Medieval drama of hundreds of years before, allowed them to handle time and space in all their dimensions.

In 1969, the Living Theatre split up into cells. Most of those cells have remained active, and Beck and Malina seem to be everywhere, turning up in New Haven one week and in San Francisco on the following week, to demonstrate and discuss the achievements of Living Theatre with convening members of the American Theatre Association. It was a long pull for a small experimental theatre group, and before it split up the Living Theatre had to be one of the most exciting companies in the Western world. To some degree the revolution they sparked is still going on.

The Poor Theatre of Jerzy Grotowski

Jerzy Grotowski, along with Ludwik Flaszen, the group's literary advisor, founded the Polish Laboratory Theatre, formally The Laboratory Theatre of the Institute of Actor's Research, sometime prior to 1959, in Opole, Poland. Grotowski was searching for new truths about theatre, and his followers, few but devoted, willingly involved themselves in a laboratory situation in which the results of each theatrical experiment would be analyzed and codified into a philosophy. It took nearly five years for this early experimentation in acting to be completed and objectified into a program, "Actor Training, 1959-1962," and nearly eight years for the resulting disciplines of the Laboratory to escape from behind the "Iron Curtain" into the rest of Western Europe. Peter Brook, the director of England's Royal Shakespeare Company, invited Grotowski and his group to England in 1967, and the results were far-reaching indeed. The Western world was shocked and amazed to realize that such "radical" ideas could be the result of a small theatre group working in conservative and commu-

Crow (Mark Metcalf) passes his gypsy life onto Hoss (Clyde Burton) in this scene from The Tooth of Crime. *Produced at Stage West, West Springfield, Maine.*

nist Poland. Peter Brook overcame his shock, if not his amazement, praising Grotowski for being unique in the sense that no one since Stanislavski had investigated the nature of acting so completely, with such depth and thoroughness.

Europe and especially the British were not quite ready to accept Brook's accolades about the Laboratory Theatre, and the United States was even less so; therefore, it was a venture that took some courage when, in 1969, Grotowski inevitably crossed the Atlantic to America. Generally speaking, our theatregoing audience was already having difficulty in understanding the philosophies about visceral theatre that were then being explored by Meagan Terry, Sam Shephard, Jean-Claude van Itallie, Maria Irene Fornes, and others. For that reason it was small wonder that the work of this group, which performed only in Polish, was loudly praised by a few Americans and as roundly condemned by a much larger number.

Peter Brook, in his video-taped introduction to a film of the Laboratory production of *Akropolis*, analyzed Grotowski's techniques for American audiences. Brook felt that the barrier of language communication, the actors speaking only in Polish, should present no problems to the viewers, and that the discipline of the performers would form in the audience an understanding of life's rhythms, ever-shifting but under perfect control. The visceral response to these rhythms is communicated almost musically to the audience, in much the same way that jazz communicates, and this leads to a visceral response to and contact with the performers.

The text—that is, the verbally meaningful material delivered in a language that is foreign to most American audiences—is delivered through ritual rhythms and discipline. Grotowski's players commit their extreme acts before witnesses, the audience, and, like a person who commits suicide by jumping from a building after a crowd has gathered, they *need* those witnesses but do not necessarily need to communicate with them. The Polish Laboratory Theatre has little to do with communication in any traditional sense. This concept is, indeed, a radical one in terms of theatrical history, because theatre has always existed to communicate. For the Laboratory, however, the audience does not have to understand technically, or be moved to action, in order to perform the function of witness.

The Laboratory's basic approach to theatre attempts three primary accomplishments: 1) to evolve a definition of that which is quite distinctly the craft of theatre, not of other arts; 2) to provide performers with an acting technique that is based on discipline and frees the body and mind completely; and 3) to arrive at an understanding of the actor-audience relationship.

Grotowski's collection of writings on theatre is titled *Towards a Poor Theatre*, and it is an appropriate title because, according to Grotowski, that is the one thing that theatre can be and film and television cannot: *poor*. Theatre, like the art of acting, must be stripped of all that is not essential to it. There must be no illusionary and exotic lighting effects. With a stationary source of raw light, the actor can work deliberately with shadows and bright spots. There must be no makeup. The actor transforms himself in front of the audience, using only his highly trained body and his craft. With proper muscle control, an actor can create a *facial mask* that is not a trick of makeup. There must be no costuming. Since costume has no autonomous value in itself, it, like everything else in theatre, can be created by the actors who, if they have proper control, can show themselves to be wearing any desired costume, even if they are in fact dressed only in swimsuits. There can be no realistic settings or set pieces. By controlled use of gesture, actors can turn anything or nothing into that which they wish an audience to perceive. There must be no music other than that which the

Harry Hamlin plays the disturbed boy Alan Strang in the American Conservatory Theatre's production of Equus, *at the Geary Theatre, San Francisco. Directed by William Ball.*

actors create. The total performance, in this way, becomes the music of the ensemble, and all sound created by the ensemble is music. These, essentially, are the fundamentals of Grotowski's poor theatre.

The Laboratory approach to acting has been, of course, modified by experimentation through the years, but some generalizations can be made. First, it must be clearly understood that the heart of Grotowski's theatre is the personal and scenic technique of the actor. For Grotowski an actor cannot be taught a technique. The approach must be strictly negative, in which the actor's resistance as an organism to a "psychic process" is eliminated. This process, dubbed by Grotowski the *via negativa*, eradicates the actor's mental, psychological, and physical blocks, so that there is no time lapse between impulse and body reaction.

In Grotowski's system, impulse is reaction, and what the spectator sees is only a series of visible impulses. Through the continuous uninterrupted performance of a set of physically and mentally highly demanding exercises, the actor develops "involuntary" skills; that is, he does not "want to do something" but becomes incapable of not doing it, which is the exact opposite of theatre's traditional "bag of tricks." All of the Laboratory's exercises and the resulting involuntary processes work toward creating a formal articulation and disciplined structuring of a role. Gesture, within these exercises, becomes an uncommon and extremely disciplined *sign*, which is the Laboratory's basic unit of expression. In this sense, technique leads to theory, and not the other way around, as is so often the case. Grotowski's productions do not lead to an audience awareness, but are products of the actor's awareness, which is transmitted through a technique that eliminates all of the traditional blocks.

To mention briefly the third accomplishment of the Laboratory, examination of the actor-audience relationship, it must be pointed out that Grotowski completely eliminates the stage-auditorium physical plant in order to rearrange the theatre. That is done in a manner that enables the creation of an actor-audience relationship that is distinctive and appropriate to each individual production. Frequently caught up in the action of the play, not by choice but through this special physical arrangement, the spectator may find himself in the acting area, where he also begins to play a part in the performance. But he had best understand the "mystery" before taking part in the work. Most Grotowski audiences prefer to remain witnesses. The physical arrangement does not always permit action to take place among the spectators. In one production, Grotowski found it stimulating to seat the audience above the action and behind a high fence, through and over which they could surreptitiously peep at the work taking place.

The roots of Grotowski's theatre obviously lie deeply within such reasonably traditional theatrical approaches as mime, Stanislavski, Noh theatre, Brecht, Artaud, and Indian traditional drama, but it should also be understood that constant experimentation and unification has bred a totally new approach that seems to delve deeper into the basic beliefs of those European and Eastern models through an attempt to logically combine

A scene from South Coast Repertory's production of The House of Blue Leaves *by John Guare. Directed by Martin Benson; scenic design by Susan Tuohy.*

them. Looking backward at sources, however, does not clearly define Grotowski's impact upon today's theatre. Many young companies, experimenting with his exercises, are finding them useful in the development of actor discipline and ensemble unity. It is also interesting to note Grotowski's obvious influence on such older artists as the "new" Jean-Louis Barrault, who, in an interview of several years ago, spoke about the necessity for the actor to free his mind and body completely and to revel in this newfound freedom.

There is, today, a tide of antitheatre (seemingly ebbing) that utlizes some of Grotowski's methods and philosophies. The ultimate success of this new antitheatre movement will, however, be decided not by the needs of its audience but by the talent and discipline exercised by the ensembles in approaching their own individual goals.

Finally, the experimental qualities of Grotowski's productions often tend to obscure the fact that, in terms of the drama it elects to play, the Laboratory leans a bit toward the conservative. It is this last aspect, this marriage of contemporary techniques and approaches to the great works of drama, that makes Grotowski and his Polish Laboratory Theatre so interesting and so important.

The Open Theatre of Joseph Chaikin

In 1963, by way of a series of experimental workshops, Joseph Chaikin initiated a program devoted to exploring new forms in theatre. Since that year the Open Theatre has been one of the most important of the little-theatre groups, testing its theories and practices before semiprivate audiences in small New York and European theatres, until its demise, at the end of the 1967 season. Gradually the Open Theatre began emerging as one of the best and most disciplined experimental companies in the United States. This reputation, besides the company's generally recognized excellence, owed much to the fact that its founder is both a philosopher and a moralist. Overwhelmed by the necessity to explore the fears and frustrations of life outside the theatre, much of Chaikin's work has developed a behavioral bias; for Chaikin it is behavior rather than ideas that provides insight and understanding.

Starting in 1959, Chaikin became one of the principal actors of the Living Theatre company, appearing in plays by Pirandello, Brecht, Gelber, Goodman, and William Carlos Williams. Thus, he learned from experience the demands that such drama can make, not only artistically but in terms of theatrical craftsmanship. Twice he started acting workshops within the Living Theatre company, but the continuing state of emergency attending the Living Theatre's early performances kept students away. Finally, with a group of Nola Chilton's ex-students, Chaikin found the opportunity to

A nightclub scene from The Death of Bessie Smith. *Directed by John Alberts.*

explore innovative acting and staging techniques for nonnaturalistic materials.

Chaikin was definitely the moving force behind the Open Theatre, and it was his own personal popularity that drew the company and held it together. Throughout its existence, however, Chaikin maintained what one might call a diplomatic relation with the company's internal affairs. Disliking personal politics, he avoided direct intervention in the various relations between actors and a workshop leader, or director, or writer. This pattern of nonintervention is important since it shaped philosophically the work of the troupe.

Participation in the workshop was not limited only to actors, for playwrights, critics, and directors also took part. The roster of such participants indicates part of the reason for the company's success, including such people as directors Peter Feldman, Jacques Levy, and Roberta Sklar; writers Megan Terry, Jean-Claude van Itallie, and Michael Smith; and critics Gordon Rogoff and Richard Gilman.

Chaikin knew enough, or had learned enough from his stint with the Living Theatre, to start the theatrical exploratory work from where the Open Theatre actors "already were"—from the Method and from certain variations on the Method worked out by Nola Chilton, who had evolved certain exercises to help actors deal with nonnaturalistic materials. Chilton had used, for example, a principle of physical adjustment as an actor's way-into-character for absurdist plays. Her exercise, called "Weapon People," provided a route of march into nonpsychological characterization by providing the actors with weapon images. This helped the performers to make physical adjustments to pure abstraction, and this physical adjustment principle seems to have led to Chaikin's *sound-and-movement technique*, which was the Open Theatre's basic unit of expression. The technique was a transmission of energy and a passing of kinetic material between two actors who come together and thereby create a dramatic event by inhabiting the same kinetic environment.

In the development of the Open Theatre's postnaturalistic theatre technique, sound-and-movement was the first step toward a series of exercises designed to promote in the actor the principle of seeking the essential physical expression of an emotion or attitude. In other words, the Open Theatre company sought to apply to acting technique the general principle that art is the image, rather than the result, of a process of investigation carried out by its creator. This concept was basic to Chaikin's workshop research throughout the history of the company.

In addition to the exercises and techniques that Chaikin evolved in his workshop, the Open Theatre also borrowed freely from the techniques of other theorists on the art of acting, particularly Viola Spolin, Jerzy Grotowski, and Joseph Schlicter. It became a principle of the workshop that members would teach each other what they had learned elsewhere, and among the first things the company took up were Viola Spolin's theatre games, which Chaikin had encountered in the summer of 1963 while working with the Second City Company in Chicago. The exercises included "Walking in Space," "Touching the Air," "Passing and Receiving," "Molding an Object," "Imaginary Objects," "Machines," "Focus," "Mirror Images," and "Transformation" (a radical change in the circumstances of a given improvisation, made by the actor's own improvising).

The basic strategy of Chaikin's work over the years was to make things visible in action. Thus, the workshop approached theatre not through talking but through doing. Discussion was minimal, and the emphasis was on improvising. By structuring the improvisations, Chaikin was able to structure the inquiry into the subject, and the result was always a scene that emerged from an inquiry conducted in totally theatrical terms. "The Odets Kitchen," for example, was an investigation of the reality behind (or perhaps below) surface behavior. Jean-Claude van Itallie, then a new writer and member of Chaikin's workshop, wrote a short naturalistic scene in which a mother, a father, and a daughter are stuck in their tiny New York apartment on a rainy day. Mother irons, father watches TV, daughter mopes. At first the three actors merely performed the script as written, labeled "the outside." Then they began to explore the internal aspects of these characters through improvisation. Since these improvisations made use of the actors' intuitions it tapped their own internal reactions and processes and made available material that is difficult to reach by rational pathways. In the "outside" production of the script, Mother Odets might express satisfaction at finally getting the ironing done. This expression of relieved satisfaction did not necessarily take place, however, in the "inside" improvisation, where the actress might display pain, as a burn from the hot iron, or intense frustration, as from the monotony of ironing.

The Open Theatre, urged on by several of its supporters, rented the Sheridan Square Theatre for two performances in December, 1963, and the Martinique Theatre for two performances the following April. The program for the performances contained the following explanation of the group and its purpose:

> What you will see tonight is a phase of work of the Open Theatre. This group of actors, musicians, playwrights, and directors have come together out of a dissatisfaction with the established trend of the contemporary theatre. It is seeking a theatre for today. It is now exploring certain specific aspects of the stage not as a production group, but as a group trying to find its own voice. Statable tenets of this workshop: (1) to create a situation in which the actors can play together with a sensitivity to one another required of an ensemble, (2) to explore the specific powers that only the live theatre possesses, (3) to concentrate on a theatre of abstraction and illusion (as opposed to a theatre of behavioral or psychological motivation), (4) to discover ways in which the artist can find his expression without money as the determining factor.

For the season of 1965-1966, Ellen Stewart (whose theatre was Cafe La MaMa) arranged for the troupe to appear at her theatre during one week of each month. As a result of her interest the Open Theatre was able to present its first full-length play developed improvisationally by a writer working with the troupe. *Viet Rock* was the first work to harness the frenetic energy of the early improvisations, and came directly out of the workshop that Megan Terry ran on Saturdays from 1965 to 1966.

The Alley Theatre in Houston presented Jacques Brel Is Alive and Well and Living in Paris, *featuring J. T. Cromwell, Judy Rice, Denise Le Brun, and Art Yelton.*

During the winter and spring of 1967, the Open Theatre came slowly to a stop, in large part because Chaikin felt the time had come to change direction—to explore America's internal problems of war, civil rights, and student dissension—and so the workshop closed at the end of the season.

The Joyous Theatre of Peter Brook

Peter Brook, born in London in 1925 and educated at Magdalen College, Oxford, where he founded the Oxford University Film Society, has staged plays at the Birmingham Repertory Theatre, at Stratford-on-Avon, in London, in New York, and on the Continent. Since 1962, he has been a director of the Royal Shakespeare Company. American audiences have had the opportunity to see his productions during several tours.

In his book on dramatic art, *The Empty Space*,[6] Brook divides the whole of theatre into four groupings: the Deadly, the Holy, the Rough, and the Immediate. Deadly theatre, by Brook's definition, is the type seen most commonly, linked to the critically and artistically despised commercial theatre. Brook feels that theatre is declining all over the world (a highly

[6]Peter Brook, *The Empty Space* (New York, 1968).

Brecht's savage examination of the rise of Adolph Hitler, less than subtly disguised as a Chicago crime lord, is titled The Resistable Rise of Arturo Ui. *Produced at The Actor's Theatre of Louisville, Kentucky, featuring Andrew Davis as Arturo Ui.*

questionable judgment), mainly because theatre not only fails to elevate or instruct, it hardly even entertains. He compares today's Deadly Theatre to a jaded prostitute, and the theatre-going public to a customer who must pay far too much for too little pleasure.

> *The Deadly Theatre finds its deadly way into grand opera and tragedy, into the plays of Moliere and the plays of Brecht. Of course nowhere does the Deadly Theatre install itself so securely, so comfortably and so slyly as in the works of William Shakespeare.* [7]

The Deadly Theatre approaches the classics with a set formula as to how they should be done, and this formula is essentially a repetition of the same style that has been badly used for decades. In fact, "style" is the one word that for Brook best describes the Deadly Theatre, since the Deadly Theatre has none. Such theatre may be avoided only by separating the eternal truths from the traditional and often superficial variations. The Deadly Theatre is not, however, *dead* theatre; it is alive and thriving all over the world, season after ongoing season. With this type of theatre, the basic question as to why theatre exists is never asked. If it were asked, even though it is rhetorical and basically unanswerable, Deadly Theatre would at long last die.

[7]Brook, *Ibid.*, p. 10.

The Holy Theatre has been defined by Brook as being, essentially, the invisible-made-visible. This definition or concept grows out of the notion that the stage is a place where the invisible can appear, made tangible through theatre's ability to penetrate surfaces and probe the realities that are hidden beneath. The Holy Theatre satisfies people's hunger for something beyond their daily existence, and it is this "something" that acts as a buffer against the often painful reality that exists outside the theatrical situation.

In the Holy Theatre the ceremony comes first, followed by the structure that provides the dramatic framework which supports and contains the ceremony. For Brook this ceremony should be an ever-changing ritual that feeds our lives. Today, he feels, the theatre is just a watered down imitation of old rituals that were once highly meaningful but have lost their significance in the toils of time. The Holy Theatre cannot consist of forgotten, meaningless ritual; it must be immediate, springing from people's spirits and souls as they celebrate some aspect of life. The prophet for the Holy Theatre, Brook feels, was Antonin Artaud, who railed against the sterile theatre, promoting in its place a theatre that would work like the plague (by infection), by analogy, by magic; a theatre in which the play, the event itself, stands in place of the text. Brook also calls on Jerzy Grotowski in support of his search for Holy Theatre. He sees Grotowski as a visionary who believes that theatre cannot be an end in itself; who sees theatre as a vehicle, a means of self-study, and as the potential salvation of humankind. The leaders of world theatre must be made to realize that for theatre to survive a Holy Theatre must be achieved.

The Rough Theatre, for Brook, is the kind of theatre that is closest to the people. The Rough Theatre can function without style, since style can exist only if one has leisure to develop it, and the Rough Theatre is too immediate for leisure. Such theatre is an almost depressingly proletarian art form in which, for Brook, dirt provides its roughness and its edge; where filth and vulgarity are natural and obscenity is joyous. In this theatre the spectacle becomes socially liberating in the sense that by its very nature a theatre of the people is antiauthoritarian, antitraditional, antipomp, and antipretense. It is a theatre of noise and boisterous action. One of the few director-creators who achieved a Rough Theatre, according to Brook, was Vsevelod Meyerhold, the Russian genius whose theatre had the highest of aims: to return theatre to its original state.

Despite his wish not to look backward, Brook finds that the Elizabethan theatre is the most perfect example of the Rough and the Holy Theatres joining together to create a statement. His thesis seems to be that we must find a way to move forward, which will lead us back to Shakespeare, since Shakespeare most perfectly combined the squalor of the ages with deep and metaphysical themes.

Under the catch title "The Immediate Theatre," Brook relates what is essentially his theatrical autobiography, the most important aspect of which is his belief that today's theatre, unlike the theatre of the nineteenth century, cannot attach itself to any one particular style. Today the world is

Walter Rhodes as McKyle and Frederick Sperberg as the 14th Earl of Gurney in the Asolo State Theatre's production of The Ruling Class *by Peter Barnes.*

moving at an ever-changing pace, and in all directions: backward, forward, and sideways. And this movement can be basically good, not destructive, and it is not merely restlessness or fashion. At certain moments, as a result of fortunate decisions and honest effort, all comes together and the Theatre of Joy emerges, a theatre which combines the Rough Theatre and the Holy Theatre. But once that moment is gone it cannot be recaptured by slavish imitation, which will only allow the Deadly Theatre to creep back in. Instead, the search must begin anew for the fun of theatre, and when that is found the Theatre of Joy will again emerge.

The theatrical experimentation of the past two decades is far from over, even though several of the most important experimental companies have disbanded. In almost every significant population center—which is to say, any city with a population capable of providing an audience—one or more little-theatre groups are wrestling with concepts of what theatre is and what it should be. In the Black ghettoes an experimental form of consciousness-raising theatre is taking place, and in the California vine-

Movements in Contemporary Theatre

Los Endrogados, *a play by Luis Valdez, performed by* El Teatro Espiritu de Aztlan. *Directed by Caesar Flores.*

yards the Chicano theatres, using all sorts of experimental techniques to make their point, are urging the field hands into a unified stand against whoever or whatever is currently deemed to be the oppressor.

Such theatrical experiments are not always (or perhaps even rarely) successful as art, but they are full of energy and commitment and will have their effect on the traditional theatre. What that effect will be is uncertain, but it will be exciting to watch.

seven

The Physical Theatre

Today, in terms of theatre architecture (primarily the shape and size of the stage and its arrangement in relationship to the audience) we have more variety than at any other time in theatrical history. Arena stages, referred to as *theatre-in-the-round*, can be found not only in year-round operation but especially in such summer-stock situations as California's Sacramento Music Circus. Elizabethan-style thrust stages can be found in generally accurate historic re-creations at such theatres as San Diego's Old Globe, or in a more contemporary form at theatres similar to the Tyrone Guthrie Theatre in Minneapolis. *Proscenium-arch* stages are common, in various sizes and shapes, with and without aprons or forestages. There are also historically accurate re-creations of the traditional Classical Greek stage, such as the Hearst Greek Theatres in Los Angeles and Berkeley, California. In addition, the past twenty years have seen such experimental theatrical forms as stadium staging, with the audience seated in opposing banks of seats, much like spectators at a football game, and the action taking place between them and at each end of the "stadium"; pincer or caliper staging, which usually extends narrow playing areas out on either side of the conventional proscenium-arch stage; Medieval-style mansion staging, where the action moves back and forth along a line from mansion to mansion area; and even perimeter staging, where the audience is seated in the center and the action moves about the perimeter of the auditorium, sometimes taking place simultaneously at several different points on the playing area.

Perhaps the most interesting aspect of all these various types of stages is that no individual form is entirely original in this century. All are either re-creations or adaptations of forms that often date back thousands of years. Thus, an understanding of the history of the physical stage can aid us today in making the best possible use of our existing facilities, and can also be of value in developing our own original contributions to the physical stage.

The Greek Stage

The earliest ancestor of the Classical Greek theatre was almost certainly a circular area of hard-packed dirt, probably a threshing floor with a low thick post in the center to which teams of oxen were hitched and driven about in a circle to tramp out the grain. When this threshing floor was doing duty as a theatrical area, the audience stood grouped about the circumference of the circle, in the same manner that people of any time and

A drawing of the Greek theatre at Priene as it existed circa 150 B.C. This represents the Hellenistic period of the theatre in which the orchestra was reduced and joined to the scene house, with the actors performing primarily on an elevated stage above the lower level of the scene house. (From Armin von Gerkan, Das Theatre von Priene, *Munich, Germany, 1921.)*

place have tended to gather to watch an event. In time this circular area grew into the most prominent aspect of the sophisticated Classical Greek theatre: the *orchestra* or dancing place.

As the plays grew longer and more complex, and as the crowds grew larger and the threshing floor could no longer accommodate them, an orchestra was laid out at the foot of a hill, where the audience could see and hear better, and an altar or *thymele* took the place of the central hitching post. At first wooden benches were set up on the hillside for seating, but eventually the slope was graded and in many cases seats were cut into the hillside itself and faced with stone flags, which provided permanent (if slightly uncomfortable) seats for the ever-growing audience.

At some time prior to 458 B.C., a scene house, or *skene* was built behind the orchestra. The word "skene" translates as hut or tent, which seems to indicate that in the beginning this scene house must have been a reasonably flimsy, temporary structure, designed primarily as a changing house. Soon, however, it grew into a rather impressive edifice. The *proscenium* was the façade of the skene, and its architectural embellishment probably provided most of the scenery for the plays, especially before the middle of the fifth century. The plays of that period, as far as can be determined, all seem to have taken place before a palace or temple, so the architecture of the skene would be appropriate. The roof of the skene contained an acting area of its own, the *theologeion*, from which the gods and heroes could speak, from which the Watchman of Aeschylus' play *Agamemnon* could address the audience, and from which Medea in Euripides' play could seem to be escaping from vengeance in her dragon-drawn chariot.

The skene contained two major mechanical devices: the *machine* and the *eccyclema*. The machine was a crane, anchored to the top of the scene building, whose purpose was to raise and lower flying figures in chariots or on the backs of birds and flying animals, and to introduce and remove gods. The *deus ex machina*, "god from the machine," was a device apparently popular with many playwrights, especially with Euripides, which allowed the writers the luxury of a miraculous conclusion for their plays. The god appeared on high, suspended from the machine, and resolved all the problems that the playwright had created. The eccyclema was a movable wheeled vehicle or platform that, at its most sophisticated, ran on tracks much like a modern railway car. It rolled out from behind the scenes with the actors mounted on it to depict, in tableau, events that happened offstage or before the action began.

The skene was flanked, on either side, by *parascenia*, which were forward-projecting wings somewhat resembling the wings of contemporary theatre. Between the parascenia and the *theatron* (auditorium) were long passageways, *paradoi*, used for entrances and exits of the chorus, entrances and exits of wheeled vehicles, such as chariots, and, before and after the productions, the entrance and exit of the audience. In front of the skene was a low stage of some sort: the *logeion*. There is little agreement as to its size, although it presumably ran the full length of the scene building

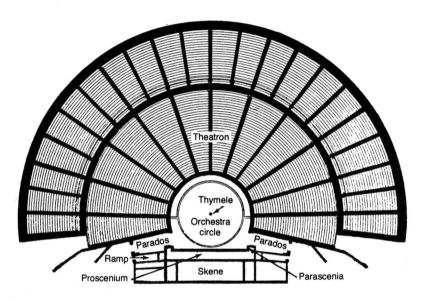

The Greek theatre at Epidaurus showing the symmetrical seating and the full orchestra of the Classical period. (Based on material in Dörpfeld and Reich, Das Griechishe Theatre.*)*

and was shallow enough not to encroach upon the orchestra. Neither is there any real evidence as to its height, though it was probably rather low, only high enough to elevate the actors 3 or 4 feet above the level of the orchestra. There is also no way of ascertaining when this stage was added to the original building, and some scholars believe this stage area to have been little more than a set of broad steps leading up to the central door of the skene.

The most important Greek theatre during the fifth century B.C., the great period of drama, was the Theatre of Dionysus at Athens, and the development described above closely follows what must have been the development of that specific theatre, with the hillside slope being the Acropolis itself. Probably the most impressive aspect of that great theatre was its seating capacity. Fourteen to seventeen thousand people could be accommodated in the theatron, or seeing place, and some scholars have raised that estimate to as high as twenty thousand.

Certainly one of the most interesting aspects of the Greek theatre was the relationship it established between the actors and the audience. The audience rimmed the action on three sides, while the skene provided a kind of backdrop through which players could enter and exit, and which could contain, though unseen by the audience, a part of the action. This forms a pattern that we will see repeated, though usually on a smaller scale, throughout the history of physical theatre.

The Roman Stage

The first permanent theatre in Rome was erected by Pompey in 55 B.C. During all of its early period, Rome had an antitheatre faction, and there is a story that Pompey, to get his theatre constructed, had to pretend that it was a temple to Venus Victrix and that the seats were merely steps leading up to a small devotional area mounted behind the last row of the auditorium. Such a pretense would be exceedingly thin, and the story is probably apocryphal, but in any case Pompey's theatre broke the ice and eventually there were nearly 125 permanent theatres throughout the Empire. The date of Pompey's theatre, however, places it nearly two hundred years after the beginning of serious Roman drama, and more than one hundred years after the date of the last surviving comedy. These facts mean that the major Roman theatres were all built after what seems to have been Rome's greatest dramatic period. Of the tragedies written in Rome, only those of Seneca survive, and they were written after the first permanent theatres were constructed. As far as can be determined, Seneca was the last of the significant Roman dramatists.

During the two hundred years of drama that preceded Pompey's theatre, a number of temporary theatres were built, none of which survive, and the information we have on their shape and size is extremely limited. Most scholars, attempting to reconstruct them, seem merely to come up with temporary wooden versions of the later stone theatres. That may not be far from the truth, however, for we have no reason to believe that when the Romans finally agreed to the construction of permanent theatres they felt any need to depart from a basic design that had served them well for nearly two centuries.

In any case, the Roman theatres that have survived are clearly modifications of the Greek theatres of the Hellenistic period, and, generally speaking, they follow a rather specific pattern. Unlike their Greek ancestors, the Roman theatres were often free-standing structures that stood on level ground rather than being cut into a hillside. In some cases, when available, a hillside was used, but corridors were cut into the hillside to match the corridors and stairways beneath the auditoriums of the free-standing structures, so that, whether built on level ground or excavated into a hillside, the Roman theatre showed slight variation.

The stage house, or *scaena*, was joined to the auditorium or *cavea* to form a single structural unit. The paradoi of the Hellenistic theatre were roofed over to provide enclosed corridors, or *vomitoria*, that emptied into the orchestra and the *auditorium*. The orchestra was reduced to a perfect semicircle and served a variety of functions: seating dignitaries; flooded for mimic sea battles; and even encircled by a marble balustrade for gladiatorial bouts.

Directly in front of the scaena was the stage, or *pulpitum*, about 5 feet above the level of the orchestra. The front of the stage was laid out along the diameter of the orchestra. In the early theatres a trough at the front of

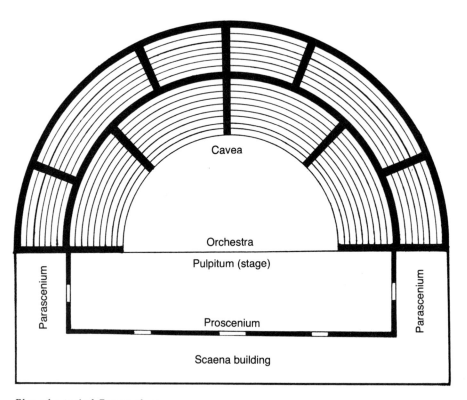

Plan of a typical Roman theatre.

the stage provided a receptacle for the curtain, but in the later stages other means were developed for handling the curtain, or it was done away with entirely. The size of the stage tended to vary in terms of the size of the total structure, but even the smallest of the Roman stages, 100 feet long by 20 feet deep, is quite large compared with contemporary stages, and the large Roman stage, 300 feet by 40 feet, again in comparison with the modern stage, is absolutely gigantic.

The front surface of the stage house, called the *scaenae frons*, was a decorative architectural façade with columns, porticos, and niches that often contained statues. That was also true of the front stage elevation. In the wall of the scaenae frons were three to five doors. In comedies these became the doors of houses opening onto a city street, represented by the stage. In tragedies the scaenae frons represented the exterior of a palace or temple, and the architectural allure was often enhanced by painting or gilding.

Concern for the comfort of the patrons led the Romans to perfect a method for cooling their theatres by blowing air over fountains of cold water. They also managed to provide their audiences with shade by mounting huge movable awnings, tended by sailors, on top of the exterior walls.

The basic pattern of the Roman stage, as it developed, was away from the pattern of its Greek ancestors. In most cases the orchestra was little used, except for gladiatorial bouts and miniature sea battles, and so the audience, instead of watching the action from three sides, looked directly into a stage that in every way except dimension resembled today's procenium-arch theatres.

The Medieval Stage

The earliest Medieval stage, like the earliest Greek stage, was probably little more than a circular area in which the dramatic action took place, with the spectators grouped around the play in the same manner that spectators still group themselves to view an event when audience-performer relationships have not been prestructured in some way. This specific type of staging holds true only for the folk drama, represented in England by the Saint George and Robin Hood plays; the Cornish drama; and perhaps for some of the morality plays. All those forms of drama tended to die out at the end of the Middle Ages, and the arena form of staging had to wait almost five hundred years before it would be revived.

Far more important, in terms of later staging practices, was the *liturgical drama* that began developing in the churches during the ninth and tenth centuries. Liturgical drama originated and flourished in monasteries on the Continent, especially at Limoges and Fleury, in France; Saint Gall, in Switzerland; Richenau, in Germany; and Ripall, in Spain. Along the way these little Latin playlets illustrating some aspect of the liturgy took root all over civilized Europe, and so it comes as no surprise that the earliest extant liturgical play, complete with directions for performance, is found in the *Regularis Concordia* of Saint Ethelwold, Bishop of Winchester in England. Those plays continued within the church for nearly three hundred years, played by the clergy themselves and occasionally making use of such lay participants as choirboys. For sets they made use of the various facets of the interior architecture—nave, altar, high altar, choir loft, stations, etc.—with some occasional use of imported set pieces.

It was not until the dramas moved outside the church in the late twelfth century, however, that significant staging practices got under way. On the Continent, *mansion staging* became highly popular and quite complex. It began in the church, with small mansions representing such special areas as Heaven and Hell and a number of earthly spots in between. Those mansions could not have been large, however, and no production could have used many of them without more open space than most churches could provide. Therefore, removal of the plays from the church and the development of a vernacular drama were necessary to major staging efforts.

The mansions were, in fact, small wood and canvas constructions somewhat like booths at a fair. Generally speaking, they were not large, even in the most extravagant cases, though they were often complex and colorful. The actors, as a result of the limited space inside the mansions, performed primarily on the *platea*, the area in front of and (in a limited sense) on either side of the mansions. The arrangement of the mansions varied. In some cases they were set up in a line—against an exterior church wall or even on the stage of the Hôpital de la Trinité in Paris, where such works were played for more than one hundred years. Heaven and Hell, the two most common mansions, occupied the two end positions when the mansions were set up in a row, with Heaven at stage right and Hell at stage left. In some cases the mansions were set up around the perimeter of an essentially enclosed area, such as an innyard or the town square. In such cases the audience was grouped in the center area and followed the action as it moved from mansion to mansion.

The mansions were colorful, highly decorated, and mechanically quite complex. The *masters of machine*, mechanics responsible for developing the technical effects that were often part of the mansions, were apparently highly skilled craftsmen who achieved results that are impressive even by today's standards. Concealed torches provided imaginative lighting effects, angels "flew" between Heaven and Earth, and the star of Bethlehem, sparkling and shiny, passed over the audience to hang suspended above the manger. Hell was often represented by the head of a monster, belching smoke from a gaping mouth and peopled by devils who issued forth to drag protesting sinners kicking and screaming down to eternal torment.

The Passion Play of Valenciennes (1547) provides a beautiful illustration of Medieval mansion staging. The mansion at stage right is Paradise, featuring God surrounded by angels and saints. At stage left is Hell Mouth, with Satan, his devils, and damned souls. In between are mansions necessary for telling the story of Christ, even including a lake for Peter the Fisherman. (From Gustave Cohen's Le Theatre en France au moyen age, *Paris, France 1928-1931.)*

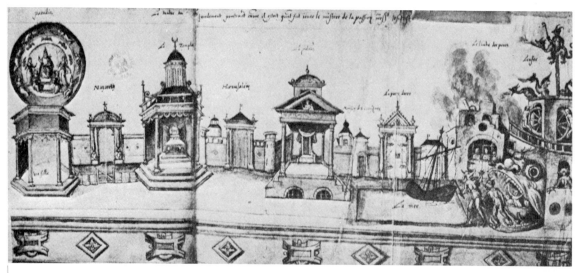

The Physical Theatre

Along with the mansion stages, the Medieval period also saw the development of the *wagon stages*, especially in England and Spain. Unfortunately, no definitive description of English wagon stages has survived. Some of the most persuasive reconstructions argue that the standard pageant wagon was probably a one-story structure with a small loft. In such cases, the wagon served primarily as a background, with the action taking place on the flat bed of a second wagon, several of which were permanently drawn up at specific spots along the route of the procession. Several other conjectures, such as two-story wagons with acting areas on both the upper and lower levels, or single-story wagons with acting areas on the ground in front of the wagon, have received some support. While all those theories have their proponents, it is almost certain that the wagons varied widely in structure, each designed to the requirements of its own special play and then modified over the succeeding years.

Those wagons, to achieve the technical effects dictated by the scripts, must have had a machine loft with some kind of flying equipment, and certainly a trap in the floor to allow trees to sprout up, fountains to gush, and actors to appear and disappear. In addition, some of the wagons must have had a reinforced flat playing area on the roof to allow Deus to appear and speak from on high.

The variety of Medieval stages and stage arrangements was great indeed, but in nearly all cases there was an interesting similarity. The audience and actor relationship was always the same, with a pageant wagon drawn up behind a flat-bed open wagon that acted as a forestage; with a single wagon drawn up by itself, and the players acting both on the

Drawing of a probable arrangement of Medieval English pageant wagon and acting area. (Based on material in Wickham's Early English Stages, *Columbia University Press.)*

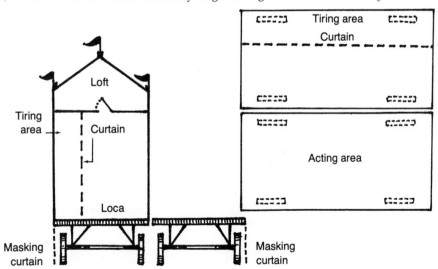

wagon and on the ground before it; or with a mansion that allowed an acting area within the mansion and on the ground directly before it. In each case the audience is grouped along the three sides of the primary playing area, much like a miniature version of the Classic Greek theatre.

The Elizabethan Stage

In the year 1576, the first two permanent theatres in England were opened for business. The first to open, and probably the more important in terms of theatrical history, was called The Theatre, a square building enclosing an unroofed courtyard and stage. This playhouse was designed to present plays for the general public. The second permanent structure was the first Blackfriars Theatre, restructured from rooms in a monastery and designed for a primarily aristocratic audience. Those two types of theatre were generally respectively referred to as *public* and *private*, and because they were substantially different it is necessary to consider them separately.

Generally speaking, the public theatres are considered to have developed out of two primary ancestors. The first and most important ancestor is the innyard, because in many ways the essentially Medieval English inn is quite similar in shape and basic appearance to the Renaissance English playhouse. These inns followed a standard pattern in terms of structure, with rooms grouped about three or four sides of an innyard entered by passing under an arch. Most of the theorists of innyard performance propose a stage with a booth or mansion at the rear (to serve as a stage-house), set up at one end of the yard. Raised bleachers around the perimeter of the yard provided seating, as did windows opening into the innyard. The flat area in front of the stage, that is, the center area of the yard, could accommodate patrons who wished to stand or who could not afford to purchase seats within the inn or on the bleachers. That describes in a surprisingly accurate way the basic structure of the Elizabethan public theatre. The second most likely ancestor, after the innyards, has generally been considered to be the arenas where bull and bear baiting took place. Such influence seems unlikely, however, for maps of London drawn during that period show the arenas as circular structures, fenced in, and without seats or galleries. In terms of the Elizabethan stage area itself, the most likely ancestor seems to be the pageant wagon, probably with a flat-bed wagon drawn up before it to serve as an acting area.

The basic pattern for the English public playhouse was established by James Burbage's theatre, known simply as The Theatre. This pattern was modified and improved in later playhouses, and, by 1599, when the Globe Theatre was built, the theatres had become quite complex, with hidden stage machinery, working lofts, traps, etc.

Essentially, the Elizabethan theatre was a building, either square or hexagonal, with an unroofed central courtyard. In most cases it was three stories high; that is, high enough to contain three levels of galleries for seating patrons. At the far end of the yard, opposite the main entrance,

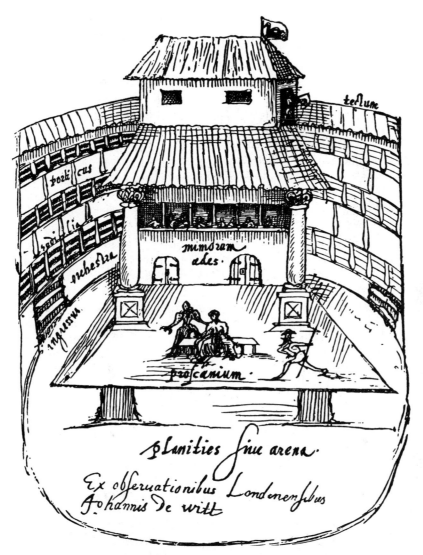

A contemporary drawing of the interior of the Swan Theatre by the Dutch traveler and scholar de Witt. His sketch shows only two doors in the backstage wall, but stage directions for plays at the Globe Theatre clearly indicate a curtained alcove between the two doors. De Witt's sketch also shows a balcony, used by actors, above the stage.

was the stage. Over the back part of the stage, supported by two pillars, was the *shadow*, or *heavens*, a roof that protected the back area of the stage from rain or even direct sunlight, and that provided a loft from which to raise and lower scenery. The size of the stage undoubtedly varied from playhouse to playhouse, and there is no way of ascertaining the exact dimensions in most cases. The building contract for the Fortune Theatre has been preserved, however, and thus we can base our guesses on the solid facts available for at least one of the theatres. The Fortune was 80 feet square on the outside, and the inner courtyard was 55 feet square. This means that there was, in the courtyard surrounding the stage, a standing area of 27½ feet in front of the stage, but only 6 feet of standing space on either side.

At the rear of the stage was a façade containing two doors that served as entrances and allowed set pieces to be brought onstage from the tiring house. The two doors also helped, as did the doors in Greek and Roman theatres, to localize the actions; thus, in *Romeo and Juliet* the Capulets and their servants would use one door, and the Montagues and their people the other. Also, the rear of the stage provided a "discovery" area, sometimes called the *inner below*, usually screened off, and used to display larger set pieces and interiors and to locate scenes. There is much disagreement about the second level of the rear playing area. The sketch of the Swan Theatre shows only an open gallery, but some feel that there must have been a real alcove in the second level corresponding to the alcove discovery area at stage level.

Even less is known about the private theatres than about the public theatres. The first Blackfriars Theatre was opened in 1576. It was leased and subsequently used by Richard Farrant, Choirmaster of the Chapel Royal, who directed a company of boy actors in public performances. The lease was broken, in 1584, by a series of lawsuits, and it was not until twelve years later, in 1596, that James Burbage, whose lease on the site of The Theatre was due to expire, acquired the buildings and converted them into a playhouse. The residents of the Blackfriars area immediately secured an injunction against its use by companies of adult actors, and so the second Blackfriars remained a children's theatre until 1608.

In spite of its history as the primary private theatre of the era, the dimensions of the second Blackfriars are widely disputed. It probably occupied a rectangular room that measured about 100 feet by 46 feet. One end of the room (perhaps up to 35 feet) was masked off for use as a tiring room. In front of this tiring room was a stage of no more than 46 feet by 25 feet, elevated about 3 to 4 feet, and separated from the front row of seats by a low railing. The audience was probably seated on tiers of wooden seats around the perimeter of the room, and on wooden benches in the center of the room facing the stage.

It is interesting that, especially in the English public theatres, the actor-audience arrangement is very nearly the same as for the Medieval and Classical Greek theatre. That is, the audience rims the action on three sides of the playing area, which is backed with a façade and a shallow alcove. The private theatres, on the basis of the probable arrangement of the second Blackfriars, may have departed from the thrust staging arrangement, going to a form of end staging, but of that we cannot be entirely sure. It remained for the proscenium-arch stage to revise an audience-actor arrangement that had lasted for nearly two thousand years.

The Proscenium-Arch Stage

The first modern stage survives in the *Teatro Farnese* at Parma—called "modern" for our purposes because it is the earliest existing theatre with a permanent proscenium arch. Exactly where the proscenium arch came from, or even when it was introduced, is open to debate. As noted in the chapter entitled "The Designer," what seems most probable is that the development of perspective drawing, and its growing use in scenic design, led artists to treat the stage structure in the same manner as they did their paintings: putting it in a frame. The Medieval mansion stage had conquered time and space by the simple expedient of ignoring such mundane

The stage of the Teatro Olimpico. *A growing interest in Classical theatre was furthered by the discovery, in 1414, of the Latin manuscipt of Vitruvius' work on architecture and its subsequent publication seventy years later, resulting in the construction of the* Teatro Olimpico. *Begun by Andrea Palladio in 1580, the theatre was completed by Vincenzo Scamozzi in 1584. It had a steep, shallow, semi-elliptical auditorium that provided good sight lines, as well as diminishing street perspectives behind three archways at the back of the stage and two at the sides. (From Giovanni Montenari,* Del Teatro Olimpico, *Padua, Italy, 1749.)*

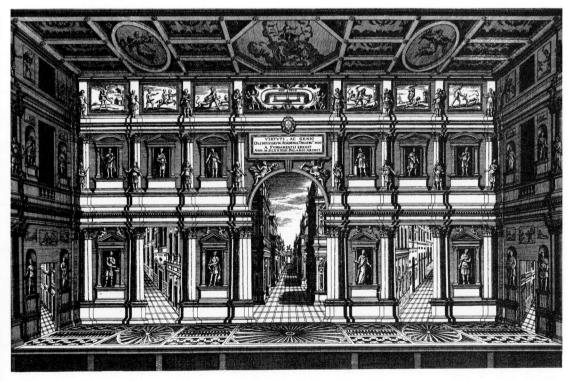

aspects of theatre; by showing all times and all places simultaneously and letting the actors and the materials of the play indicate specific time and date. Once perspective settings became popular, however, the scenic designer was restricted to a single view as seen from a fixed point. The fluidity of the Medieval stage and the Renaissance stage had been lost.

Beyond the increasing demand for perspective sets, there was also a growing demand for realistic spectacle. The staging excesses of the Italian Renaissance *intermezzi* had whetted audience appetites for spectacle, and the proscenium-arch stage, with its practical curtain that could be drawn to hide the changing of scenery, fulfilled this requirement.

The artistic results of the proscenium-arch stage were enormous and not slow in making themselves felt. In the past the relation between actors and audience had been an immediate one, even in a theatre as large as the Theatre of Dionysus, for no physical barrier separated the two. In a few cases scenes might be played in a large doorway in the façade behind the orchestra, or in an alcove in the façade behind the thrust stage, but those were brief scenes integrated into a total action that took place, essentially, in the midst of the audience. Now, however, as a result of the proscenium arch, the action had to be placed behind the opening, and no matter how physically close the spectators might be to the action, a psychological barrier was set up. The lighting, too, tended to exaggerate this separation. Where before the audience area and the stage area were equally bright, now the auditorium was dim and the stage light.

During the late sixteenth century in Italy, the professional theatre seriously got under way. The introduction of opera, earlier in the century, accelerated this development, at least in terms of staging and architecture, because from the beginnning opera tended toward elaborate staging. The highest form of that early development came in Venice, where the San Cassiano Opera House was so spectacularly successful that, by 1641, three others like it had been built. Those houses each had a proscenium-arch stage, complex stage machinery, and elaborate perspective sets, as well as boxes, pits, and galleries. The San Cassiano Opera House became the basic model for most of the new theatres that would be built in Western Europe during the following two hundred and fifty years, and the form remained dominant until the end of the nineteenth century.

To speak meaningfully of the shape and style and function of physical theatres, no matter in what period, and not take some note of the plays being produced in those theatres, would be a difficult if not an impossible task, and certainly an unfruitful one. The effect that the playwrights and their plays have had on the various theatre structures, and, reversing this pattern, the effect that the theatres have had on the playwrights and their plays is in many ways similar to the old saw about the chicken and the egg. In the case of theatre we know which came first; at least, we can be reasonably sure that the play (or dramatic rite or ritual) existed before any special structure or even playing area was built to house it. Once primitive drama actually got under way, however, we can speculate with some degree of certainty that specific, controlled physical conditions were soon developed to house and enhance the dramatic activity. Thus, playing areas with at least some attendant scenery and props were certainly developed early in theatre prehistory.

Once the play and the playing area were brought together, each began influencing the other. For example, knowing that the play he was writing would be produced in the great Theatre of Dionysus at Athens, a playwright would almost certainly write his play to take advantage of the surroundings and the physical equipment available, and the size and seating arrangement of the theatre would likely affect the dialogue. Thus, the physical theatre shapes the drama intended for it. On the other hand, because playwrights seek constantly to delight, amuse, shock, or instruct audiences, they tend to make ever-growing demands upon the theatre and

In Italy the evolution of the picture stage and scene-changing devices was rapid and highly successful. After the prisms of the Greeks came angled wings, nestled in grooves, which slid on and off the stage. This 1620 design by Joseph Furttenbach shows how well this device worked. (From Joseph Furttenbach's Architectura Civilis, *1628.)*

its technical capacity. Thus, the drama manages to affect the physical theatre.

For thousands of years now, in its various periods and styles, drama and the physical stage have changed and developed together. Future developments are problematical at best, depending on our understanding of theatre's past, and also on the growing technology that will be so very important in shaping our future.

eight

The Director Takes the Stage

Today there are almost as many understandings of the directorial function as there are directors. Perhaps all that can truly be said, by way of introduction, is that contemporary directors have potentially more authority than directors have had during any other period in the history of theatre. Not all directors accept or even want such authority in all aspects of production. Bertolt Brecht, for example, when he was directing, sat and waited for the actors to show him the meaning of his own play, but strong authority is available for those who are willing to accept it, a group that seems to include the majority of directors.

Such deference to the director was not always known, although at various points throughout theatrical history the director has certainly had substantial authority. During the Golden Age of Classical Greek theatre, tragic dramatists usually directed their own works. In Aeschylus' lifetime authors acted in their own plays, trained the Chorus, wrote the music, choreographed the dances, and in general supervised every aspect of production. That was true, apparently, for most writers of tragic drama. In

Brecht's Mother Courage *was produced by the McCarter Theatre Company. Directed by Michael Kahn; settings by David Jenkins; costumes by Lawrence Casey; lighting by John McLain.*

Greek comedy, on the other hand, it was quite common for the authors to turn all directorial duties over to someone else, who, because he received his appointment directly from the author, presumably had equivalent authority.

We know almost nothing about the director in Roman theatre, though the Roman theatricians followed Greek practice in so many other ways that we can conjecture with some safety that they followed Greek directorial practices as well. However, from the time that the Roman theatres were closed in the sixth century A.D. by the Emperor Justinian until the latter part of the nineteenth century, the position of theatrical director fell off in importance and, in fact, was often split up and handled in a variety of ways. The Medieval cycle plays, generally a series of short, almost fragmentary plays, produced sequentially in terms of their Biblical origin, seem generally to have had a variety of directors, each responsible for a limited aspect of the production. Groups such as the trade guilds in England took responsibility for producing these little plays, many of which demanded extensive technical effects, and production authority seems to have been parceled out as it was needed. Thus, the masters of machine were responsible for seeing to the production of realistic technical effects, and the performers, most of them amateurs, apparently worked out their own blocking and business, except in cases where certain motions, movements, or stage positions had become traditional, or when professional minstrels were hired to play major roles. One can surmise that the amateur performers usually deferred to the opinions of professional entertainers in most matters relating to the mounting of a production.

The Elizabethan theatre consisted of permanent professional companies of actors and playwrights who owned shares in their own companies, and were able to do without the position of director. The working professionals and entrepreneurs were apparently able to work out their own movement and business (in the few cases where it was not inherent in the script) on an amicable workmanlike basis. Scholars suspect that the Elizabethan playwright, as in Greek times, took a particular interest in seeing to details of the production not covered in the script. It is impossible to imagine that Shakespeare, for example, as a practical theatre professional and businessman, could watch one of his plays being produced haphazardly, without taking an active part in the production. In fact, Hamlet's advice to the players gives us every reason to believe that Shakespeare did, indeed, take a hand, at least in coaching the actors.

In the seventeenth century, Moliere apparently took on many of the duties that we now think of as belonging exclusively to the director. He filled the positions of author, actor, and manager of his own company, which meant that he shouldered the entire responsibility of making the company's shows a success, season after season. His remark that "actors are strange creatures to drive" indicates that in spite of his other, formal responsibilities, he certainly did not ignore stage direction.

The modern movement toward a strong director first began to be felt in eighteenth-century Germany, when playwright Christoph Gottsched joined forces with Carolina and Johann Neuber in an attempt to revitalize German theatre. Frau Neuber in particular sought to raise the level of

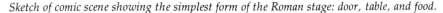

Sketch of comic scene showing the simplest form of the Roman stage: door, table, and food.

performances by way of careful rehearsals, thoroughly blocked, and the abandonment of improvisational techniques that allowed actors to move and speak pretty much as they wanted. The Schröders, Sophie and later her son Friedrich, continued this practice, insisting on thorough rehearsals in which the actors were told exactly what to do and how to do it.

In the mid-eighteenth century in England the actor-director David Garrick began considering ways to make mounting a play less of a slap-dash business, and his solution was to consider the production as a whole, concentrating not just on the acting but on the combination of all those aspects that make theatre what it is. In Drury Lane he insisted that the young gallants get off the stage, where they still commonly posed while the play was taking place. He also installed footlights and took care in selecting proper costumes, props, and painted drops. Perhaps most important of all, for the first time he insisted on taking great care in the casting of even the most minor roles.

In the late eighteenth and the early nineteenth centuries, actors such as William Macready and Charles Kean, were following Garrick's lead,

A scene from a musical adaptation of Two Gentlemen of Verona *by John Guare and Mel Shapiro. At the Trinity Square Repertory Company, Providence, Rhode Island.*

David Garrick, the greatest actor of his age, in a scene from Venice Preserved *by Tom Otway. (From a painting by Zoffany.)*

trying to institute professional casting practices, fully scheduled (and attended) rehearsals, and ensemble acting techniques. Producers like Madam Vestris and designers like Henry Planché were moving toward realistic sets with historically accurate furnishings and props. It was in Germany, however, that all of these varied aspects of production were at last assembled under the guidance of a powerful central director.

The Modern Director Takes Control

On May 1, 1874, the Duke of Saxe-Meiningen, Georg I, presented his theatrical company to Berlin in a production of Shakespeare's *Julius Caesar*. That event was of particular importance because it introduced the world to the first modern director, the *régisseur*, who exercised complete control over all aspects of an entire production. The play was enormously successful, both popularly and critically, and the historically accurate sets and costumes, the controlled acting, and the carefully choreographed crowd scenes were to become the trademark of the Meininger Company.

To achieve his total theatrical effect the Duke had developed a pattern for production that was long emulated, highly influential with later innovators such as Stanislavski and Antoine, and, in essence, still often followed, especially in productions featuring large casts. That is, the labors of production were carefully divided, with the supervisors of each area responsible directly to an all-powerful director. The Duke himself was the director, taking on the responsibility for general supervision, determining the outlines of the production and the forms of presentation, and resolving all conflicts. His wife, Helene (the former Anglo-German actress Ellen Franz), chose the plays, adapted the texts, and served as both mistress of speech and acting instructor. Ludwig Chronegk, a comic actor who had joined the Meininger Company in 1866, proved to be capable of remarkably clear communication with actors and actresses, cutting directly to the core of a role, and, as a consequence, he became a powerful assistant director, acting as intermediary between the Duke and his performers.

From the first rehearsal the Company worked with the proper scenery and furniture, even though that sometimes meant long waits when newly conceived approaches necessitated rearrangement of a stage setting. The

A sketch by the Duke of Saxe-Meiningen for his production of Heinrich von Kleist's The Battle of Arminius.

A scene from Mrs. Warren's Profession *by George Bernard Shaw. At the University of Illinois, Urbana-Champaign. Directed by Clara Behringer; set design by Bernhard Works; costumes by Ellen Ryba.*

performers were to be fully prepared to act from the first rehearsal. There was no building to a part, no gradual growing. From the very beginning the play was to be rehearsed with the same vocal strength and spiritual depth that would be used on the evening of performance, and no matter how often a scene was repeated, relaxation was never allowed. All Meininger plays were rehearsed as if they had never been staged before, and, as a consequence, the plays were firm only in their general outlines. There was no preconception, and the play was always ready for innovations worked out in rehearsals. Suggestions could come from any quarter, and if they seemed valuable they were tested immediately. Another essential of the Meininger approach was a strong emphasis on ensemble production. There were no stars; even guest performers were made temporary members of the Meininger Company and were expected to play any role assigned.

One of the most striking and widely acclaimed features of the Meininger was the construction of crowd scenes. Recognizing the necessity of using untrained *supers* to fill out such scenes, the Duke advised that directors should take great care to distinguish early between those who could be trained and those who were untrainable or dubious. They should rid themselves of the untrainable and use the dubious only as fillers. The crowds should be divided into small groups, each with a skilled actor as its leader; the leader would be in charge of the physical and vocal responses of group members. This approach contributed greatly to the individualization of responses from within the various small groups that made up the crowds.

Following the pathway blazed by the Duke, and impelled by the ever-growing demand for realistic theatre, directors became more and more concerned with controlling all elements of production in an attempt to present a unified whole. At the end of the nineteenth century the Duke's methods were being expanded and new methods explored by such leaders as André Antoine, with his *Théâtre Libre* in Paris; Otto Brahm and the *Freie Bühne* in Berlin; and, later, the great Russian director Constantin Stanislavski at his Moscow Art Theatre; all of them deeply impressed by the Meininger approach. The aim of that exploration, however, remained the concept of artistic unity. If all those pioneers agreed on little else, they held in common the one belief that to achieve theatrical unity there must be a *single* creative authority in total charge of every production: the director.

The Director in Today's Theatre

In the United States especially, the director wields a power that is almost total. Within the confines of the theatre his authority is so close to absolute that his position might well be compared to that of a captain of a ship at sea. "It has been said that Paris is the playwright's city; London is the actor's city; and New York is the director's city."[1] This statement may be debated, especially in view of the work performed by such experimental and demanding non-American directors as Peter Brook, but certainly the American director is the center of theatrical activity in the United States.

Primarily, the director is responsible for unifying all aspects of a production, for bringing order out of chaos, and for making harmony out of discord. That last musical reference is used advisedly, for in one sense the function of the director can be compared to that of an orchestra conductor. The conductor plays no instrument and the director does not act, but both are responsible for determining interpretation, which means that

[1]Edward A. Wright and Lenthiel H. Downs, *A Primer for Playgoers* (Englewood Cliffs, New Jersey, 1969), p. 175.

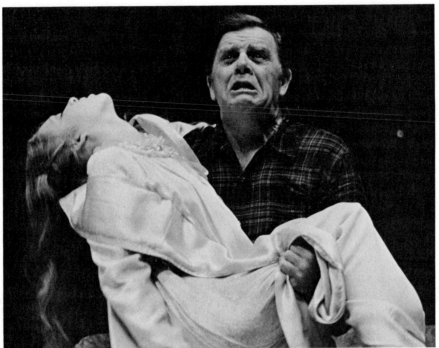

Pat Hingle and Deborah Offner star in A Grave Undertaking *by Lloyd Gold. Produced by the McCarter Theatre Company; directed by Michael Kahn.*

they must control such common aspects of production as tempo and emphasis. Both must think in terms of the total effect of the performance on the audience, and both are responsible for welding the contributions of many artists into a unified and aesthetically pleasing whole.

To accomplish the job successfully, directors must undertake a staggering variety of tasks and bring all of them to fruition. They must, in many cases, choose a script. In professional theatre, of course, directors sign on to direct specific scripts already settled on by producers, but the decision about whether or not to direct still belongs to the individual artists, and if they agree to direct scripts that they feel are unworthy, then they have chosen badly. In community theatre and educational theatre the responsibility for choosing a script usually rests with the individual director.

Following script selection, directors must analyze the scripts in much the same manner as literary critics, and then carry this analysis one step further by determining how, in terms of stage techniques, they can bring what they have discovered in the scripts to life. In the case of a new script, one that has never been produced on stage before an audience, they must also act as script consultants for the authors. In other words, they must also be play doctors, helping the authors revise those aspects of their new scripts that may look good and read well in print, but somehow do not play.

The Manitoba Theatre Center production of Arthur Miller's The Crucible, *featuring Edda Gburek, Jacquie Presly, Jill Harris, Alexe Duncan, Cynthia Parva. Directed by Arif Hasnain; sets and costumes by Joseph Cselenyi; lighting by Neil McLeod.*

The Director as Critic

Once the script is selected, either by direct choice, as in educational theatre, or indirectly by agreeing to direct it, as in professional theatre, the director takes on the immediate function of critic-interpreter; that is, the director must first determine what is in the script, what it is all about, and then work out methods of transmitting that material to an audience.

Taking a play apart, closely analyzing the material, determining the relationships of scene to scene and character to character, and then putting it all back together again and considering it as an artistic unity, is a highly difficult task, but a necessary one. Some would-be directors have tended to shy away from such detailed analysis, feeling that it is academic and thus dry, dull, and boring, with little to recommend it in terms of the somewhat more visceral aspects of performance. Nothing could be further from the truth. Examining the playscript for all of its various truths is every bit as exciting as the search for truth in any field of endeavor. It is heady stuff indeed, and directors who have no interest in pursuing the spiritual, philosophical, and aesthetic truths inherent in their scripts will likely be pedestrian directors at best.

For the director preparing to direct a show, the end result of script analysis is interpretation of the work of the playwright to an audience. In this sense, interpretation and criticism are one and the same, and they can both be reached by the technique of explication; that is, finding out what *exists* in the script, what *happens* in the script, and *why*. The succeeding material is not intended as an outline of the only way to approach a play—

Sandy Duncan, Lucie Arnaz, and Stockard Channing as high school cheerleaders in Jack Heifner's comedy Vanities *at the Mark Taper Forum, Los Angeles. Directed by Garland Wright.*

there may be as many approaches as there are directors—but whatever the order, most directors complete the following tasks.

After determining the general outlines of the script, what happens and why, the director usually tries to ascertain the *controlling idea*. This controlling idea usually derives from a philosophical or sociological concept, and an understanding of this idea and the concept from which it springs is necessary to achieve a clearer understanding of the work. Also it helps the director in determining where to place the emphasis in his or her production. Examples of works with strong controlling ideas or concepts can be found in any of the plays of such widely separated dramatists as Shakespeare and Bertolt Brecht. In *Romeo and Juliet*, for example, the philosophical backbone of the play is, essentially, Shakespeare's belief in or acceptance of the "great chain of being," which translates into the necessity for maintaining a strict personal and social order. Major sociopolitical wounds in a country or body politic disturb this natural order, and evil results. The schism created by the Montagues and Capulets is such a wound and must be healed through tragic action: the deaths of the young lovers.

A third step in this critical analysis consists of determining the mood, the poetic tone and emotional context of the material, as well as discovering how that mood can be transmitted to an audience. To some degree

Edward Albee's All Over *at the Hartford Stage Company, Hartford, Connecticut. Featuring Pirie MacDonald, Anne Shropshire, Anne Lynn, Humphrey Davis, David O. Petersen, Margaret Thomson, Myra Carter. Directed by Paul Weidner.*

artists are always craftsmen, with certain tools and techniques at their disposal. Discovering the way artists have used those tools and techniques tells the director much about the work itself and also suggests methods for making the audience aware of the various levels and meanings of the piece. In terms of the playwright's art, words tend to be the first and foremost tool, and the playwright often uses them subtly and to great advantage. T. S. Eliot, for example, in the opening choral ode of his verse drama, *Murder in the Cathedral*, provides a series of death images—"sombre," "death," "darkness," "danger," etc.—which totally influence audience perception without every becoming obtrusive. Arthur Miller, in *Death of a Salesman*, uses a similar technique to a somewhat different end. Whereas Eliot was concerned primarily with creating a charged mood or atmosphere, Miller was concerned primarily with telling the audience something about Willy Loman. Thus, in the early scenes of his play the word "lost," or phrases that indicate the quality of "lostness," occur and recur. As a result, the audience knows, early in the play and seemingly intuitively, that Willy is lost in time and space and an ever-burgeoning population. The director's job is to understand how Miller accomplishes the feat so that the actors can be directed in a way that makes the best possible use of what is essentially a technical device employed by the writer.

After determining the prevailing mood of the work, the director pays careful attention to formal structure, which relates closely to mood and meaning. The structure of most traditional plays can be illustrated geometrically; that is to say, given a baseline that illustrates the beginning and end of a work, the rising action can be traced upward to the climax and the descending action traced downward to the end of the play, the result being a triangle which depicts the outline of the form.[2] In the works of Shakespeare, for example, the climax or high point of the action usually comes near the play's geometric center; take any play of Shakespeare, count the number of pages, divide by two, and the chances are that you will be close to the climax of the play. Thus, your diagram will be a regular delta triangle (△). On the other hand, for French tragedy of the seventeenth and eighteenth centuries the climax is likely to be early in the play, giving a skewed diagram (◁). Such information is valuable to the director because it indicates something about the material of the play itself. French classical tragedy, it can be seen, emphasizes the results of the tragic action and not the material leading up to the tragedy. Thus the plays become laments over what has happened. In contrast, works that emphasize events leading up to the tragic action will be diagrammed as (◁). Again, the type of pattern indicates to the director how and where to put emphasis. In this last case, the emphasis is obviously on the suspenseful elements of the plot that result in the tragic action.

The Freytagian diagrams illustrated above are often used more by the literary critic than the theatrical director. In most directing texts, where

---

[2]The concept of rising action, climax, and falling action is based on the work of the nineteenth-century German critic, Gustav Freytag.

climax is equated to emotional peaks, the script is usually diagrammed as a series of climaxes, rising ever higher to the crisis, which usually occurs near the end of the script.

Once the formal structure of plays are discovered, the directors analyze the individual scenes to see how they build and how they contribute to the final denouement. Directors are alert to such elements as word order and sentence structure within the individual scenes, and all the physical action, both written and implied. Once they become aware of the meaning, philosophy, mood, and form, they proceed to analysis of the characters themselves.

One of the most difficult tasks for directors is character analysis, and to a large degree it must be shared with the performers, who should be given leeway in developing their own characterizations, at least to the degree that they do not conflict with the directors' total concepts. For directors and the performers alike, character analysis means not only determining any special behavioral characteristics but also understanding what characters do and why they do it. To achieve that end some directors

A scene from Lillian Hellman's The Autumn Garden *at the Long Wharf Theatre, New Haven, Connecticut.*

The Cleveland Playhouse production of The Yellow Jacket, *at the Euclid-77th Street Theatre, Cleveland. Featuring Jonathan Farwell, Eugene Hare, Dan Desmond, George Simms, and Richard Halverson.*

find it helpful to use a technique that has attained popularity with actors themselves: *scoring* each of the roles. The scores developed by directors are usually only minimal in comparison with the individual scores developed by performers, but they are enough to establish character and determine how each of the characters relates to the others and to the material as a whole. Directors will also help performers find the spines of the characters they are playing and establish primary goals or superobjectives for each character.

The Director as Craftsman

Once the script has been thoroughly analyzed, the director consults with his designers and begins the casting and rehearsal process, where art and craft and criticism all come together to produce theatre. The starting point in this process is usually the audition, where the prospective performers appear before the director and, through a series of scenes, cold readings, improvisations, or a combination of all three, demonstrate their ability to perform. The ideal end result of all this, of course, is that the persons

David Dukes plays Leo and Carrie Nye plays Gilda in Noel Coward's Design for Living *at the Goodman Theatre Center. Directed by William Woodman.*

displaying the highest level of ability should be cast in the available and appropriate roles.

The ideal often fails in reality, however, for a number of reasons. Physical typecasting has remained of real importance to directors because for many theatregoers what they see is at least as important as what they hear. Thus, a young, slim, handsome actor will find it almost impossible to get himself cast as Falstaff, no matter how great his acting ability. The large, overweight actor will find it equally difficult to get himself cast as a romantic lead. Also, certain physical types are often cast because they complement each other visually. Thus, a director casting a play with a large farcical content may be looking for actors or actresses who will provide a visual "Mutt and Jeff" quality.

Another problem that directors face when casting directly from auditions is that some performers seem to reach the peak of their ability in the audition situation, whereas some who seem very bad in tryouts will grow immensely in rehearsal and performance. To solve such problems some directors insist on a second step in casting: the interview. In an interview it is possible to question a performer concerning past experience, desires, and future aspirations. For some directors that is the most important part of the audition process; like horseplayers, they believe that a track record is the only meaningful measure of ability. That attitude, perhaps unfair, is to some degree acceptable in professional theatre, where large sums of money are often invested in the hope of even larger profits and where show backers may legitimately resent directors who gamble their investments with unknown actors in major roles. Such an attitude, however, is completely unacceptable for educational theatre, where the director must be concerned at least as much with the development of the students as with the overall success of his production.

After casting is complete and the rehearsal period begins, directors conduct one or more read-throughs of the script and give their cast the information they think will be important to the process of character building. They may give only the broad, general outlines of the production, they may give specific hints for developing each of the major characters in the script, or they may give nothing, preferring that the actors themselves come forth with suggestions for their characterizations. Most directors avoid being too specific in terms of individual roles, feeling that if all directions for character type come from a single source, then the result will likely be a flat sameness to all the characterizations.

Following the read-throughs, most directors go directly into blocking or composition rehearsals. Those are too highly complex to deal with here but, essentially, what the director does is move the actors about the stage, or have the actors move themselves, in a manner that is visually meaningful in terms of the content of the play and that visually illuminates each individual scene; that in some way comments on each situation and complements the verbal materials of the playscript. Additionally, the composition must be aesthetically pleasing in itself. That is, at any point during the production of the play, the location and posture of the performers should,

Theatre: A Contemporary Introduction

Tennessee Williams' The Purification *at the Alley Theatre, Houston. Anthony Manionis as the Boy and Margo McElroy as the Mother. Directed by Nina Vance; set design by William Trotman; costumes by Barbara C. Cox.*

against the physical materials of the set, provide an exciting, meaningful, and well-arranged composition.

Some directors tend to think of composition in terms of motion. Others think in terms of still-picture, or camera, composition, making use of movement only to get the actors from one composition to another. In any case, composition on stage is a particularly difficult and demanding art, because the director is working in three dimensions, with live actors, usually in front of a stationary backdrop, and each of his compositions not only must be aesthetically pleasing but also must help explicate and support the scene and, thus, the total play.

Along the way, throughout the rest of the rehearsals, directors fulfill a multitude of tasks. They orchestrate the total work, making sure that the ideas and materials the actors bring to their roles fit properly with the total concept. They take care to develop pace and emphasis. They coach the actors and actresses in their lines and movements, working carefully with phrasing and pronounciation, and in educational theatre they also function as acting *teachers*, imparting styles and techniques. Perhaps most important of all, in terms of the actors, they try to establish an atmosphere of trust in the whole company that will allow the actors to cast off those emotional controls that we develop to hold ourselves in check in doubtful situations.

Somehow, in the midst of all this activity, directors manage to consult with the scenic designers, pointing out basic needs, aesthetic demands, and any special requirements. Directors do the same for the costume designer and the lighting designer, giving them the basic materials they need to fulfill their own special function, and then taking the responsibility for approving the final designs. During all of this, they may very well be called on to consult with the front of the house management about publicity, and with the technical directors and crew heads about special technical problems in mounting the show. They will also find themselves acting as confessors, psychiatrists, and, when the show opens, cheerleaders.

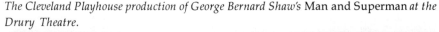

The Cleveland Playhouse production of George Bernard Shaw's Man and Superman *at the Drury Theatre.*

A scene from The Hostage *at the Cincinnati Playhouse. Moultrie Patten as Pat, Linda Dunlevy as Theresa, and Joyce Krempel as Meg. Directed by Geoff Garland; set design and lighting by Neil Peter Jampolis.*

The patterns just outlined are probably never followed exactly by any single director, but basically most directors perform all of those functions in their own special ways. There are as many directing techniques as there are directors, and many directors even vary their methods to suit the special problems that are presented from script to script. The director's task is clearly a huge one, requiring an artist who is flexible, able to adjust from script to script and from cast to cast. Perhaps the best way of understanding the enormity of the director's task is to examine how several of the great modern directors have handled the problems of producing a show.

The Hot L Baltimore *by Lanford Wilson, as produced at the Mark Taper Forum, Los Angeles. Featuring Jennifer Salt and Barbara Colby.*

The Director at Work

DAVID BELASCO (1853–1931), an American director best known for the meticulous realism of his productions, was in every way a practical man of the theatre. As author, co-author, or adapter of some seventy plays, and as director, designer, and theatre technician, he combined sentiment, romance, and sensational action under a veneer of realistic dialogue and stage business.

The appeal of Belasco's dramas was directly to the heart. He aimed to arouse and indulge all the popular sentimentalities of the American people, and so the problem that he always set himself was how to get it across, into the hearts of his audience. Belasco himself freely admitted this, writing that

> the complete play is impressive and fulfills its purpose only to the extent that it carries an audience back to its own experiences. If my productions have an appealing quality, it is because I have kept this important fact constantly in mind and have tried, while concealing the mechanism of my scenes, to tug at the hearts of my audience. [3]

Belasco's stage settings, the famous "Belasco realism," also exerted an influence on the style of acting in his productions. He began his career when the scenery for most plays consisted of backdrops, wings, and borders, on which were painted a pretense of reality. Early in his career he began to question the effectiveness of this kind of scenery, for he noticed how eagerly an audience responded to real touches and how much these seemed to add to the illusion of the play. In one of his early productions in San Francisco, he indulged his passion for literalism by filling the stage with livestock and reproducing several of nature's more violent moods. In another drama he introduced a real car, a real baby, and real food on the table. The public was delighted with all these effects. Belasco continued to supply more and more of them. He was determined to bridge the gap between the life he saw around him and life's artificial representation on the stage.

At the zenith of his career he came as close to his ideal, perhaps, as it is possible to come. His settings were marvels of solid walls, illusionistic lighting, and authentic properties. He would allow nothing to be built out of canvas stretched on frames; everything had to be real. The play *Du Barry* displayed furniture and ornaments actually used by Mme. Du Barry. During the season of 1912-1913, Belasco produced *The Governor's Lady*, which was notable chiefly for the reproduction on stage of a Childs restaurant. Another play featured rugs, furniture, and wall paper that had been removed from a cheap theatrical boarding house in New York City. Such authentic settings influenced performers to improve the realism of their movements, gestures, delivery, and reactions. And such realistic excesses

[3]From Garff B. Wilson, *A History of American Acting* (Bloomington, Indiana, 1966), pp. 202-203.

William Swetland and Geraldine Fitzgerald in Arvin Brown's production of O'Neill's Ah, **Wilderness** *at the Long Wharf Theatre, New Haven, Connecticut.*

Theatre: A Contemporary Introduction

A scene from the San Diego City College production of Jean Giraudoux's The Madwoman of Chaillot. *Directed by Lyman Saville; settings by Robert Green; costumes by Gloria Kendall, Carol Riordan, and Robert Green.*

prompted disciples of the new theatre to cry out against the "hideous reality" of Belascoism.

Furthermore, the lighting was designed to heighten the reality of the scenery. Belasco was a pioneer in this field. As early as 1877 he experimented with locomotive headlights, and had used colored silks as a medium for changing the hue of stage illumination. Later, in his New York theatre, he maintained a lighting laboratory and spent large sums on experimentation. He did away with footlights because they were unnatural, and he evolved a system of diffused lighting from above which better simulated the light of the sun.

And Belasco's realism was not always intended merely for the delectation of the audience. Sometimes its sole purpose was to help actors and actresses identify with the mood of the play and the characters they were representing. If performers were supposed to make an entrance from a stairway, for example, Belasco built the stairway complete, whether the audience could see it or not. He believed it helped the actor get the spirit of his entrance.

In retrospect, we can see clearly that Belasco was a highly influential figure, helping to bridge the gap between the old style of mounting a play and the new stagecraft inspired by Adolphe Appia and Gordon Craig. In acting, consistent with his other contributions and influenced by them, he championed a contemporary realism that exploited personality and emotion and is still found, to a degree, on many American stages.

ANDRÉ ANTOINE (1853–1943) and his *Théâtre Libre* have become so synonymous that it becomes necessary to point out that Antoine was also an actor, producer, and director, as well as the founder of the French Free Theatre. His principal contribution to drama came through use of the *Théâtre Libre* to freshen the stale air of French theatre by introducing new French play-

Bowling Green State University produced No Place to be Somebody *by Charles Gordone. Directed by Allen S. White; set design by Milton Bradley; costumes by Verdya Bradley; lighting by Stephen Bailous.*

wrights and foreign playwrights with new types of drama. Perhaps equally important, this resulted in his development of new acting techniques, directorial concepts, and staging practices to handle the new drama.

Antoine was quick to perceive that the old style of acting was inappropriate to the new plays, so he began training amateurs according to his own ideas. He taught them not to recite, but to act as though they were that character and lived in that setting, in other words, to live their parts and to identify with the scene on stage, not the audience. He taught them that the play is more important than any single actor or actress, and that each scene has movement that is part of the total movement of the play itself. Impressed by the Meininger's crowd scenes, believing them pictorially right but vocally wrong in their semichoral effect, he had his actors in crowd scenes speak at different times to produce a more authentic sound.

Antoine felt that the director fulfills the same function in the theatre that descriptions do in a novel, and he divided the work of directing into two parts: 1) finding the right decor for the action, and the proper way of grouping actors; and 2) interpreting and guiding the flow of the dialogue. He believed that environment determines the movement of the characters, and that all rehearsals should be held on a finished set. The set should be authentic, something seen before, a landscape or an interior. In an interior, the whole house should be sketched in the original design, so that the exits, halls, and connecting rooms are all architecturally accurate, and all this detail, plus furnishing, should be done within all four walls. When that has been completed, a wall is removed and the set design is complete.

> *Once this work is done, can you see how easy and interesting it is after examining the landscape or an interior from every one of its angles, to choose the exact point at which we shall have to cut in order to remove the famous fourth wall, while retaining a set that is most authentic in character and best suited to the action.* [4]

After viewing the Meininger Company and Irving's Company, in 1888, he sought even more realism, and in an attempt to reproduce environment exactly, he even went so far as to hang real carcasses of beef on stage for a play about butchers. Even at that time (that is, during Antoine's active theatrical life) a reaction against realism was starting, mainly with Aurélien Lugné-Poe, yet Antoine's belief in the importance of environment helped establish the idea that each play required its own setting. Later on, at the *Odéon*, though still using realistic methods, Antoine did modify this extreme.

Antoine could see only too clearly from his own experiences that directing and producing were two separate careers. He felt that the director was an artist and should not be burdened with the problems of making or paying out money, while a producer was a businessman. At that time the producer often assumed both the producing and directing functions, usu-

---

[4] André Antoine, "Causerie sur la mise en scene," in *Directors on Directing*, ed. by Toby Cole and Helen Krich Chinoy (Indianapolis, 1963), p. 95.

Rubek (Ronald Bishop) and Maia (Nancy Sellin) share a quiet moment in a scene from When We Dead Awaken *at Stage West, W. Springfield, Maine.*

ally turning the script over to someone on his payroll, often one of the performers, to begin rehearsals, and stepping in later to take over. In reference to this arrangement, Antoine said:

> *. . . directing is a career by itself—an amusing but subtle kind of diplomacy. Then too, when you realize that the director must also understand the author, feel his work, transcribe it, transpose it, and interpret to every one of the actors the part assigned to him, you will understand why I am so desirous of developing this personnel which we do not now have.*[5]

[5]*Ibid.*, p. 94.

MAX REINHARDT (1874–1943) had, as a director, the tremendous asset of organizational capability. Without it he could never have staged his vast productions, such as *Oedipus* and *Faust*, produced in European circus buildings where enormous sets and audiences could be handled. Reinhardt had started early to perfect the techniques he would need to achieve his success. He came to the *Deutsches Theatre* at age thirty-two, a successful acting career already behind him, prepared to be a master *régisseur*. By the time he began directing for the Brille, a private society that put on cabaret-style entertainments, Reinhardt had developed a concept of what the *regiebuch*, or director's production-book, needed to be for him. It was a total blueprint for a play, including gestures, movement, and line readings, carefully worked out before rehearsals began. The *regiebuch* included sketches of blocking and stage pictures, philosophical statements about motivations, and instructions to various people. Such painstaking planning allowed the director to "see" his entire production before rehearsals began, so that he had a constant measure of how well the play was developing from the very first day. When rehearsals began, copies of the *regiebuch* would be made and given to the various assistants, for uniform control of the productions.

A scene from Sean O'Casey's The Plow and the Stars *at the Asolo State Theatre, Sarasota, Florida. Featuring Henson Keys, Robert Murch, Barbara Reid, and Stephen Johnson.*

Natalia (Brenda Curtis) and Shpigelsky (John Wylie) confront each other in this scene from Turgenev's A Month in the Country at the Cincinnati Playhouse. Directed by Michael Murray; set design and lighting by Neil Peter Jampolis; costumes by Elizabeth Covey.

His rehearsals were conducted in such an efficient, businesslike manner that early in his career Reinhardt was accused of being dictatorial. It is also said that he mellowed over the years, growing more gentle and flexible in his approach. In any case, because of his organization and control his productions were virtually always highly polished and he was able to draw fine performances out of less than excellent actors and actresses. The ensemble effect of his company remained a trademark of the Reinhardt style.

VSEVELOD EMILIEVITCH MEYERHOLD (1874–1940), after four years as an actor under Stanislavski and a number of years in the provinces as the primary Russian exponent of theatrical symbolism and modernism, was appointed, in 1907, as one of the directors of Russia's Imperial Theatres. There, in an attempt to revitalize the conservative and rather crusty productions for which the Imperial Theatres had become known, he began directing shows that featured an increased flamboyance, spectacle, and overt theatricalism, and a reduction of the cerebral symbolism that had marked his earlier work. He became greatly influenced by the circus, the music hall, and the spectacular, while emphasizing tragic farce and the comic grotesque. His chief concern seemed to be away from a *literary* style and toward a *theatrical* style, which allowed him freedom to draw on a greater range of theatrical literature than was usual in the Imperial Russian Theatres. He worked as director for the Imperial Theatres, as drama director at the Alexandrinsky,

Sketch of "constructivistic" set model for Meyerhold's production of Ostrovsky's The Forest.

and as opera director at the Marinsky. And under the comic pseudonym of "Doctor Dappertluto," he staged private productions. In all cases he aimed to create new forms and new approaches to "nonrealistic consciously stylized art." His prime concern became the relationship of performer to scenery, and, in turn, the relationship of that combination to the audience.

Before the revolution of 1917, Meyerhold had been committed to an essentially political theatre, but after the revolution had firmly established itself, he drifted away from political theatre and began to concentrate on aesthetic theatre. He became an experimenter-researcher of methods and modes to fit the new century. This new approach needed new performers, and Meyerhold set about to create them. He spent nine years experimenting in his Meyerhold Studio, and the result was the *cabotin*—troubadour, minstrel, mime, histrione, juggler—a twentieth-century version of the traditional wandering minstrel that Meyerhold felt was essential to producing the retheatricalized new theatre.

Meyerhold's experimental approach led to two of his most interesting discoveries: biomechanics and scene constructivism. Biomechanics, which was directly opposed to the theories of his old mentor, Stanislavski, held that the actors and actresses special traits were their abilities to react to external stimuli applied to their reflexes. This theory was even put forth in a remarkable stage algebra, in which the performer was the totality of the organized and the organizer:

$N = A_1 + A_2$ (where N = actor; A_1 the artist who conceives the idea; and A_2 the executant who executes the conception of A_1.[6]

It appeared to some that Meyerhold was creating mere automatons, but the director believed that with biomechanics he was creating a performer who was highly disciplined physically, a dynamic representation of the new "Soviet man": robust, efficient, dexterous, and cooperative.

Constructivism was another product of Meyerhold's experimentation, though he put less emphasis on it than on biomechanics. Essentially, constructivism was the transposition to the stage of a form that, in the pictorial arts, had developed, like dadaism and cubism, to break the mold of realism, even of the most abstract sort. The movement began as early as 1914, but it was not until 1921 that Meyerhold had the artist Popova reproduce constructivism in stage terms. The sets—skeletal structural forms, in many respects pretentious—were not really Meyerhold's own creations in the way that his biomechanics-trained actors were, and he stayed with constructivism probably as much for economic reasons as artistic.

To Meyerhold, constructivism and biomechanics were not an aesthetic end in themselves. He termed them "stylistic: that is, extremes which enabled an audience to achieve detachment from the characters and their environment." He was interested in the *how* of things, rather than the *why*, which caused his theatre to become the Russian model of comedy and satire.[7]

JACQUES COPEAU (1879–1949) was one of the early symbolistic directors who helped curb the growing predominance of realism and the superficiality of theatricalism. His productions were designed to prove that the modern theatre needed no elaborate realistic scenery or gimmicks, but an ensemble of well-trained and rehearsed performers who "live" the characters and thus project the inner meaning of the plays. To achieve this effect, Copeau stressed the necessity of having all aspects of a production fused into an integral whole under one director.

Copeau was influenced by a great many people, and is generally considered to have been the greatest of theatrical eclectics because he assimilated many of the ideas of his colleagues and predecessors. He did, indeed, owe a debt to those who came before him, but it was a debt of inspiration only; he did not so much copy ideas as adopt parts of ideas for his own use. From Moliere, Copeau adopted some of the *commedia dell'arte* techniques. From Dalcroze, he gained some of his ideas about actor training, especially the importance of physical training and rhythmic dancing.

[6]James W. Symons, *Meyerhold's Theatre of the Grotesque* (Coral Gables, 1971), p. 73.
[7]*Ibid.*, p. 119.

The California State University, San Francisco production of Cocteau's The Infernal Machine. *Directed by Lynn Clark; stage design by Dorwin Gregory and Jim Ellingwood; lighting by Darrell F. Winn.*

He was influenced by Stanislavski in that their rehearsal procedures were similar: both worked in the country and both believed in the importance of improvisation. The ideas of Antoine and Copeau differed greatly, but it was to Antoine and Reinhardt that Copeau went for his ideas on the homogeneity and unity of the production. Copeau was also deeply impressed by Gordon Craig's belief in symbolic scenery and his revolt against ''painted realism.''

The major influence on Copeau was Adolphe Appia. They both strove for simplicity in design and lighting. Suggestion was important to them, and both agreed on the predominance of the actor. Together they worked to develop spatial settings, to create a major role for lighting, and to do away with painted scenery. Copeau wanted an almost empty stage, where the audience would see merely a few platforms, stairs, and screens. He wanted no footlights, and he demanded that the proscenium arch be removed to bring about a closer communication between actor and audience. Appia found in Copeau a stage director who shared his own basic concept of the art of the theatre, and Copeau found in Appia the artist who was capable of explaining to him that for which he was constantly searching.

BERTOLT BRECHT (1898–1956) has, for some students of theatrical art, in the few short years since his death advanced from the position of elderly *enfant terrible* to grand old man and theoretician of theatre. It is still too early to assess Brecht's place in theatre history, but his ideas, as they affect the director, deserve careful attention. It is interesting that those ideas were formulated after many years of writing poetry and plays, and after several years of practical experience at the Berliner Ensemble Theatre.

Brecht, in developing his theory of "epic theatre," was rebelling against Aristotle's definition of theatre as being unchangeable in terms of human nature. To break completely with traditional forms, Brecht went back to Goethe and Schiller and to epic poetry. The difference between epic and dramatic literature, he discovered, is that the epic poet presents the event as totally past, while the dramatic poet presents it as totally present. Brecht felt that society can be rationally understood only as a dialectical, historical process with all values in constant flux. For Brecht, therefore, the action of the theatre must take place in a carefully defined historical past, not in a present that is different with each performance. To aid in achieving the audience-performer separation that a totally separate past requires, Brecht developed his theory of *verfremdungseffekt*, which is usually translated as "alienation effect." The alienation effect was designed

A song sequence in Three Penny Opera. *Note the location of the orchestra above and behind the action and in full view of the audience. Directed by Jack Campbell, California State University, Fullerton.*

to keep the spectator from identifying with the characters, to constantly remind him that he is in a theatre. The spectator, thus alienated, will remain detached emotionally and so will be able to understand the didactic material in the play.

Because Brecht wanted an antiemotional, didactic theatre that would teach in a scientific manner, he frequently used the parable form for his plays. This device helped remove his characters from the changing present and put them in a constricted past where the audience could see them play out their necessary role and draw conclusions about their individual and collective behavior. However, Brecht wanted the theatre to be a study of human relationships, not merely human nature, and so the story, or parable, or fable, and not the characters is the main focus of his theatre.

Brecht always wanted to remind his viewers that they were in a theatre, not in the presence of reality. Lighting would not be used to create mood or atmosphere, and the source of light should be visible to the audience. The set should suggest the location of the action without actually representing it. Projected titles would identify scenes, and two-dimensional painted backdrops would provide any necessary scenic material. Symbolic costumes and makeup were used in much the same way that the Greeks used masks to represent certain aspects of character and personality. Musical numbers were used in reverse of present trends; that is, not to forward the action but to interrupt it, to comment on it, and to give the audience an opportunity to reflect on it.

Cat on A Hot Tin Roof *at the Asolo State Theatre, Sarasota, Florida.*

Brecht believed in the "gestural attitude" approach to the acting of his plays. For Stanislavski the gestures performed by an actor came from the inner emotion; for Brecht the attitude or gesture of a character was designed to create the inner emotion. Although Brecht did not want his audience to identify with his characters, or empathize with them, he did want them to identify with the situations and struggles of his characters. This caused Brecht to qualify his original position on emotion in the theatre. He decided that the epic theatre does not renounce emotion. Instead, it tries to strengthen or to evoke emotional response.

SIR TYRONE GUTHRIE (1900–1971) believed that "the only really creative function of the director is to be at rehearsal a highly receptive, concentrated, critical sounding board for the performance—an audience of one."[8] He stated that the director goes through a process of "psychic evocation," a process that consists of unconscious giving and receiving, from performer to director. "I don't shout or scream much, but I'm death on people who are late or slacking. Yes, I'm pretty nippy at times, like a sergeant major."[9]

Perhaps the first rule of directing, for Guthrie, was that the director should never arrive at any stage of rehearsal with set decisions. He should, rather, be open to several ways of operating, and he should remain as flexible as possible.

In the prerehearsal period several steps should be taken by a director. First, he should interpret the script. Guthrie compared the stage director to a musical conductor, and even used such musical terminology as "crescendo" for directions throughout his scripts. He felt that performance is no more than an instrument of the director, and that the director should, therefore, be individual and follow his own interpretation of the play. The worst thing that a director can do is to play it safe.

As far as casting goes, Guthrie felt that a director should have a clear idea of what he wants before he casts. Also, readings are a complete waste of time in that the good people usually do not do well whereas the pushy and the insensitive do. The performers are usually nervous at casting; thus, "their voices are upset, their muscles are tense, their diaphragms are quivery, and their throats are dry."[10] Guthrie felt that the best way to cast a play was to see the actors in their own productions. He did not, however, undervalue the casting process. In fact, he felt that casting could constitute nearly ninety percent of the director's task.

According to Guthrie, the director should come to the first rehearsal prepared to give specific movements, but as the play forms he must be willing to change his plans. He should work within an outline, but an out-

---

[8]Don Ross, "Broadway is Encircled by Dr. Tyrone Guthrie," *New York Herald Tribune* (February 12, 1956), p. 26.

[9]*Ibid.*, p. 26.

[10]As quoted by Alfred Rossi in *Tyrone Guthrie*, Ph.D. Thesis, University of Minnesota, 1965.

Theatre: A Contemporary Introduction

Lonely, old, miserable Scrooge is transformed into a joyful soul filled with the spirit of Christmas in Charles Dickens' A Christmas Carol, *adapted for the stage by Barbara Field. Jeff Chandler as Scrooge. Directed by Stephen Kanee; sets by Jack Barkla; costumes by Jack Edwards; lighting by Duane Schuler. At the Guthrie Theatre, Minneapolis-St. Paul.*

line that allows flexibility. The movements should all be concerned with expression of ideas and not with the action. They should be concerned with the subtle "delineation of emotion by the way people are placed. It is more delicate than getting them into common sense positions."[11]

Conferences with the leading actors and key personnel are important in order to exchange ideas about the "soul" of the play. The director, how-

[11]Toby Cole and Helen Krich Chinoy, *In Directing the Play* (New York, 1963), pp. 199-209.

The Director Takes the Stage

The Guthrie Theatre Company's 1973 production of Anouilh's Becket. *Directed by David Feldshuh; designed by Lewis Brown; music by Dick Whitbeck. The Guthrie Theatre, Minneapolis-St. Paul.*

ever, is always the leader. He should try, for example, to keep the designer from departing from the concept of the play through "doing his own thing." He should not dictate, but he should always be in charge. Thus, discussion during a rehearsal is bad in that it wastes the time of the minor actors. It should therefore be held in private before rehearsal.

Guthrie felt that the most important contribution of the director is establishing a creative atmosphere; that is, making the company feel as one. The director must create an atmosphere in which the actor is not afraid to experiment.

Probably Guthrie's most unique directing accomplishment was his modern-dress *Hamlet*, the opening production of the Tyrone Guthrie Theatre in Minneapolis. Some of the comments that Guthrie made to his actors during the *Hamlet* rehearsals shed light on his directing process. "Take positions. We'll worry about how you get there later." Deeper into rehearsals, while reworking Act 1, Scene 1, he pointed out that "you must act with your bodies and reactions to make up for the things we don't do with gauze and eerie lighting."[12]

Guthrie rarely took time out before doing a scene to explain how he thought the scene should be played. He felt that in rehearsing the scene

[12]All the following material relating to Guthrie's working habits, and his direction of *Hamlet* is from the work by Alfred Rossi, *Op. cit.*

the actors would discover on their own what he wanted from them. Also, he seldom spoke in analytical terms about the relationships of characters to each other. Rather, he felt that direction should be concerned with language and movement.

As for his direction of bit players and supernumeraries, Guthrie did not give everyone a specific movement to make, or even tell a player when to move; but everyone, through his explanations of the effect he wanted, was sure about what to do. That was achieved by having each individual onstage find a variety of positions and then select the proper balance. That refusal to overdirect the minor roles probably grew out of Guthrie's feeling that there is nothing duller than seeing a bit-part actor or actress move up to react and then move back to the same position.

Finally, Guthrie seemed to get more out of lines by using silence for emphasis. He felt that it is possible to illustrate action without telling actors what to do. He was specific to only a few people in an ensemble, encouraging the other members of the cast to create their own characters. Through this method of group direction he made his plays alive and fresh.

HAROLD CLURMAN (1901–) brings to the task of directing all of the many talents he developed during stints as an actor, writer, theatre critic, and, in a very real sense, social philosopher. It is this enormous breadth, this passionate interest in all things human, that has made Clurman one of the most important, and perhaps the most influential of figures in contemporary American theatre.

Dunois (Scott Thomas) and Joan of Arc (Sarah Miles) pray for the wind to change during the seige of Orleans in a scene from the Center Theatre Group's production of Saint Joan *at the Ahmanson Theatre, Los Angeles.*

A scene from the Alley Theatre's production of George Bernard Shaw's You Never Can Tell. *Directed by Ted Fellows; set design by Matthew Grant; costumes by Michael Olich.*

For Clurman, the task of the director is related directly to the roots of the theatrical experience: action. Directing is creating stage action. The drama is written; that is, the playwright has put words on paper and has visualized in a general way what he wants from a scene. He may, for example, know that

> *he wants a scene to be light and airy, suggestive of a summer day in the country and so forth, but except in a very general way he rarely knows how this atmosphere may be created through the actor's feeling and movement, through the placement of properties or the use of colors and lights. He does not know because these are not primarily his tools. . . .*[13]

But these *are* the director's tools. The old saw that "actions speak louder than words" is, for Clurman, the first principle of the stage, and for him the director is the author of stage action. Gestures and movement, light and color, are the visible manifestations of this action, and the director must be a master of this stage "language" just as the playwright must be a master of the spoken language. The dialogue and instructions of the play

[13]Harold Clurman, "In a Different Language," *Theatre Arts*, XXXIV (January, 1950), p. 19.

A scene from Sean O'Casey's The Plough and the Stars. *Directed by Gerard A. Larson, California State University, Sacramento.*

become, for the director, clues to what the playwright is seeking to express, and the director then adds action to the spoken dialogue to produce a theatrical whole that expresses the author's meaning.

> *To put it as simply as possible, the function of the stage director is to translate a play into stage terms: that is, to make the play as written, clear, interesting, enjoyable, by means of living actors, sounds, colors, movement.* [14]

ELIA KAZAN (1909–) deserted a successful career as an actor to become one of the best known and influential directors on the American stage and in American film. Perhaps the best way to begin an examination of his directorial technique is in terms of his own statement that, as a director, he attempts to "catch the thoroughly saturated essence of a type." [15]

[14] As quoted in Cole and Chinoy, *Op. cit.*, p. 380.
[15] As quoted in Thomas E. Morgan, "Elia Kazan's Great Expectations," *Harper's Magazine* (September, 1962), p. 66.

In 1947, Kazan directed Arthur Miller's *All My Sons*. It was a highly successful production and won the Critics Circle Award, though it achieved nothing like the success of Miller's *Death of a Salesman*, which Kazan directed in 1949. From those experiences, Arthur Miller attempted to define Kazan's directorial art:

> When Kazan directs, he wants to dramatize the metaphor in every human action. There is always the overt action and something under the surface. You kill a man, but in what attitude? In anger? Or as though you were praying to him? A good deal of the time, Kazan finds the inner metaphor and that is why his best work has tremendous depth. Now, other directors also try for this, but with Kazan it is in the forefront of his mind. If he finds nothing below the surface, his work tends to get clouded or seems overloaded. He is always on a quest for metaphors. That is his art. [16]

Technically, Kazan first decides what the spine of the play is, because for him all other facets of the play are merely ribs off the main spine. Boris Aronson, a scenic designer, said of Kazan, "there is nothing precious about him. No halftones or undertones. He concentrates on structure, plot, character. He strives for power and simplicity."[17]

Kazan directed four plays by Tennessee Williams, and many feel that his technique and style as a director are best revealed in the tragic actions of Williams' characters. Kazan worked well not only with Miller and Williams but with most playwrights. Indeed, the playwright Robert Anderson has pointed out that Kazan is a playwright's director.

> His point of reference is the playwright and the playwright's intention. Most plays do not come from an "idea" or a gimmick but rather grow out of the essence of a writer, what he is, feels, thinks, believes, and experiences. So that he can interpret the writer's play, Kazan sets about discovering for himself this essence. [18]

Kazan's ability to make other people believe that he believes in their work forms the basis of his professional relationships. This, plus a mixture of chemistry, sympathy, and mutual regard, make him unusually successful in getting what he wants out of writers and actors and producers alike.

In a sense, Kazan's success as a director is summed up in a short, simple statement he made about his own outstanding career: "I've always done the scripts I wanted with the actors I wanted the way I wanted. That's the way I've played the game, and I'm proud of it."[19]

[16]*Ibid.*, p. 67.
[17]*Newsweek* (October 16, 1961), p. 112.
[18]Robert Anderson, "Walk a Ways with Me," *Theatre Arts* (January, 1954), p. 31.
[19]Morgan, *Op. cit.*, pp. 66-68.

nine

The
Actor
Onstage

Certainly the most highly visible and best-known aspect of theatre is the acting. In the privacy of rehearsals the director may reign supreme, but when rehearsals are over and a show opens, the actor or actress stands in the spotlight and receives most of the glory not only from the general audience but also from most reviewers. Many people think of theatre only in terms of the performers, and they think of them strictly as onstage and in their moments of glory: the curtain calls. They rarely if ever think of the performer as actually working; and yet, acting is a craft as well as an art. To act well requires extensive training and years of hard work to perfect the effortlessness displayed onstage.

If theatre were broken down into its two major components, one would have to be the *audience* and the other, on the production side, would be the *performer*. Theatre—not film or video tape but real, live, legitimate theatre—exists only when the live actor is onstage before an audience. Other aspects of theatre production can be vital to a complete and aesthetically satisfying production, but the actor or actress is absolutely indispen-

John Forsythe and Hume Cronyn do some verbal fencing in the Center Theatre Group's original production of The Caine Mutiny Court Martial *at the Ahmanson Theatre, Los Angeles. Directed by Henry Fonda.*

sable. Directors, scenic designers, etc., can be dispensed with, and even the formal staging area can be discarded, but theatre exists only when an actor steps out before a live audience. This combination is the essence of theatre. The audience gives the actor a reason for being and raises this art to something far more than internal, psychological game playing. The actor, in turn, gives the audience an opportunity to live imaginatively, to unchain fancy, to suspend disbelief, and for a short time to experience a life beyond the normal boundaries, to experience thoughts and emotions that stand outside the usual sphere of existence.

Where do actors come from? What do they do? Why do they do it? These are questions that have intrigued both audiences and scholars for as many years as there has been theatre, which is very probably to say ever since the human race began. Obviously those questions are not easily answered; instead, we must settle for a series of responses based on understandings of our own time. Where do actors and actresses come from? They come from inside us. A mimetic drive exists within every human being, and when that drive is strong enough, and other internal needs are great enough, the performer emerges.

The mimetic impulse—the desire and even the necessity to imitate, to impersonate, to pretend to be—is buried deep in the nature of humanity, a part of our genetic inheritance. In large measure it is a learning process.

Tom Poston plays Friar Laurence in the McCarter Theatre Company's production of Romeo and Juliet. *Directed by Michael Kahn; settings by John Conklin; costumes by Jane Greenwood; lighting by Marc B. Weiss.*

Imitation is not only the way the monkey learns; it is also the way we learn. When we see a child impersonating an adult, we see the learning process at work, shaping and setting actions and reactions. In the early years such imitation is promoted; later, however, it no longer receives approbation. The small child mimicking an older brother or sister is called "cute" or "precious," but the early teenager mimicking the advanced teenager becomes a "copycat," and, as the term indicates, the reaction is one of disapprobation. Open imitation thus becomes less and less acceptable, until it is finally smothered under a layer of social strictures.

If the drive is strong or the emotional need is great, however, the mimetic instinct survives. For the actor or actress it never dies, and is never overwhelmed by social convention. In cases where it manages to remain alive, though in an untrained state, it continues to be merely mimicry, copying the observed. When the mimetic instinct is *trained*, however, whatever the school or theory, when instinct is mated with *craft*, it then becomes the basis of art.

Because acting, as an art form, is so subjective and personal, and because there are so many acting schools and theories, the art and craft of acting resists examination. Even so, certain basic understandings can be reached by examining various components of the art.

The Actor as Interpreter

On one level, theatre, by its very nature, seldom if ever encourages what some critics consider to be *purely* creative art. Theatre requires the united, interlocking efforts of a number of artists, and so the resulting product that the audience views is not an individual *tour de force* but the creative result of this combined artistry. Playwrights, from this point of view, are perhaps the freest of the theatrical artists, for the only limits placed on them are those of the language itself (not exhausted by even the greatest of poets) and the writer's own sensibility and sensitivity. The director is one step down on the ladder of pure creativity in that he must work not only within the technical limitations of the theatre but also within the capabilities of the cast and the limits prescribed by the author's script. Actors, then, must operate at the third step down, with the limitations placed on them by the playwright's script, the director's general interpretation, and the work of the scenic, costume, and lighting designers.

Within these creative restrictions actors and actresses also have certain other limiting responsibilities. They are interpretive artists who must take an original conception and, by the exercise of their own art, bring it to life for an audience. In so doing they must remain faithful to the values and ideas of the script and not use it merely as a point of departure, as an opportunity to "do their own thing." Rather, they must work to develop a deep, penetrating, critical analysis of the total script, not only of their own

The Alliance Theatre Company of Atlanta, Georgia, produced Count Dracula, *featuring Philip Pleasants and Susan Gilliss. Directed by Robert Farley.*

roles and lines but of the whole work and the roles played by the other performers. They must, then, develop ways of making their own creation mesh with the totality of the work, always remembering that, like the musicians in symphony orchestras, they are responsible to the scores (scripts), the conductors (directors), their fellow musicians (actors), and the audience.

The Actor as Creative Artist

Actors may well be the most creative of all artists precisely *because* of all the various limitations imposed on them by restrictions derived from the author, director, and numerous other factors. It is difficult enough to

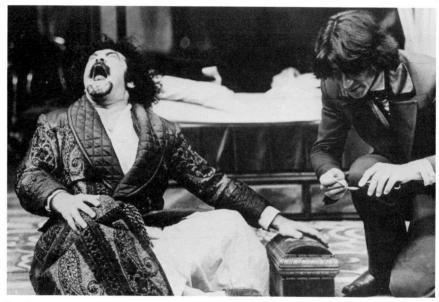

Ben Jonson's Volpone *was updated to the nineteenth century and set in San Francisco in this production at the Mark Taper Forum in Los Angeles. Avery Schreiber is featured as Volpone, with Sam Waterston as Mosca. Directed by Edward Parone.*

create totally, with no (or at least very few) limiting factors, and the difficulties facing the actor or actress make the resulting creation an impressive feat indeed.

There are many ways by which actors and actresses work to perfect roles, and because acting is such a personal art form, many of those ways are not easily defined. For most actors the creation of a character is at least in part an intuitive, subconscious process that they do not fully understand. Wedded to the conscious formal research into the script, and honed by the exploration undertaken in rehearsals under the guidance of the director, which provides the necessary opportunity to react as well as to act, the result is artistic creation at its highest level.

In the process of creation theatrical performers, unlike other artists, become totally their own tools or instruments. Painters may use brush or pallet-knife and paint, musicians use specific musical instruments, and writers use pen and paper, but actors and actresses are the only artists who use themselves totally. The dancer uses the body as an instrument, and the singer uses the voice, but the theatrical performer calls up intelligence and sensitivity, dredges emotion and memories to create, and then uses *both* body and voice (and, of course, face) to translate the playwright's work to the audience. That is what makes acting such a personal, difficult, and exciting art form.

The Actor's Equipment

To achieve the necessary control over their physical equipment, the actors or actresses usually undergo, formally or informally, a pattern of training that is highly complex and extensive, and no one aspect supersedes another or even exists as a completely separate entity, which is to say that the performer's voice and body must interact and correlate at all times.

The variety of physical types—young, old, small, large, thin, fat, tall, short—that are called for by most plays guarantees that anyone, of whatever particular size or shape, has the opportunity to act. Nevertheless, no matter how impressive or appropriate theatrical performers' physical endowments, their bodies must be highly trained and under complete control at all times. That is particularly necessary because, on the stage, they are often called upon to "speak" as expressively with their bodies as with their voices or their faces. They must be able to create a room with a gesture, and furnish it with movements. Often they may be called upon to work on a bare stage, with little more than levels and lighting to provide the physical environment. In such cases the lines of the script may indicate the setting to some degree, and the actor's body must then demonstrate this setting and even enlarge upon it. The body must also be trained to wear costumes, to be at home in them, and to use them to proper advantage. It may seem simple to exchange today's street clothes for a Medieval bishop's robes, or the costume of an Elizabethan courtier. Not so. To feel comfortable onstage while making proper use of the flowing robes of that bishop or the beplumed hat of the courtier in creating the character is not nearly as simple as it may at first seem.

Finally, the actor learns that onstage all body movement or motion is an outward manifestation of the inner state of being, and that the two are inseparably joined. The essence of acting, in one sense, is revealing the internal, and bodies sometimes become even more important than the lines the actor speaks. In some cases actors must be able to demonstrate physically a truth that stands in direct opposition to what they verbalize. An example is the character who announces loudly that he is not afraid but shows trembling limbs and terror in a posture ready for flight.

The body of the actor or actress certainly communicates a great deal, but what it communicates is, in most cases, general and emotional. The body tells an audience that the character is exhausted, or afraid, or happy, or sad. Exactly *what* led to that exhaustion, or fear, or happiness, or sadness, the specifics of the situation, is usually communicated verbally. Words, however, do transmit emotional meaning as well as facts. Words carry a great deal of emotional freight, and in the theatre there are very few words that are not charged with several levels of meaning.

For most people, the voice is something they use regularly and to which they pay little attention unless they have a speech impediment. For the actor, however, voice is a primary tool, perhaps *the* primary tool, and deserves not only care but diligent practice in its various uses. The actor

Ben Gazzara as Erie Smith in a scene from Eugene O'Neill's Hughie *at the Huntington Hartford Theatre, Los Angeles.*

who is serious about his art will work to develop voice in at least four general areas: (1) quality; (2) strength; (3) versatility; and (4) control.

Developing vocal *quality* means, in fact, not working toward a specific manner of speaking or pattern of phrasing, but toward developing a resonant and pleasing tone. That is more important than it might at first seem because, although many roles actually require an unpleasant vocal quality, the actor with a trained voice can easily achieve the desired effect. For roles requiring a rich, full voice, however, the actor who has not developed voice in terms of quality will be unable to adjust.

Vocal *strength* means, for the actor, both the ability to hold up during the long hours and over the extended period of rehearsals, and to be able to maintain full voice during production. It also means being able to *project*; that is, to be heard clearly in any portion of the house without (necessarily) seeming to shout. At times a script will call for a quiet, intimate conversation onstage, and well-trained actors and actresses will be able to accomplish this, and be heard throughout the auditorium, without the audience believing for a moment that the actors are screaming at each other.

Versatility means, vocally, an ability to meet a variety of oral demands. The well-trained actor can adopt an accent or adapt to any special speech pattern without sacrificing strength. Also, actors who are vocally versatile will be able to capture nuances of phrasing because they will have mastered articulation and tonal elements. That is to say, they will be able to pronounce words in sequence in a manner that is clear, sharp, and crisp, without ever seeming to overenunciate.

Control of the voice, like control of the body, is essential to the actor and actress because it allows them to adjust immediately from soft to loud, or friendly to unfriendly, or sad to gay, or any combination of these contrasting elements, even within the same passage. Those who have tried the "gravedigger speech" from *Hamlet* or the long opening monologue of Mrs. Zero in *The Adding Machine*, will immediately recognize the necessity for such vocal control.

Joan of Arc (Sarah Miles) kneels before the Dauphin (Richard Thomas) in the Center Theatre Group's production of George Bernard Shaw's Saint Joan *at the Ahmanson Theatre, Los Angeles.*

After the body and the voice, two of the main instruments that actors use are their own emotional sensitivity and their creative intelligence. Essentially, actors and actresses must develop the ability to focus their fancies, imaginations, and intellectual awarenesses on the specific roles they are performing, and on the context in which that role exists. In part, this requires a recognition that theatre is both a state of being and also a special and quite specific physical situation. Onstage actors need to invoke their own emotional sensitivities because they are artists who must dredge up their own memories and emotions to create a role. They are also craftsmen occupying spaces in their own workshops, which demand an intellectual awareness of the situation. The specific product of these workshops will be the effect created in the audience.

Last, but certainly not least of actors' and actresses' instruments, are the various aspects of their *craft*; that is, those external technical skills with which they work on a conscious level, both to help create a role and to enhance characterization. On the whole, these are all skills that can be learned objectively. Actors learn the various areas of the stage and its terminology, and the primary stage positions and their strengths and weaknesses. They learn historical acting styles, so that they can play, with

A scene from Agatha Christie's classic thriller The Mousetrap *at Columbus College. Directed by Hazel Hall; designed by Sandra Luker.*

The Actor Onstage

The Playboy (Jerry Sy) tells the Widow Quinn (Mary Knaus) about how he "killed" his father in Synge's Playboy of the Western World. *Directed by Alvin Keller.*

equal effectiveness, an Egyptian queen, an Elizabethan nobleman, a Restoration courtier, or a twentieth-century ship's stoker. Also, they attain at least a limited command of such stage-related skills as fencing and tumbling. Along the way, the apprentice actor will pick up such skills as applying makeup and methods of entry and exit, and even learn which hand or foot to use in performing certain types of onstage action.

The History of Acting

Perhaps the two greatest difficulties in considering the history of acting are that acting is, by its very nature, an ephemeral art form, and it is a form in which the work of art and the artist cannot be separated.

Acting is ephemeral—an art form that lasts a very short time, essentially, as long as the performance—in the sense that until very recently there was no method of recording the art, which is contained in the performance. People could view it, and recognize it as art, and later write about it, but such recollection is not the art itself, and there was no way of preserving it. Today, by means of film or video tape or even records, some aspect of the performance can be preserved, but even that falls short because it is not the art, but only a record of it. An artist paints a picture and the picture *is* the art and can exist long after the artist has died, perhaps even been forgotten. The art is what survives. The same is true for the composer or the poet or the playwright. For theatrical performers, the artists of theatre, the art begins and ends in their own living presence, and this presence is what is missing in filmed or taped re-creations of performances.

In this area of endeavor the art and the artist are inseparable, for the actors and actresses create live, out of their own beings. Their art is not something that can be passed along like a painting, that can be viewed not only by contemporaries but also by future generations. The actors' and actress' art begins and ends with each performance. Each performance is a new creation because of changes in the audience, the performer, and the reactions and errors of the rest of the cast and the technicians. As David Garrick wrote, "Nor Pen nor Pencil can the Actor save, The Art and Artist, share one common Grave."

Even though we cannot view the live performances of great actors of the past, we do know something, even about acting back in the Classical Greek period. Our knowledge is based largely on commentaries and paintings of the periods, and it is both interesting and valuable in that it allows us to trace, however imperfectly, the development of the acting art.

Greece

Acting in the Western world began in Greece in the sixth century B.C. There had been earlier acting, certainly, for dance, song, ritual, and mimesis had existed in most early and primitive societies, including the

Lewis Clark Normal School in Lewiston, Idaho, was one of many colleges producing Eugene O'Neill's Long Day's Journey Into Night. *This production featured Jack Holland in the role of James Tyrone.*

Actor dressed to play the role of a young king.

Greek. Nevertheless, acting, and thus theatre, really began when Thespis, the first actor, stepped forward to add impersonation to the musical narration and dance of the dithyramb.

In those early times there was still only a Chorus, a Chorus leader, and one person, usually the poet wearing masks to impersonate several characters. Aeschylus, the first of the great tragic dramatists, added a second performer; Sophocles added a third and diminished the importance of the Chorus. The addition of more actors shifted emphasis away from the poet presenting his own materials, to the actors performing the materials of the poet.

The successful Greek tragic actors must have been highly trained individuals indeed. That becomes apparent when it is understood that they were required to dance, sing, chant, and recite poetry, all while wearing a full mask and long, heavy robes. These physical requirements alone seem to militate against any attempt at realistic theatre, implying a highly stylized, ritualized performance. In comedy the stylization must have been a bit less extreme. Even so, comic actors also wore masks, traditional short robes, and often heavily padded costumes. Members of the Chorus, in Greek tragedy or comedy alike, often wore fantastic costumes and makeup. For example, in Aeschylus' play *Eumenides*, legend has it that when the Chorus of Furies made its appearance before the audience, men fainted, children died of fright, and pregnant women gave birth. Whether the makeup was actually that realistically horrible is questionable, but surviving pictures of the actors and Chorus members, in various types of makeup and costume, at least support the idea that the Greeks strove to achieve a certain level of reality especially for members of the Chorus.

The primary physical attribute of the Greek actor was voice. Actors were judged on the quality of the voice, its resonance and beauty of tone, and its ability to capture the mood of the characterization. Not unnaturally, since the masks hid facial expression, and the tragic costume put severe limits on physical movement. The costume restriction was apparently less severe, in comedy, but the tradition of comic exaggeration also removed the acting from anything approaching realism.

While the specifics of acting in ancient Greece may have been quite different from our own, the Greek actor, like the actor today, was responsible for capturing the emotional context of the material, and there are some indications that this was done in ways similar to those used by today's actors. There is a story, probably apocryphal, that an actor, playing the role of a tragic king, brought to the theatre the ashes of his dead son, apparently to help achieve the proper tragic mood. This technique, though macabre, is not far from some of the techniques of emotional recall so popular with actors today.

Rome and the Middle Ages

Both the early written drama of Rome and the techniques of performing in that drama were based primarily on Greek theatrical models. Perhaps the primary difference between Greek and Roman actors was the elevated social and religious status of Greek actors, in contrast to the Roman actors, who were mostly slaves, trained by managers of acting troupes, without legal or religious rights. A very few players, such as Quintus Roscius and Claudius Aesopus, rose to great wealth and fame, but those two were marked exceptions in a profession that was considered less than significant.

Roman theatre declined under the despotic conditions of the Empire period, becoming steadily more and more obscene and bloody. Finally, in the sixth century, the Emperor Justinian closed the theatres, and the Medieval period, already under way for the other art forms, began for theatre.

Throughout the early Middle Ages the profession of acting was tenuous indeed, nearly dying out as an art form and kept alive only by the performances of the wandering minstrel (the *scop* or *gleeman* or *jongleur*) small traveling companies of entertainers, and the folk themselves. The minstrel was at home in both the great halls of the feudal nobility and the

The Actor Onstage

Scene from The Woman of Andros *taken from the Medieval manuscript of Terence in the Vatican. It shows a simple setting much like those used to stage the Roman farces.*

squares of the small villages. He provided acrobatics, pantomimes, songs, and dances for entertaining his audiences. Sometimes, particularly in the later Middle Ages, he became attached to the retinue of a particular lord or nobleman, but the image of the minstrel as a wanderer contains a large portion of truth. The folk, in their little ritual dramas inherited from prehistoric ancestors, also helped to keep alive the idea of theatre and acting in a hostile age. The village amateur performer, acting the role of St. George or Robin Hood, passed along the delights and, to some degree, the techniques of playing.

Throughout that period the Church seemed to be the arch foe of theatre. Council, diet, and synod constantly denounced theatre in general and entertainers in particular, commanding them to go away and die. It is therefore interesting to discover that when true theatre was at last reborn, it found its birthplace in Medieval Christian practice. Out of the antiphonal singing of the antiphons grew little plays, designed at first as illustrations of the liturgy; and the actors in those plays were the clergy themselves. As the plays grew larger and moved out of the churches they took upon themselves the representation of the entire Christian epic, from the Creation to Judgment.

Those plays, produced at first by the Church and then later by such groups as the trade guilds in England or even whole cities on the Continent, were acted primarily by amateurs, although there are records of payments made to professional actors (minstrels) hired occasionally to play especially demanding roles, such as that of *Deus*. In France during the late Medieval period, when farce reached its peak in such works as *The Farce of Master Pierre Pathelin*, plays were acted by student groups such as the *Basochians*, an organization of law clerks, or such fools companies as the *Enfants sans Souci*.

Like the Greek stage before it, though unlike the Roman, the Medieval theatre relied on men to play all the roles, both male and female. Apparently the churchly fulminations about the immorality of acting, and a tradition that began as early as the Greeks, were still enough to make the stage unfit for women. There is little record of how those men managed their roles, although an exceptionally fine performance was sometimes noted and praised in a letter, journal, or day book that has survived. Still, acting as an art form waited for the reappearance of the professionals.

Commedia dell'arte

The sixteenth-century drama of Italy was not highly significant in the literary sense, but sixteenth-century Italian theatre, that part known as the *commedia dell'arte*, exploded out of Italy to exercise a strong influence on the whole theatrical scene in Western Europe.

The *commedia* troupes, highly trained and closely knit groups of professional actors, played their comedies (and sometimes tragedies) on the streets and in the town squares, at both rustic and urban festivals, and, eventually, in the great halls of the nobility and the castles of kings and princes. Each actor specialized in playing a stock character who had certain easily identifiable characteristics, and spent an entire acting life perfecting that role.

Perhaps the most famous aspect of *commedia* performance, and the one most admired and emulated in our own time, is that the performances were, in most respects, improvisations. That is, the players took a brief scenario that outlined the action and then provided their own dialogue and comic business, or *lazzi*. This emphasis on improvisation has unquestionably been overstated in many cases. Because of the concentration of each actor on one role, or at least one characterization, troupes ended up with actors who had played the same characters for five to fifty years and for a large portion of that time had played together as a unit (many of the troupes were, in fact, family groups). During that extended period the individual performers perfected certain "set" speeches and bits of business that would be applicable in specific situations, and the troupe members as a group learned to recognize their fellow players' "set" materials and to respond to them appropriately with their own. Thus, the players could adapt to individual audiences and "improvise" brilliantly because they were familiar with the materials of all the other actors. If one player made a move, physically or verbally, the others could automatically counter because they had done the same or similar things so many times before.

Frontispiece from the first edition of Paul Scarron's novel Roman comique, *Paris, 1651.*

Actor training in such a situation was primarily on an individual coaching and understudy basis. Young actors who displayed an appropriate or promising personality and possessed the proper physical attributes would understudy one of the stock characters, often for many years. Through observation and personal coaching they would learn the movements, set speeches, stage business, and style of their mentors. That allowed a continuity of performance from player to player within the troupe that was especially necessary to actors who were, in however limited a way, improvising their material. When an older performer left and a "new" actor finally took over a character, all the other people on stage could count on the new actor. He not only knew the lines and business of the actor replaced but also the lines and business of the other performers. This method of learning a characterization must have engendered similarities of style over generations of performers, but stagnation

French commedia *actors, or* farceurs, *on the stage of the* Hôtel de Bourgogne, *in an engraving by Bosse, 1630.*

was unlikely since the young actor taking over a characterization almost certainly gradually modified lines, movements, and business to something slightly different and more individualized.

In addition to the practical training involved in working as understudy, the actors of the *commedia* also promoted special forms of study to enrich performance. For example, Pietro Maria Cecchini, in 1628, advised those actors seeking to play the "young lover" character to read a great deal, thereby enriching their minds with "a number of noble and charming discourses pertaining to the various themes treated on the stage."[1] In addition to reading, the actor must also see to it that "his mind controls his memory (which dispenses the treasure of memorized phrases over the vast field of opportunities constantly offered by comedy). . . ."[2]

That style of theatre reached its peak in the late sixteenth century with the great Gelosi troupe, featuring Isabella Andreini (perhaps the most famous and celebrated of *commedia* performers), and maintained its ascendancy until the middle of the seventeenth century. During the next hundred years its influence declined, but it had already changed the face of the performing arts for all time.

[1]Pietro Maria Cecchini, "Frutti delle moderne comedie et avisi a chi le recita" (Padova, 1628), in *La Commedia dell'arte; storia, tecnica, scenari,* ed. by Enzo Petraccone, as quoted in Cole and Chinoy, *Actors on Acting,* p. 50.
[2]*Ibid.,* p. 50.

The English Renaissance

As the Medieval period came to an end in England a secular national drama began to emerge. The primary impetus for this drama, and perhaps for everything artistic that happened during the Renaissance in England, came from the rediscovery of Classical art and learning. Scholars, courtiers, and schoolmasters wrote plays based on ancient models, mostly Terence and Seneca, to which they added a bit of the farcical and often bawdy humor that was their heritage from the Middle Ages. When two young law students, Thomas Norton and Thomas Sackville, wrote *Gorboduc* (1561) and performed it before the Queen, English blank-verse tragedy was born. Written in the style of the Roman tragic writer Seneca, it began a vogue of Senecan tragedy, rhetorical tragedy that emphasizes emotional excess, rapine, and murder. This kind of tragedy lasted through the first twenty-odd years of the seventeenth century.

Between the 1580s and the 1620s, great actors paralleled the creation of great plays by playwrights like Shakespeare, Marlowe, and Jonson. Actors gradually circumvented the Medieval laws against their profession by seeking the patronage of the powerful nobility. Those players, under the protection of a powerful lord, gained experience by playing farce and morality plays in inns, innyards, and village squares, and eventually formed a nucleus of trained performers to produce the early plays in the deluge of drama that was about to burst upon the English scene.

Ball scene from Alliance Theatre Company production of Romeo and Juliet, *Atlanta, Georgia, 1974. Directed by Fred Chappell; designed by Lewis Greenleaf III.*

Most actors, throughout the Renaissance period, learned their skills by working as apprentices (as young boys, often playing the female roles) and eventually moving up to full membership in an acting company. Those companies owned their own theatres, distributed roles according to specific talents of performers within the company, and shared in the profits of their ventures. Playwrights wrote plays for such companies and thus wrote roles to fit the personnel they knew would be available. In that sense, the actors of the period conditioned the play itself in a way that would not be possible with open auditions. For example, William Kemp, a popular clown in Shakespeare's company, traveled to the Continent and very possibly learned some of his techniques from the *commedia* players. Thus, Hamlet's remarks against players who say more than is set down for them is often taken as a reference to Kemp's improvisational techniques.

Scene from Shakespeare's Henry VI, *Part 1, at the Oregon Shakespearian Festival, Ashland, Oregon.*

His highly physical and verbally bombastic style of performance is more guessed at than supported by hard fact, but characters such as Bottom and Dogberry that Shakespeare created while Kemp was with the company are physical and verbal types who lead to such a conclusion. Robert Armin, who followed Kemp in the company, was obviously less physical and a more subtle actor. That is testified to by Shakespeare's creation, during Armin's tenure, of such subtle, restrained clowns as Touchstone and Feste.

Of the Elizabethan actors specializing in tragic roles, the bombastic style is probably best represented by Edward Alleyn of the Admiral's Men. Thomas Nashe, writing about Alleyn, said that neither "Roscius nor Aesop, those admired tragedians . . ., could perform more in action than famous Ned Alleyn."[3] The words "in action" give a possible clue to Alleyn's style of acting. Because of Nashe's comment, and the traditional rivalry between the Admiral's Men and the Chamberlain's Men (the company to which Shakespeare belonged), Hamlet's remark about the ranting player who "out-herods Herod" has been taken as a satiric comment on Alleyn's bombastic style.

If the supposition that Shakespeare was referring to Alleyn is correct, then Richard Burbage, the leading tragic actor of Shakespeare's own company, must have been restrained by comparison, probably speaking his lines as Hamlet, and thus Shakespeare, commanded—"trippingly on the tongue," without "mouthing it" or ranting so loudly as to "split the ears of the groundlings" or overdoing movement and gesture. Unfortunately, few documents have come down to us that comment directly on Burbage's style, and only his versatility has been generally accepted.

The greatest period in English drama had, essentially, come to an end before 1620, just as the great Classical period in French drama was in the wings, ready to make its entrance.

French Classical Period

The Renaissance in France, as in England, emphasized the rediscovered Classical materials. During the early years of this period the religious drama, of major importance during the Medieval period, began to die out, eventually being suppressed by civil decree. Finally, of the early drama only the popular Medieval farces such as *Pierre Pathelin* continued to be played. A company of players specializing in religious drama, the *Confrerie de la Passion*, had held exclusive rights to perform in Paris, and when religious drama was ended by decree, in 1548, they were recompensed for potential loss of income by renewal of their exclusive right to perform plays in Paris. Unable to perform their own religious drama, but holding an exclusive license to perform in the city, the *Confrerie* became an agency to which any theatrical group had to apply for permission to play within the city limits. Permission could be granted if the group would pay a hand-

[3]From *Pierce Penilesse* (1592).

some performance fee, and this meant that the *Confrerie* exercised enormous control over development of the acting art in France.

Of the groups that played, not only in Paris but throughout France, the Italian *commedia* companies were the most common during the closing years of the sixteenth century and the early years of the seventeenth. It was not until several native French companies established themselves that a real spread of performance styles emerged.

The most famous of those early tragic actors was Montdory (Guillaume Desgilberts, 1594–1651), an actor who specialized in heroic characters and apparently played them with enormous physical exertion and vocal gymnastics. This style won Montdory great critical and public acclaim, to the point that when Corneille's *Le Cid* was under attack by Cardinal Richelieu and the French Academy for ignoring the Classical unities, many critics began attributing the play's huge public success to the performance of Montdory in the title role of *Le Cid*, the character Rodrigo. This highly physical style, however, eventually proved Montdory's undoing, and while playing Herod (apparently "out-heroding Herod") he was struck by an apoplectic fit that paralyzed his tongue.

Jodelet (Julien Geoffrin Bedeau, 1600–1660), Montdory's comic counterpart at the *Théâtre du Marais*, specialized in playing farce. His acting style

A scene from Doctor for a Dumb Wife *by Moliere-Anatole France. Adapted and directed by Edwin Duerr; designed by Viktor Schreckengost. Western Reserve University.*

A scene from a production of Beaumarchais' The Marriage of Figaro. *An engraving after Saint-Quentin, 1785.*

is said to have been of the broad slapstick sort that might be predicted for anyone specializing in farcical roles. With this style, however, he combined a flair for acrobatics and, one may surmise, the perfection of timing on which such a comic style so totally depends.

Following Montdory's retirement, several tragic actors attempted, apparently, to outdo the grand old man in terms of theatricality. Montfleury (Zacharie Jacob, 1608–1667) and Bellerose (Pierre Le Messier, ?–1670) introduced a new style that took Montdory's bombast and added to it a flamboyant and mannered artificiality. Montfleury's greatest claim to historical notice is that he and his affected style were unmercifully satirized by Moliere.

In 1658, performing before Louis XIV, the acting company of Moliere

(Jean Baptiste Poquelin, 1622–1673) achieved a triumph that made them the first troupe in France. Moliere had abandoned the study of law to join a small theatrical group, the *Illustre Théâtre*. When the group failed, Moliere, the Béjart family, and also some other members of the group went into the provinces to perform, remaining there for thirteen years while Moliere perfected himself as actor and playwright and drilled the company in the techniques of acting and the necessity of ensemble performance. It was the reputation of his troupe for avoiding the excessive and unnatural, as much as Moliere's own plays, that brought audiences first to the court theatre, the *Petit-Bourbon*, and later to Richelieu's old theatre, the *Palais Royal*.

After Moliere's death and Louis XIV's establishment of the *Comédie-Française* in 1680, the history of French acting is bound up in the development of what might be called the *Comédie-Française* style; that is, a style that was mannered, finely declaimed, colorful, and essentially nonrealistic. The two major exceptions to this were Michel Baron, who developed his realistic style under the tutelage of Moliere at the *Palais Royal*, and Adrienne Lecouvreur, whose simple, natural style of speaking lines, eschewing the chanting and declamation that had taken over the French stage, allowed her to bring to the stage a feeling of warmth and humanity that had gotten lost in the artificiality of the period.

The Modern Actor

In a very real sense, modern acting begins with an actor, David Garrick (1717–1779), and a book, Denis Diderot's *The Paradox of Acting* (published posthumously in 1830). The aspect of Garrick's performance that excited the most comment during his own lifetime was his "naturalness." That is not to say that he was "naturalistic" within our own understanding of the term, and in fact Garrick's style would probably strike a contemporary audience raised on a diet of theatrical realism as mannered and artificial. But in terms of his own period he was considered the epitome of reality onstage. The period just before Garrick, from the middle of the seventeenth century onward, had been one of formalized, stylized performances, modeled after the French Classical style of acting as promoted by the *Comédie-Française*, so Garrick's style was something that was very new indeed.

Breaking new ground in any art is never easy, and for Garrick the development of his style, which seemed so natural and easy and alive to his audiences, was a matter of hard work, great concentration, and enormous study, all of which was directed toward a complete understanding of himself and his fellow human beings. Garrick felt that such understanding was the primary requirement for acting. In his "Essay on Acting" he points out that "the only way to arrive at great excellence in characters . . . is to be very conversant with human nature, that is the noblest and best study, by this way you will more accurately discover the workings of spirit (or what other physical term you please to call it) upon the different modifications of matter."[4]

---

[4]David Garrick (London, 1744), p. 2.

A scene from Brian Friel's Lovers *at the University of Montana, Missoula. Directed by Jeanette Chastonay. Featuring Dale Raoul.*

It was at least in part the emphasis that Garrick placed on reading and observing that led Denis Diderot (1713–1784) to write *The Paradox of Acting*, a book that provoked a never-ending debate between proponents of the emotionalistic school of performance and proponents of the realistic school. Diderot himself was never an actor, at least professionally, but he was deeply interested in the theatre. He wrote plays (not very well), and brought to his theatrical enthusiasms the same care and dedication that made his *Encyclopédie* one of the most successful scholarly works of all time.

Garrick's methods of performance and, especially, his methods of preparing for a performance had deeply impressed Diderot, following a meeting of the two men when Garrick visited France in 1773. Diderot found in the great English actor a kindred soul, a man who so thoroughly planned and rehearsed every aspect of a performance that nothing was accidental, nothing left to chance. Garrick's famous dictum that a good actor could as easily make love to a wooden table as to a beautiful woman supported this essentially rational approach to performance and, in Diderot's view, had the added virtue of assuring a standard of perfor-

The Cat and the Canary *by John Willard, produced by San Diego City College. Directed by Lyman Saville; set by Robert Green; costumes by Carol Riordan.*

mance from night to night that did not exist when actors relied too heavily on their own emotional resources.

Diderot's premise in *Paradox* was that the actor should never "feel" his role, but should instead remain constantly aware, an unmoved and disinterested onlooker. His primary reason for this belief is one that relates to his concept of *control*. An actor must always remain in complete control of his performance because audiences change, and sometimes even theatres change, but the actor must go "on" night after night (sometimes several times in one night) and sustain his performance. The emotional actor who is full of fire at the matinee may very well be as cold as ashes by the time he gets to the evening program, burned out by the passions of the earlier performance. Also, these performances may well be played under quite different physical conditions. Thus, Diderot pointed out,

> *You give a recitation in a drawing room; your feelings are stirred and . . . you burst into tears. You were carried away, you surprised and touched your hearers, you made a great hit. All this is true enough. But now transfer your easy tone, your simple expression, your everyday bearing, to the stage, and I assure you, you will be paltry and weak. You may cry to your heart's content, and your audience will only laugh.*[5]

[5]Denis Diderot, "The Paradox of Acting" (1830), in *The Paradox of Acting—Masks or Faces* (New York, 1957), p. 14.

The Actor Onstage

Diderot had, of course, aroused a powerful outcry with his contentions. Constant Coquelin (1841–1909), the great French actor for whom Edmond Rostand (1868–1918) wrote *Cyrano de Bergerac*, fully supported Diderot's thesis that the actor should never feel his role, but remain in total control. A large, handsome man of great stage presence and energy, Coquelin was also an actor who gave total attention to even the most minute details of performance. In so doing, he did not intend to exclude emotion from the stage; he merely felt that it must be dominated by intellect. Tommaso Salvini (1829–1915), on the other hand, the finest Italian actor of his period and perhaps of any period, stood diametrically opposed to Coquelin. An energetic, passionate performer who achieved his greatest

Shirley Knight as Blanche DuBois in the McCarter Theatre Company production of A Streetcar Named Desire. *Directed by Michael Kahn.*

success in the difficult role of Othello, Salvini believed that the actor had to feel his role completely in order to move an audience emotionally. Salvini did not want to banish intellect from the stage, but insisted that it be subservient to emotion.

The man who, in a sense, resolved this conflict, was Constantin Stanislavski (1863–1938). Both a theorist of great importance and a practical man of the theatre, Stanislavski was, in combination, an actor, producer, and director. With Nemirovich-Danchenko, Stanislavski became one of the founders of the Moscow Art Theatre, in 1898, and there he acted in, directed, and produced plays from all over the western world, though with special emphasis on his fellow Russians Anton Chekhov and Maxim Gorky. As a character actor and director he was able to examine his own performances from two points of view, and it was this double vision that led him to look for ways by which an actor might create each role freshly and not become dependent on stale theatrical trickery.

As an actor, Stanislavski knew only that some of his performances were better than others. As a director, however, he knew that some of his performances were truly memorable and others ranged from mediocre to poor. He determined that this was concomitant with unrestrained emotional performance, the problem on which Diderot had founded at least half of his *Paradox*. And yet, unlike Diderot, he had no wish to take

The "crown scene" from Shakespeare's Richard II. *Directed by Alan Stambusky at University of California, Davis.*

emotion out of acting. The problem was to feel the *right* thing, and to feel it *consistently*, from performance to performance. To accomplish this he developed a system that required great physical and mental discipline, and that took into account all aspects of performance. This system is thoroughly explained in two of his books, *An Actor Prepares* (1936), which deals with internal preparation, and *Building a Character* (1949), which deals with such external aspects of performance as stage techniques, voice production, body movement, etc.

What Stanislavski did was hardly new—for many years actors had used most of those techniques, consciously or unconsciously and never all at the same time. What he did was exciting and new, however, in the sense that he managed to put all those techniques together into a workable pattern or system that helped a performer not only "get at" the internal and external aspects of his role but do so consistently and at a desired level of intensity.

The Stanislavski system, promoted in the books and by the tours of the Moscow Art Theatre, provoked great controversy, especially in America. Nobody was totally unaffected. Performers loved it or hated it, but none were indifferent. The controversy stemmed from the fact that the seminal work on internal preparation appeared so many years before the book on external preparation that it was studied and emulated in isolation from its missing companion piece. Thus, to many people outside of Russia the system seemed to be internal only, to disavow the necessary stage techniques and the practical demands of acting as a craft as well an art. In the United States the system, or the Method, came into prominence when the Group Theatre adopted it in the late 1930s as part of its reaction against what the members of the Group felt to be the stylized, stereotyped performance techniques common to the New York stage and the London west-end.

In 1947, the Method as practiced by the Group Theatre was taken over and made almost a household word by the Actors' Studio, founded by Elia Kazan, Robert Lewis, and Cheryl Crawford (and later Lee Strasberg, the present director). The Method was gradually refined and changed to suit the temperaments and beliefs of the various directors, but by whatever name and however modified, as practiced by the Group Theatre and later by the Actors' Studio it managed to turn out a highly impressive roster of talented, well-trained actors such as, from the Group Theatre: Luther Adler, Franchot Tone, John Garfield, Lee J. Cobb, Morris Carnovsky, Elia Kazan, and Harold Clurman; and from the Actor's Studio: Marlon Brando, Montgomery Clift, Tom Ewell, John Forsythe, Mildred Dunnock, Karl Malden, and Maureen Stapleton.

Finally, no matter what system is followed in the learning process, acting is a highly internal and thus a highly intuitive art form, which makes it very difficult for performers to discuss. When actors analyze their art and craft they tend to explain a great deal about their own personalities as well. Still, some actors have been quite verbal about the basics of their profes-

Peter Grimes, *an opera by Benjamin Britten, as produced by California State University, Northridge. Directed by David W. Scott; set design by Michael Fontana; costume design by Chris Goulding.*

sion, and it can be most enlightening to look at how the greatest of recent actors have set about the job of acting. The three actors who are discussed in the following section are people who entered the profession by way of the stage, and who learned its techniques in the expectation that they would probably spend the greater part of their lives onstage before live audiences. Two of them have also had distinguished careers in film, but they are still stage-trained and stage-oriented, and their success makes it clear that the stage is still the best training for an acting career, including film or television.

The Actor at Work

EDWIN BOOTH (1833–1893) is still considered by many scholars and historians of theatre to be the greatest actor that America has ever produced. He was also a major innovator in theatre architecture and staging, and one of the first theatre managers in this country to cross the line into the job we now call "director." He was a man touched personally by the most unforgettable crime of his century, his brother's assassination of President Lincoln. Booth was visited by major personal tragedies, and tortured by alcoholism. He outlived the prime of his creative powers by nearly twenty years, and his last performances were pathetic. Yet, when he died the eulogies from the greatest theatricians of the day put him in the rarefied company of Garrick, Marlowe, and the playwright he most loved, Shakespeare.

Booth, in acting style, appears to have verged on modern realism, to have been natural in manner rather than declamatory and affected. He often used the device of turning his back to the audience, something that was *never* done by actors, especially when standing at the front of the stage near the audience. But his greatest talent was the ability to draw the script into himself and synthesize it into a character, a person. He did this best with Hamlet, and his daughter, looking back over those early years, had a sound idea of why that was so:

> It was long before I could thoroughly disassociate him from the character of Hamlet, it seemed so entirely a part of himself. Indeed, in that impersonation, I think, his confined nature and pent-up sorrows found vent. He told me that the philosophy of Hamlet had taught him to bear life's vicissitudes. [6]

The acting of Booth was superior in most roles. His Iago, Richard III, and Richelieu were considered outstanding. Yet Hamlet was always his most nearly perfect characterization. The word "naturalness" appears over and over again in the reviews, as does the word "believability"; these in an age when declamation, gesture, and emotion were usually an actor's most prized characteristics.

Before his death, which ended an era, Booth briefly touched a new technology. In 1890 he recorded two Edison cylinders; audio tapes of those recordings are at the University of Southern California. He also had some association with realistic theatre as it now exists and, according to the critic William Winter, loathed it. He felt that accuracy, or realism, is useful only as far as it supports the "romance of art."

No one can experience Booth's Hamlet ever again, yet it was his "living" of that beleaguered prince that brought about his greatest fame. He did a great Hamlet because he knew what Hamlet meant to him, and what theatre and art meant to him.

[6]Edwina Booth Grossman, *Edwin Booth* (New York, 1894), p. 2.

LORD LAURENCE OLIVIER (1907–), English actor, producer, and first director of the National Theatre of Great Britain, is one of the best-known and most highly admired actors of modern times. Certainly one of the finest tributes to his skill and passion as a performer was made by Franco Zeffirelli, commenting on Olivier's creation in the role of Othello:

> I was told that his was the last flourish of the romantic tradition in acting. It is nothing of the sort. It's an anthology of everything that has been discovered about acting in the last three centuries. It's grand and majestic, but it's also modern and realistic. I would call it a lesson for us all.[7]

In an interview with Kenneth Tynan,[8] Olivier made a number of points regarding his attitudes toward and beliefs about the art and craft of acting. For Olivier, acting is, in essence, the art of persuasion, and the first person who must be persuaded is the actor himself; that is, he must be persuaded that there are aspects of the character within himself, and then he must use those aspects to create the character. To achieve that he must make ultimate use of observation and intuition. He must scavenge up every scrap of "human circumstance; observe it, find it, use it some time or another."[9]

Just the reverse of those actors who create totally from the inside out, Olivier creates primarily from the outside in which is heresy for the Actors' Studio supporters but has worked very well for such great (and dissimilar) actors as Olivier and Louis Calhern. Olivier describes his own process of creation in this way, referring specifically to developing his role as Shakespeare's Richard III: "I began to build up a character, a characterization. I'm afraid I work mostly from the outside in. I usually collect a lot of details, a lot of characteristics, and find a creature swimming about somewhere in the middle of them."[10]

Once the "creature" is found, however, and identified, Olivier feels the absolute necessity of making use of stage techniques to create, to make physical, the creature for the audience, and every part of the actor is necessary to the act of creation. For Olivier

> . . . it's a fusion of every single part of you that has to go into it. The mime actor doesn't need the voice; the film actor hardly needs the voice, hardly needs the body, except to use it as a marvellous physical specimen in such roles as demand that attribute. The stage actor certainly needs the voice, certainly needs all the vocal control, all the breath control, all the techniques of the voice, certainly needs all the miming power imaginable, certainly needs the hands, certainly needs the eyes—he needs them all.[11]

If Olivier has worked to accomplish anything in his illustrious career, one attribute stands out, something that has little to do with the practice of

---

[7]Quoted in Cole and Chinoy, *Op. cit.*, p. 409.

[8]Printed in *Great Acting*, ed. by Hal Burton (New York, 1967), pp. 11–40.

[9]*Ibid.*, p. 23.

[11]*Ibid.*, p. 24.

acting but a great deal to do with the art of being—he has worked to make the art and craft of the actor not merely a part of the financial aspect of entertainment but a part of the life of the people. In that ambition he has achieved great success.

GERALDINE PAGE (1924–), by almost any definition, must be considered one of America's major contemporary actresses, with such successful roles behind her as Alma in Tennessee Williams' *Summer and Smoke*; Nina Leeds in Eugene O'Neill's *Strange Interlude*; and Olga in Chekhov's *Three Sisters*. In a 1964 interview with Richard Schechner,[12] she made apparent a part of the foundation of her artistry. Her approach to a role seems, on the surface at least, to stand in direct opposition to that of Olivier, partly because she has been so closely identified with the Actors' Studio and its techniques.

And yet, in spite of the seeming differences, there is much that is similar. For example, when questioned about whether she draws on her own experience in preparing a role, her response was an immediate affirmation, just as Olivier's would be. It is the way that this "drawing upon" works that identifies the difference between these two performers. Olivier's method seems to be primarily conscious, whereas Page's seems to be largely below the conscious level. As she points out, "A line can go by me for weeks on end and then, suddenly, the association will pop into my mind. I hopefully assume that the associations are there unconsciously; otherwise I wouldn't be able to understand my own reactions."[13]

This drawing upon one's own experience should not, however, be confused with emotional recall, which is a conscious method for calling up emotion. Rather, Page tries to keep the emotional doors open, not forcing anything up and not trying to screen anything out, but remaining in a constantly receptive state.

> *Nobody can, eight times a week, lay his whole soul on the stage and have it fully express the play. You cannot do it, no matter what kind of nut you are. Therefore, I think it's best to know how to do it the other way. But at the same time, don't paint yourself into a corner; leave enough space so that when things come to take you, you're free to let all the props fall on the floor and go. And then, when the spirit's left you, keep the technical stuff there and make it send the messages to the audience.* [14]

Along with that intuitive approach, Page also works hard in the related area of improvisation, in exploring and expanding and understanding a role. She feels that if the lines are said as written, without a chance to

---

[12]Geraldine Page, "The Bottomless Cup," interview by Richard Schechner, ed. by Charles Mee, Jr., *Tulane Drama Review* (Winter, 1964) IX, pp. 114–130 passim; as reprinted in Cole and Chinoy, *Op. cit.*, pp. 635–640.
[13]*Ibid.*, p. 637.
[14]*Ibid.*, p. 640.

improvise, at least in rehearsals, the actor is often forced to leap from "mountain crag to mountain crag" without any opportunity to explore the hills and valleys along the way. Improvisation provides the opportunity to stretch the fabric and explore the folds and thereby discover the links that are not at first apparent.

ten

The
Designer

Not very many years ago if someone referred to a theatrical designer the assumption could safely be made that the reference was to a "scenic" designer; that is, to one who designed stage sets (and usually costumes). As the physical mounting of a show has become technically more complex, however, more and more often the artistic assignments once given a single designer have been split into five primary design functions: scenic, costume, lighting, makeup, and audio. Those are not always, or even often, assigned separately. Scenic and costume design are still quite regularly handled by a single person, as are lighting and audio design, and makeup design is all too often left up to the talents of the individual performer. As the technological demands of theatre grow, however, those separate design functions are increasingly given to individual designers.

A Brief History of Theatrical Design

The Classical Period

In its earliest periods the physical design of plays was essentially non-existent. Design was fundamentally unnecessary for the Greeks, for they performed before a purely architectural setting in the light of the sun, dressing in costumes specified by tradition and wearing masks that varied only slightly from play to play. The lack of emphasis on stage design is evidenced by the fact that Aristotle, in his listing of dramatic elements, placed spectacle sixth and last in order of importance. Following the lead of the Greeks, Roman theatre, as far as can be determined, added little to theatrical design. The Romans also used standard architectural façades as backdrops for their play productions, with occasional lapses into designs that made use of such set pieces as crosses for crucifixion scenes. One fragment from a Roman mime indicates a set with a river onstage with enough water for nine nude "barbarian women" to bathe in. Whether that indicates a real set or only the flooding of the orchestra (which apparently was fairly common) cannot be determined.

Medieval Period

Certainly the roots of our concept of design in the contemporary theatre must be found in the Medieval period. While the Medieval styles and methods of presentation differed greatly from anything onstage today, the emphasis on scenic and costume design was extensive. The mansion sets of Medieval drama were, apparently, quite spectacular and as highly realistic in their spectacle as Medieval technology could support. Even when the wagon stages rolled across the English countryside, there is evidence that competition between the trade guilds that sponsored the various plays in the cycles led to some spectacular technical and scenic effects, such as sprouting and rapidly growing trees, gushing wells, and the appearance of Deus (God) on his golden throne. In terms of costume, most of those plays were richly mounted. Some of the costumes, such as the red wig and yellow robe of Judas, became standardized. Saved souls were costumed in white, and damned souls who capered at the entrance to Hell, or Hell-mouth, were in black. The Virgin Mary was usually in blue, and we are told that Pilate and Herod wore splendid clothes and carried clubs. Evident in all that activity is a great deal of design work.

The Renaissance

The Renaissance, particularly in Italy, expanded the ideal of scenic design and moved it toward the concept of pictorial representation that is still with us today. For example, in 1508 at Ferrara, a play by Ariosto was produced on a perspective set with its landscape containing a collection of "houses, churches, towers, and gardens." Later productions featured pillars, statues, altars, and temples. And we are told that all this was done so that "the streets looked as if they were real, and everything was done in relief, and made even more striking through the art of painting and well-conceived perspective."[1]

From the Italian Renaissance we have also received technical instructions, by way of Sabbatini, on "How to Make Dolphins and Other Sea Monsters Appear and Spout Water While Swimming"; "How to Produce a Constantly Flowing River"; "How to Divide the Sky Into Sections"; "How to Make a Cloud Descend Perpendicularly With Persons on It"; and even detailed instructions on how to make the cloud descend at an angle.

The prototype of the contemporary stage, with proscenium arch, was completed at Parma (the *Teatro Farnese*) in 1618. Almost all of the aspects of scenic design that followed its construction are devoted to the realistic possibilities that the proscenium stage affords. Exactly where the proscenium arch came from is unclear. Some scholars feel that the involvement of the great Italian painters in scenic design led to adapting the picture frame to the stage. The supposition lacks concrete proof, however.

In England, Renaissance stage design took a step backward from the Medieval representations when the professional companies undertook playing on a thrust stage in front of a simple (compared with the Greek and Roman) architectural façade. We know that limited scenic representation was attempted, for we have lists of scenic properties that were owned by such companies, but there is nowhere any mention of a stage "designer." Thus, we can assume with some safety that, following the practice in other areas of theatrical endeavor, design was the province of the whole company, not a specific person. That is not to suggest that the English as a whole totally neglected scenic design. In fact, one of the most influential designers of all time, Inigo Jones, was hard at work during the English Renaissance, though his designs were created for court masques rather than for commercial theatre companies.

The Seventeenth and Eighteenth Centuries

As more and more plays were produced behind the proscenium arch, with the resulting demand for sets that gave the appearance of reality, producers began to feel an obligation to represent shifts in scene on a realistic level. Thus, a shift from Birnam Wood to inside the castle at Dunsinane had to be clarified visually. This necessitated a number of advances, at first not so much in scenic design as in the ability to shift scenes quickly and efficiently. Several methods were devised for accomplishing this, all requiring some revision of traditional design concepts. The wing and groove system made use of portable angle wings, composed of wood and canvas, that could slide back and forth in grooves at the sides of the stage. The chariot-and-pole system was a mechanical device that shifted scenery with a moveable pole that stood up through a channel in the stage floor. In

[1]Quoted in Alessandro d'Ancono, *Origini del Teatro Italiano* (Torini, 1891), II, p. 102.

An early eighteenth-century illustration of a production of Farquhar's Beaux Stratagem.
(*From* The Works of the Late Ingenious Mr. George Farquhar, *London, England,*
1711.)

some theatres, backdrops and even wing flats were designed to "fly,"
sinking and rising to shift scenes swiftly.

Subsequent changes throughout the eighteenth, nineteenth, and
twentieth centuries have been, on the whole, changes in manner and
method rather than in type. For example, although electricity changed
theatre lighting profoundly, expanding effects achievable in a safe and
efficient manner, there was no substantial change in the philosophy of
lighting. Only in recent years, since the advent of the lighting designer,
have there been real changes in the concept of lighting a show.

The history of theatrical design is a complex one, too complex to deal with efficiently in one book, let alone one chapter. Therefore, perhaps the best way of bringing the whole field into focus is to look at what the designers in each of the major areas do, paying special attention to the requirements of the field.

Scenic Design

Lee Simonson once defined the scenic designer as a "member of a group of interpreters," which implies that the responsibility of the designer, along with the director and designers from other areas, is to provide a cohesive visual production that adheres to an *appropriate* interpretation of a dramatic script. That is to say, the scenic designer creates a physical environment that fits the concept set forth by the director, that works in terms of the special needs of the actors (to make entrances, exits, etc.), and that coordinates with the ideas of the lighting and costume designers.

Artistically, the scenic designer studies the script closely, making careful analyses on both a practical basis (determining exactly what special items are necessary to get the actors on and off, and to complete all of the actions called for in the script) and also a purely subjective, artistic basis (seeking to understand or "feel" the mood and atmosphere of the play). In consultation with the director and his fellow designers, the scenic artist gradually evolves a concept that aims at being aesthetically pleasant and yet practical in terms of the needs of the show.

After completing a design, coordinating it with the costume and lighting designers, and receiving the approval of the director, the scenic de-

William Raoul's touring set for Hamlet. *Designed for the Montana Repertory Theatre.*

signer is faced with a number of practical tasks that must be completed if the planned design is to be executed onstage. The designer is expected to provide a scale model or rendering, or both, to the director so that the director can begin visualizing scenes and planning the blocking. Most directors prefer to receive a model of the set, since that helps them think of blocking in terms of depth and sightlines and even allows them to move chess pawns or buttons about on the model to check their compositions.

The scenic designer provides groundplans for the director, the stage manager, and the head of the construction or shop crew. A groundplan is essentially a scaled drawing of the set as seen directly from above, locating walls, furniture, doors, windows, etc. Such plans are invaluable to everyone concerned, since they show how the set will fit onstage. Generally, on the basis of the groundplan and set renderings, the technical director will provide the shop crew with construction drawings. If there is no technical director, as is sometimes the case, then the scenic designer or assistant scenic designer will provide construction drawings in addition to elevations that show just how the raw set is to be painted.

After those technical requirements have been met, the scenic designer selects furniture and (usually) props. That may not be a problem in a theatre that has a large storage area filled with appropriate furniture items,

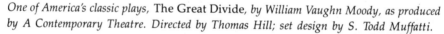

One of America's classic plays, The Great Divide, *by William Vaughn Moody, as produced by A Contemporary Theatre. Directed by Thomas Hill; set design by S. Todd Muffatti.*

The Designer

Creating scale models of his set designs is part of the scenic designer's responsibility. An idea of the size at which the designer works, and the delicacy of his models, can be gained from this photo of designer S. Todd Muffatti holding a tiny chair in front of a scale model of his set for The Inspector General.

or on a show where the budget allows expensive rentals. Low budgets are the rule rather than the exception, however, so the designer must often do extensive shopping at used furniture or secondhand stores. Shows that have specialized furniture or prop requirements can use up a large portion of a designer's time and energy.

After the basic construction on the set has been completed, the designer supervises the scene painting, checking colors and making sure that such aspects as masking and toning have been properly accomplished. The designer also supervises placement of furniture on the set, making certain that the arrangement fits specifications and checking to see that it works visually in terms of the audience. Arrangements that looked fine on paper and even in the model sometimes fail to work in full size. That can happen when practical reasons force the designer to use furniture that is only an approximation of his originals in size and shape. Also, period shows containing such special costumes as hoop skirts can often necessitate some rearranging of the furniture.

After the painting is done and the furniture is arranged, the designer "dresses" the set. That means adding the intimate touches that bring a bare set alive, giving it its character, mood, and atmosphere. As an example of how such dressing works, a traditional box set of a big-city apartment belonging to an elderly couple might have old-fashioned pictures in oval frames and samplers hanging on the walls. The bookshelf might contain hardcover works, some of them sets with matching bindings and spines. Doilies would be on the tables, throw rugs on the floor, and perhaps covers on the arms of the chairs. Such details vivify a set and make it appropriate in terms of its occupants. On the other hand, the same apartment occupied by college students might have travel posters and photos of rock stars on the walls, paperback books and journals not only in the bookcase but scattered about on the chairs and tables, a portable typewriter on one of the end tables, and a few appropriate items of rumpled clothing on the furniture.

Finally, scenic design is one of the most difficult, and yet one of the most personally rewarding, of all arts. It requires that an artist design in three dimensions, using color that will work properly with the costume-designer's concept and will look right under the colored lights that the stage requires. The set must also be efficiently lit by the lighting designer, and have as few acoustical dead spots as possible. When it is completed, it is a purely plastic creation that must maintain its artistic focus as actors in costume move through it, changing spatial relationships, form, and balance by the placement of their bodies, and varying the color by the placement of their costumes against the background. Sound will issue from the

Schultz cartoons were featured in the setting of You're a Good Man Charlie Brown. *A touring set designed for the Montana Repertory Theatre by William Raoul.*

The Great Diamond Robbery *at Oregon State University, 1961. Directed by Don Henry; designed by D. Palmer Young. The melodrama is today's legacy from sentimental tragedy.*

set, and it will be washed with a variety of colored lights prepared by the lighting designer. And through all this it must maintain its artistic integrity.

Perhaps that is why scenic design is so rewarding. The results can be very satisfying, indeed, because the designer is one of a community of artists who are all working together toward a common end.

Costume Design

In many ways, designing costumes for the theatre is the boldest, most exciting area of clothing design. Costume designers are called upon to work in many different historical styles and modes. They create costumes at least close to being historically accurate, support the mood and atmosphere of the play, and identify and characterize even the most minor performers. As can be seen from the functions that these costumes must fulfill, the costume designer is not totally a free agent. The costume designer's purpose is not merely to create beautiful clothing but to create clothing that fills a special need within the limits of the artistic whole.

In fulfilling this function the costume designer, like the other design artists, first consults with the director to determine the objectives of the play, and then with the scenic designer to consider color, so that in the finished production the colors of the costumes will work in relationship with the colors of the set. The colors, however, do not have to complement

Costume design for Pantalone. The University of California, Davis, production of The Three Cuckolds. *Directed by Robert Sarlos; costume designs by Gene Chesley.*

The Designer

each other in the traditional sense. A decision may be made on a considered, artistic level to use colors that clash. The costume designer must not, however, select colors that make the actor fade into the background when he walks onstage.

The two requisites for the costume designer, beyond technical skills in art, are a feeling for character and a sound knowledge of historical styles. The feeling for character is necessary to keep incongruities from arising to distract the audience or destroy a characterization or both. For example, to costume Hamlet in happy colors, or Algernon (in *The Importance of Being Earnest*) in somber garb, would be to distort those characters almost beyond recognition. Perhaps of even greater importance to the designer is a thorough knowledge of historical styles. That knowledge must be tempered, however, because in some cases it can be dangerous. For instance, a film version of *Macbeth*, produced in period costumes accurate for the times in which Macbeth was supposed to have lived, failed miserably with the

The final scene of Harold Pinter's The Homecoming *at California State University, Fullerton. Directed by Jerry V. Pickering; scenic design by Mike Chapman; costume design by Jan Herscovitch.*

audience despite some brilliant acting and inventive camera work. The failure was due in large part to the costumes. General audiences, that is, the audiences that attend films rather than stage productions, have been conditioned to expect Shakespeare's English history plays to be performed in the costumes of the English Renaissance, making horned helmets and sheepskin jerkins quite unacceptable, though historically accurate.

Having completed the designs satisfactorily, the designer must next select the fabrics out of which they will be constructed. The texture of material can be almost as important to a designer as color. The obvious way in which textures can work for the designer is the use of specially knitted fabrics to simulate chain mail in historical costumes. Beyond that, however, texture is also important in terms of how a fabric works under the stage lights. Coarse, soft fabrics, for example, tend to break up light and thus look more substantial and richer than fabrics that reflect light. Color, however, is the most important consideration in selecting fabrics. Some knowledge of traditional color symbolism is therefore highly important. The successful designer will know that red is a vibrant color, that blue or white is innocent and virginal, that green is the color of certain types of supernatural creatures such as woods sprites or elves (which explains Robin Hood's traditional costume), and that browns or earth colors symbolize peasants or farmers or those who are in some ways close to the earth. That may sound obvious or very silly, but audiences have been color-conditioned since birth, and when a woman appears in a white gown or a man walks onstage in a red costume, it sets off a preset response in the minds of most viewers

Finally, as a word of caution to the costume designer, contemporary styles are very powerful indeed, and most designs must be tempered with such styles in mind. Anyone viewing a production of *Julius Caesar* and then looking at Roman drawings and paintings that show similar costumes, would find significant differences. The theatre costumes would all have a more tailored look. In fact, the show costumes are *stylized versions* of Roman originals.

Lighting Design

The responsibility of completing the visual picture on stage and presenting this image to the audience lies with the lighting designers, who must illuminate the performer, complement the set, and enhance the costumes and makeup. In so doing, designers must reinforce the themes and create moods while simultaneously providing sufficient illumination to make the performers visible from the most distant seats in the house. Not only must lighting designers be keen artists with a true aesthetic feel for all the various production elements, they must also possess a high level of organizational ability.

The Designer

Mark Lamos is the damned Faustus and Michael Gross is Mephistophilis in Christopher Marlowe's drama about a man who sells his soul to the devil in return for unlimited earthly delights. At the Guthrie Theatre. Directed by Ken Ruta; sets by Ralph Funicello; lighting by Duane Schuler.

Few theatres can allow the luxury of ample time for experimentation, a fact that forces the lighting designer to think out ideas and commit them to paper before preparing designs. Minimum time is thus wasted during rigging, focusing, and rehearsal situations. The lighting designer, during the preplanning stages, works closely with the director, the other designers, and the technical director. Following discussions with the director, the designer establishes all the lighting cues for the production and communicates instructions for their execution to the stage manager and the technical director. The lighting designer also supervises the drafting of all charts, schedules, and cue sheets relating to the production, and devises any special electrical effects that might be controlled through the switchboard.

The designer supervises the rigging and focusing sessions and coordinates with the master electrician regarding the training and dry-run rehearsals of all lighting cues, so that the lighting can run fairly smoothly during the first and subsequent technical rehearsals. During the technical rehearsal phase, the first rehearsal is generally for purposes of timing and execution. The designer works closely with the director, technical director, and stage manager, so that these rehearsals will achieve their desired end.

Aesthetic judgments are communicated directly to the master electrician by the lighting designer. Timing and coordination matters are communicated to the technical director or the stage manager for execution. Starting with the second technical rehearsal and lasting generally until the final dress or preview, the lighting designer works on the aesthetic phase of the design. Prior to that point, most lighting activity has been mechanical. Now the designer finishes his whole composition, balancing and integrating each effect into a unified whole. When finished, the lighting should enhance the production without calling attention to itself.

Possibly the most appropriate compliment that can be paid to a lighting designer would be no compliment at all. If the lighting design stands out, then it has failed to become a part of the total composition.

Makeup Design

In times not far past (and in some cases even today), makeup was not considered to be a design function. All actors took basic work in the application of makeup, or learned it as part of their apprenticeship by observing senior performers apply their own. Makeup designers have been considered important principally for films, which deal in close-ups and often shoot scenes six weeks apart that in the film are only minutes apart. Some theatre productions—usually large-budget, Broadway-type shows or shows where prosthetic makeup is an absolute necessity—have assigned makeup designers to serve the major performers, but such shows have been few.

The actual fact of getting into makeup is a psychologically exciting aspect of theatre for the performers. Many actors and actresses, including such fine performers as Lord Laurence Olivier, find that makeup helps them to "get inside" a character. Not until they get into makeup do they fully feel the character they are portraying.

Basically, makeup falls into two categories. The first, simplest, and by far the most common is "straight" makeup. This means that there is no real attempt to change the actor's features, to add age or deformity or any other special characteristic. The assumption behind straight makeup is that the actor as cast resembles the part to be played, which is to say, the role has been typecast and the function of the makeup is merely to project the actor's own features to the audience against the competition of amber stage lights. Straight makeup consists of applying a coat of base, usually somewhat more toward the red tones than the usual complexion, and then adding subtle highlighting to the natural shadows and eyebrows. This straight makeup may be followed by a light application of powder, usually of a somewhat lighter shade than the base, and, for some, a touch of lip rouge.

Prosthetic makeup constitutes the most complex classification. It usually requires the basic straight makeup plus prosthetic devices such as wigs or beards. It may include enlargement or reshaping of a facial feature with "nose putty," a soft, plastic substance that can make the nose larger, the

Professional actor Kirk Mee without makeup, and then in makeup as Lord Talbot in Shakespeare's Henry VI, *Part 1, at the Oregon Shakespearian Festival, Ashland, Oregon.*

ears cauliflowered, the brow beetled, or the chin jutting. Prosthetic make-up also requires more deft shading, with facial lines or planes given extra emphasis.

The above deals with what makeup is but does not explain the function of a makeup designer. This designer works to assure that the makeup fulfills its proper function. For every character in a show (except perhaps some minor straight makeups) the designer creates a makeup schematic. These schematics begin with a drawing of the basic facial structure, which is then divided into planes. The exact shade of base is determined, as well as the shades and amounts of rouge and shadow necessary to complete the design. Areas to be "worked on" are carefully delineated, and where a feature is to be changed (for example, a Cyrano de Bergerac, who needs an outsize nose), the exact proportions of the finished product are designed to scale.

Dion Anthony, wearing mask, from a scene in the California State University, Fullerton, production of Eugene O'Neill's The Great God Brown. *Directed by Alvin Keller; scenic design by Darrell F. Winn. Masks especially designed for the production of Abel Zeballos.*

A scene from Edna St. Vincent Millay's Aria da Capo. *Produced at the University of California, Santa Barbara. Directed by Linda Mitchell.*

In addition to the above, the makeup designer provides original drawings of such items as masks and either completes or supervises completion of the finished products. Such tasks are more common than one might at first suppose, because of the production of classical shows, *commedia* performances, and contemporary works such as Eugene O'Neill's *The Great God Brown*. Also, the makeup designer plans and executes such unusual tasks as providing prosthetic limbs for such shows as *Knickerbocker Holiday*, in which the Governor General, Peter Stuyvesant, has a peg leg. Last but not least, the makeup designer is always on hand before shows and dress rehearsals to supervise the makeup crew and to help apply the especially difficult prosthetic materials.

Audio Design

Audio design is only presently getting started as a major theatrical design function. In the past, when sound was simply the unamplified voices of the actors, sometimes together with a pit orchestra, as in musicals, audio design was totally unnecessary. Today, however, sound designers are swiftly coming into their own with the growing monetary necessity for large houses that require sound amplification for actors, and the expanding use of sound effects and other mechanical sound.

Rules for audio design do not exist at present; they are in the process of being written. The need for audio design is recognized, however, by any theatergoer who has attended a play where a record played onstage blares out of speakers at the back of the auditorium, or who has seen an actor gesture toward guns supposedly firing in the distance, while the shots come from speakers in a quite different direction.

Design theory is far too wide, and design practices vary too greatly for either to be discussed at short length with any real degree of accuracy. Therefore, the topic is probably best approached by looking closely at four of the great designers of contemporary theatre, examining their theories and practices for clues and approaches to the basic problems of theatrical design.

The Designer at Work

ADOLPHE APPIA (1862–1928), together with Gordon Craig and their latter-day disciples, created a revolution in scenic design during the first three decades of the twentieth century. Appia was the first of these new scenic artists, not only in time but also in the fact that he was ahead of all of them in writing down the new principles. He advocated a spatial design that emphasized the role of the actor, stating that "the proportions of this role determine the form of the setting through *three-dimensionality* (the point of contact between the living actor and the inanimate setting)."[2] Appia's theory was that the nature and extent of the three-dimensionality was the determining factor controlling spatial arrangement, which, in turn, controlled the lighting and scenery.

Appia further believed that a harmonious relation must be established between feeling and form; that is, a perfect balance must exist between the idea the artist wishes to express and the means by which it is expressed. He pointed out that the idea as presented onstage to an audience must automatically differ from that written into a play by the playwright because so many artistic aspects in theatre become involved in the production process. The dramatist, to express an idea fully and truly to an audience, would have to exercise complete control over each individual aspect of the theatrical arts, which is impractical in production situations. In fact, the dramatist is usually unable to exercise any degree of control over a production because the drama is a result of the collaboration of a number of artists who function independently of the author's dramatic intention. Specifically, the dramatist does not control the scenic designer, who designs the

---

[2]Adolphe Appia, *Music and the Art of Theatre*, trans. by Robert W. Corrigan and Mary Douglas Dirks, ed. by Barnard Hewitt (Coral Gables, Florida, 1962), p. 26.

The Designer

inanimate elements of production, such as lighting, scene painting, and spatial arrangement of scenery on stage. Nor does the dramatist control the costumer, who has total responsibility for costume appearance. In fact, the playwright does not even dominate the actors unless, of course, the playwright happens also to be the director.

Such conditions subject the theatrical production to several styles that are often widely divergent and that depend on the whims and tastes of a number of individual artists. This complexity in the staging of a play acutely diminishes the integrity of the drama as an art form. Appia was aware of arguments to the effect that, even without control of all production aspects by the dramatist, drama is nevertheless capable of performing an expressive artistic function because it can be continually restated in new ways to please the taste of new audiences. This capability of continual restatement provides the unchanging dramatic text with greater breadth, unending depth, and longer life. Appia supported those arguments, finding that the scenic form of drama cannot escape the ever-changing tastes of the time. Thus, he pointed out, the *mise-en-scène* cannot be an expressive medium *as a work of art* and still reflect the dramatist's ideas.

Searching for a creative principle that would allow him to design sets compatible with each individual dramatist's original conception, Appia turned to the operatic works of Richard Wagner, the German composer, poet, and dramatist, and to the productions at Bayreuth, where he found the unifying element of music. Appia theorized that music is the source

As Appia grew older his sets became more simplified and severe, as can be seen in this sketch of his 1923 design for Ibsen's Little Eyolf.

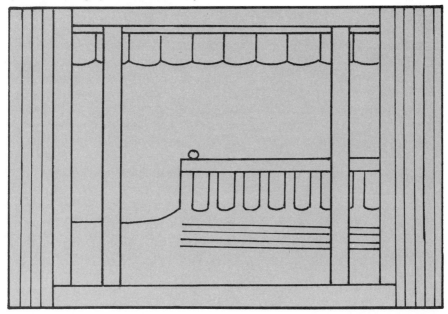

Theatre: A Contemporary Introduction

from which drama springs, and that drama consists of two primary elements: time and space. Time is expressed through words and tones determined by the text (score and libretto). Space is determined by actors (singer-actors), setting, lighting, and painting. Nevertheless the actor is the sole intermediary between the text and the physical form. The actor is the focal point of the audience and, as such, must be the focal point of the designer.

To provide this focus on the actor, Appia conceived a setting in three dimensions that allowed the actor to be perceived in space rather than against two-dimensional paintings. These settings were arranged in three parts: the lower section consisted of the stage floor with platforms placed upon it; the middle section was the one most prominent to the audience; the upper section consisted of borders and backdrops. He considered the lower section to be the most critical.

Appia's objections to the realistic and naturalistic settings of his time were that such set pieces as trees, columns, pillars, and rocks were never truly connected and integrated with the rest of the set, being moved on and off as needed but never part of the whole unit. Also, he did not like the elaborate and spectacular painted scenery then in general use, preferring

The creatures of the forest are threatened by the invasion of the Machine in Chuck Kading's Crisis in Chucklewood, *an ecologically oriented play for children. Directed by Don Henry at California State University, Fullerton.*

instead a stark simplicity. Using ramps, stairs, pillars, plain walls, drapes, and platforms at varying levels, he created three-dimensional arrangements that had a feeling of unity. In support of these settings, Appia introduced lighting methods designed to eliminate borders and footlights, accentuating the use of spotlights to obtain complete plasticity. All of these innovations constituted a drastic and complete break with the ornately painted flat wings, shutters, and borders, arranged to give the audience a sense of angle perspective, which had been inherited from the Italian Burnacini and Bibiena families of the late seventeenth and eighteenth centuries.

The approach to costumes which Appia developed was based on endowing the actor's form with a harmonious relationship not only with the poetic musical proportions but also with the rest of the stage picture. Close study of costumes prior to 1900 convinced Appia that opera costuming was elaborate and ornamental without any special significance, and that play costuming was so completely subordinated to historical concept that it was difficult for actors to attain a unified effect when seen against the ornate settings. His theory was that costumes should be freed from these two problems so that they could assume their proper function of serving the actors.

Appia's designs for use of stage lighting were attempts not only to illuminate the stage generally but also to mold the three-dimensional actors and scenery, to provide color to the scene, and to create mood and atmosphere.

Appia's followers include such great names in theatre as Stanislavski, and American designers Robert Edmond Jones, Donald Oenslager, Norman Bel Geddes, and Jo Mielziner. This shy, retiring, self-taught scenic designer, often ridiculed and unrecognized in his own time, is responsible for generating some of the greatest and most far-reaching changes in the history of modern theatre.

EDWARD GORDON CRAIG (1872–1966) came to theatre naturally. His mother was the celebrated actress Ellen Terry and his father was Edward William Godwin, an architect with a passion for the theatre. Craig loved the theatre all his life. He hated formal schooling and considered the Lyceum Theatre his real school and the actor-manager Henry Irving his real schoolmaster. He learned elocution backstage and studied Irving onstage. At the Lyceum, where he remained for eight years, Craig gained a practical knowledge of stagecraft and became a fairly proficient actor. He grew restless and a bit distressed, however, when he realized that he was constantly comparing himself with Irving and that he could never be more than a fair imitation of that great actor.

As a result of this dissatisfaction, Craig left the Lyceum and for the first time began to read seriously. He became interested in poetry, especially that of John Ruskin, whose antirealism helped turn his thinking away from the beliefs of the Lyceum and its preoccupation with realism. For the next three years Craig read widely and began to formulate his

Gordon Craig's design for Electra. *(From Craig's* On the Art of the Theatre, *London, England, 1911.)*

aesthetic principles. He absorbed ideas from various people, often quite different. From the romantic poet William Blake came his fascination with symbols; from James Pryde he learned that art was not imitation but re-creation; Goethe suggested to him that the function of art was to express the inexpressible and that theatre must be visually symbolic; from Tolstoy came the notion that realistic theatre was the negation of art; and from Nietzsche he learned that all aesthetic activity implies a state of ecstasy.

It was Pryde, along with William Nicholson, who influenced Craig in one of his earliest artistic endeavors: woodcutting. Those two men, known as the Beggarstaff Brothers, so influenced Craig that his first carvings ended up as imitations. However, through concentration on his craft, he learned not to waste time reproducing detail, to appreciate line and simplicity, and to be sparing with his resources. Also during this period, and certainly as a result of working with woodcutting, Craig developed his love for black and white as the central colors of all visual art. He found these colors to be the most essential, especially black, which he felt had roots in the deeper springs of nature itself.

By 1900, Craig was deeply involved in the fight against stage realism. He had studied in the art galleries of London, discovering the simplicity of the Italian architects and painters and the artistic importance of color and light as opposed to form. At the time Craig also read an article about the Roman theatre at Orange. The article described a huge wall, containing a central portal, that stood at the back of the stage. The wall emphasized vertical lines, its sculptured quality providing a strong contrast between light and shadowed areas, and it allowed the actors to be perceived in relationship to the simple, strong, architectural form.

Another idea that appealed to Craig was Wagner's music-drama, with its blend of music, poetry, and acting. Because Wagner advocated a new style of theatre architecture to accommodate his creations, Craig was compelled to develop some new forms himself. One of his projects had no boxes, no circles, but a floor that sloped gently toward the stage, and scene changes masked by darkness and not covered up by a curtain. He also devised a small box at the back of the auditorium from which the director could run the show. He made no provisions for footlights; all lighting was from the side or above.

Craig realized the nature of art and the importance of both imagination and discipline. Art was not accidental; it had to come from conscious effort. With these thoughts in mind, Craig became stage director at the Lyceum, in 1899, for the production of Purcell's *Dido and Aeneas*. Staged in 1900, this production was the beginning of a movement in the production of poetic drama. In it Craig had all light coming from above, except for two spotlights at the back of the auditorium which could focus directly on the actors. Because he so much disliked the star system, Craig used mostly amateurs, and partly as a result of such casting it took him an unprecedented six months to complete the rehearsals for this production. In terms of set, he tried to work with the usual scenic painters but finally dismissed them, utilizing a purple-blue sky-cloth, no borders or wings, no customary landscaping, and minimal furniture. He tried to suggest mood, wanting the audience's imagination to run free, undaunted by detail.

In a production dealing with the birth of Christ, no attempt was made to·copy a stable because Craig wished to suggest the divine presence through the use of light. Instead of the traditional doll in the manger, a light shone from the depths of the crib, illuminating the faces of the actors gathered around the Virgin and Child. Never had this type of effect been used before.

As well as designing and directing, Craig was also writing. His first book, *The Art of the Theatre* (1905), met with tremendous enthusiasm in Europe. He wrote about what he was currently working on, made catalogues of his work, and eventually sold collections to libraries and institutions all over the world. In his first book, Craig surmised that until the status of the director was improved there could be no forward movement in theatre; the director had to have complete control of every aspect of the production, for this was the only way to achieve artistic unity.

One of Craig's most famous ideas (infamous among actors) was his concept of the *Über-marionette*. Because he believed that actors were slaves to their emotions, he was looking for some method to ensure that intelligence remained the primary controlling factor for actors onstage. The answer seemed to be a superpuppet, with strings pulled by the director. Craig postulated that in order to give good performances, actors had to be in complete control of their instincts so that their imagination and ability to create could lead them through the parts. If the actors lost control, their performances became disjointed sequences of accidental scenes. Craig did not wish to replace actors onstage with wooden figures, but he did want to cast out their weaknesses from the stage. Still seeking to achieve this, he also experimented with masks to dehumanize the actors, thereby making them conscious of their movements and gestures, so that they would have to rely on their intelligence to re-create rather than reproduce.

At the same time that Craig was writing and theorizing, he was also designing (and creating "plays") for the theatre of the future. *The Steps*, a design done in "four moods," was an outright dismissal of spoken drama and dramatic literature. It consisted of a series of scenes that were called "moods," each showing a flight of steps going across the stage with figures and light and dark patches appearing in different positions on them. It was the architectural fact of the steps themselves in which Craig was interested, and not what the actors were doing on them. The players might dominate the steps for a time, but eventually they would leave and the steps would remain. Actors (people) come and go, but art is eternal.

A unit set was employed for this University of Portland production of Golden Boy. *Directed by Alvin Keller; set design by Veryl Leech; costumes by Carolyn Silverthorne.*

Imagining the stage floor as a chess board, Craig developed the idea of a stage with each square an elevator that would be able to rise and lower to any number of positions, thus providing an almost infinite variety of levels and playing areas. Along with this came his idea of using screens, equal in size to the squares on the floor and colored in monotones. The designer could employ them to create "places" on the stage, giving them color, shape, and animation through imaginative use of light. When Craig finally went to Moscow to produce *Hamlet* with Stanislavski, he used his screens, which were cream and gold canvas stretched over wooden frames. These screens were arranged to hint at streets and niches, when aided by the imagination of the spectator, and they were supposed to glide from one position to the next without closing the front curtain. However, they did not work well and the front curtain had to be closed for set changes. Though the production was clearly not what the two men wanted (theirs was an uneasy collaboration at best) *Hamlet* was a success and the two great theatricians parted with at least mutual respect.

In 1913, Craig finally developed the school he had been wanting so long: the Arena Goldoni. The school was to be set up in two successive operations. First should come the selection of fifteen to twenty salaried technicians who would learn Craig's theories and later act as his assistants. The second part of the operation would be the acceptance of twenty to thirty paying students. He had no intention of allowing his students to become parrots of his ideas. Rather, the school was to help them realize their powers of creative imagination by urging them to use their minds and fancies as a source for creation. Unfortunately the school lasted but a short time, forced to close by the problems created by World War I.

Unlike his contemporary, Appia, Craig put all elements of theatre on the same creative level, insisting that they all contribute to the total production. His major premise was that neither the script nor the acting alone constituted the art of theatre. The art lay in the whole production. He worked toward this end until his death.

ROBERT EDMUND JONES (1887–1954) was highly influential in the American theatre between 1915 and 1950. During those years the theatre abounded with examples of his work and with comments not only on his theories of design but also on his philosophy of theatre as a totality. The brilliant, inventive, and imaginative theatre that he helped to create can be seen in the settings of Jo Mielziner, in the plays of Arthur Miller, and in the acting of young and exciting theatre groups all across the country. He created a theatre that was symbolic, elegant, poetic, and eloquent, in those respects the exact opposite of the realistic theatre that surrounded him.

Robert Edmond Jones was born December 12, 1887, in Milton, New Hampshire, and grew up in an atmosphere of gentility, learning, and the puritan ethic. He read books, studied music, and learned to draw and paint. As a boy he had read plays, Shakespeare in particular, but until he attended Harvard he had never seen a professional play, and when he finally did, a whole new world opened up. He sought an education in drama, though he did not consider it as a potential career until he found that he could combine his painting with theatre by way of stage design. He graduated from Harvard in 1910, and, in 1913, went to Europe, first to Florence and then on to Berlin, where he studied the work of Max Reinhardt.

At the outbreak of World War I, Jones returned to New York, where he was soon at work designing a set for the first production of the Washington Square Players. In 1915, he was selected by Harley Granville-Barker to design the set and costumes for a short play which was the curtain-raiser for Barker's production of *Androcles and the Lion*. Jones created a Reinhardt-style set in black and white, with costumes in reds, orange, and yellow. It was an auspicious beginning to a long and important career.

Over the next few years Jones designed several sets for Arthur Hopkins, worked regularly with the Provincetown Players and the Theatre Guild, and also did free-lance work. During this period he became closely associated with Eugene O'Neill, directing several of his plays and creating sets for *Desire Under the Elms* and *Mourning Becomes Electra*. He was also a celebrated teacher, working with such talented students as Lee Simonson, Donald Oenslager, and Jo Mielziner. He designed a skeletal Tower of

Robert Edmond Jones' design for the Theatre Guild production of Shakespeare's Othello. *(From the souvenir program of the original production.)*

London for *Richard III*, a "mirrored confection" for *Love for Love*, and a delicate Oriental gem for *Lute Song*.

Jones believed in teaching by example, in fusing his own personal sense of magic and excitement into his sets and allowing students to learn by observation, by participation, and by osmosis. In *Mourning Becomes Electra*, seeking a contemporary equivalent for the Greek tragic spirit toward which O'Neill was striving, he created a brooding neoclassic house to evoke the tragic image. He designed sets reflecting his basic belief, perhaps by way of Appia, that the actor must be the central focus of theatre, that it is the actor's representation of the author's words and actions that brings the play to life, and that it is the function of the scenic designer to support the actor in this representation.

Theatre, Jones believed, existed in its magic and poetry, and thus he often went to Shakespeare to illustrate his theory. His sets were designed to evoke an image of a place and the "feeling" of that place. In Shakespeare he found the perfect example of this approach, with an actor at the Globe Theatre providing all the setting necessary with the words, "In fair Verona where we lay our scene. . . ." Jones envisioned Hamlet standing on that same stage, looking out through the open roof at "this brave o'erhanging firmament, this magestical roof fretted with golden fire." This was the language Jones loved—"golden fire"—and it gave him the image he needed to create a theatre of poetry in design, avoiding the mundane, always pursuing the magic.

In lighting, Jones found an infinitely versatile tool for creating mood and emotion. Lighting, he felt, was the most primal of theatrical devices because it touches the animal in us, awakening our atavistic fear of darkness while arousing our inherent attraction to color. In *Richard III* and *Macbeth*, he made use of sharply defined light and shadow to highlight the hopes and fears of the characters. In *Love for Love* he used a mirrored set, sparkling with light, to reflect the polished brilliance of Congreve's wit. He even looked forward to the day of mixed-media productions, when film would become an integral part of lighting, enhancing the actor's characterization.

In costuming he believed in designing from the inside out, in much the same way that an actor designs a role. Beginning with the basic personality, with the inner workings of the character, the designer must work out toward a costume as rich in imagery as any other aspect of the physical set.

Perhaps the most interesting characteristic about Jones was his ability to translate his magical, poetic theory into practical terms, creating workable settings for such basically commonplace locales as a barroom or a New England farmhouse. Unfortunately, in terms of his use of color, black-and-white reproductions of his renderings only hint at what audiences must have experienced. Critics have described his sets as "lustrous," and the muted tones of the farmhouse in *Desire Under the Elms* are said to have reflected the harsh yet beautiful quality of New England during Jones' youth. In any case, Jones' generalized (though enthusiastic) theory

Theatre: A Contemporary Introduction

The Eastern Michigan University production of Robert Anderson's I Never Sang for My Father. *Directed by Parker Zellers; scenic design by Gary Decker.*

worked, over and over again, and not just for Jones himself. His approach is still to be seen in today's theatre, in the cubic set of *Company* and in the sets which Arthur Miller demands for his plays (and which Jo Mielziner provided).

For Jones the ultimate concept was *theatrical* as opposed to *realistic*. Certainly as a concept this was not entirely new; while Jones was in college, Meyerhold was already assailing the detailed realism of Stanislavski's sets for the Moscow Art Theatre, and many American critics were fuming over what they called the vulgar realism of David Belasco's productions. When he began designing for the theatre, the "new stagecraft" was already an established fact, yet it took Jones to bring the theatre of symbolism and images to popular attention in this country.

The Designer

JO MIELZINER (1901–1976) was one of the foremost theatrical designers of the past several decades. In addition to an impressive array of scenic, costume, and lighting designs, he made highly important contributions to the field of theatre as an architectural consultant, lecturer, and author. In spite of his enormous success as a designer, Mielziner sometimes tended to dwell on his frailty as a fallible human being in the world of art. He freely admitted his past mistakes, and it is perhaps this openness that permitted him to speak so clearly and distinctly about his successes, with no touch of aggravating self-esteem, and with unusual clarity and concision for an artist discussing his work.

Mielziner was born in Paris in his father's Latin Quarter studio, and he grew up handling clay and paint and absorbing the artistic atmosphere of turn-of-the-century Paris. His father was Leo Mielziner, an artist who worked mainly in portraits. His mother, Ella Mielziner, was, during those early years, a correspondent for *Vogue*, covering the artistic life of Paris: theatre, music, and painting. She was an avid theatregoer, and Jo and his brother were exposed to the dramatic arts at an early age. In fact, it was at

A scene from George Bernard Shaw's The Devil's Disciple *at the University of California, Berkeley. Directed by Edwin Duerr.*

his mother's suggestion, during his apprenticeship as an artist, that Jo sought a position as theatrical scene painter. The Mielziners moved to the United States, where Jo attended the Pennsylvania Academy of Fine Arts. This education was helped along by a series of scholarships, and Jo eventually gave up all other studies to devote himself to art.

During the early years in America Jo's older brother, Kenneth, was having a degree of success in juvenile leads. He talked Jo into taking a job as an apprentice in the Bonstelle Stock Company in Detroit, where he worked in various positions such as actor and assistant stage manager. From Bonstelle, Mielziner went to the Theatre Guild in New York to continue his apprenticeship, eventually ending up as apprentice to Lee Simonson, and later to Robert Edmond Jones. Mielziner's first position on Broadway was as actor and stage manager for a Theatre Guild production at the Garrick Theatre, in 1923. Almost a year later he designed his first Broadway show, *The Guardsman*, produced by the Theatre Guild and starring the Lunts. Following the success of this first production, Mielziner had an almost unbroken series of outstanding designs.

In all his written works, Mielziner demonstrated a deep concern for the beginning theatrical designer and tried patiently to let the upcoming artist know about the pitfalls that are to be encountered. Especially valuable in this sense is his warning about the six sins of omission that he himself committed during his early years as a designer.[3]

The first sin was mistaking means for ends, which is to say, allowing egotism to rule instead of having proper concern for the unity of the production. Mielziner's design for *Anatol* was an example of overstatement to a point of gaudiness. It not only distracted from the unity of the production but slowed scene changes, damaging the pacing and overall effect of the play.

The second sin was in turning to the theatre merely as a method of earning a living. Again, Mielziner's ego played a part in creating the problem. He enjoyed seeing his settings realized onstage and under lights, almost to the point of resenting the actors screening his creation from an admiring audience. It is always interesting to hear artists confess to their faults, if only because so many people seem to think that all fine artists are great from the beginning, doing nothing more than developing their art. Mielziner did indeed develop, but he also learned.

Sin number three was not learning early enough about the importance of collaboration between the major creative artists. Theatre is at all times and in all ways a collaborative art. Mielziner had to learn the importance of the total theatrical production, comprised of the individual contributions of the scenic designer, the lighting designer, the costume designer, the actors, and the director.

Number four was a failure to develop early the substantial critical ability necessary to get beneath the surface of the playwright's descriptions. When at last Mielziner began to read plays with deeper insight, he

[4]Jo Mielziner, *Designing for the Theatre* (New York, 1965).

was able to put more into a setting than the mere requirements of the script embellished by his own ego.

The fifth sin of omission was a failure to recognize the need for collaboration, not only with the major designers but with the whole of the production company. Finally recognizing this necessity, Mielziner developed a concept in which the designers, producer, actors, composer, lyricist, choreographer, dancers, etc., all work together like the spokes of a wheel. The hub of the wheel is the dramatist, and the rim of the wheel, and one who sees to it that each spoke does its own share of the lifting and pulling on behalf of the dramatist, is the director. All the spokes of the wheel must work in unison to make a production a success.

Sin number six was the failure to recognize the complicated nature of the physical structure that houses drama. This last became an area of great interest to Mielziner, who became deeply involved in studies of the problems of designing theatre facilities. He designed many theatres and consulted on a number of others. His book on the subject, *The Shapes of Our Theatre*, is a study of the history of theatre structure, containing fascinating ideas regarding solutions to problems that will be faced in the future.[4] Besides covering the prerequisites of solid architectural planning of theatres, Mielziner's book also discusses many of the typical follies that can and have resulted in unworkable theatre structures, or stages that are extremely awkward to use. His book probes deeply into the problems that will likely face future theatres. How will they be designed? "No vital, truly contemporary theatre can be conceived by traditional knowledge alone; on the other hand, the designer whose sole credo is 'innovation' is either dishonest in proclaiming unequivocal divorce from past tradition, or is apt to produce an ill-conceived theatre design."[5] For Mielziner, the truly creative theatre architects will look to the past as well as to the future for solutions to their problems.

Jo Mielziner's contribution to theatre covered more than fifty years and includes a collection of outstanding scenic designs that is almost unrivaled. In addition to his design contributions, he provided books, articles, and lectures that cover the whole range of theatre's physical aspects. Finally, after the 1940s, he worked diligently to improve the design of theatre facilities, ensuring that theatres to come will be more useful and more efficient in every way. Someday this last may be considered his greatest contribution.

[4]Jo Mielziner, *The Shapes of Our Theatre* (New York, 1970).
[5]Mielziner, *Op. cit.*, p. 131.

eleven

The
Film

Let us firmly establish it now: film is *not* theatre. It is purely its own art form, taking acting techniques that have existed in theatre for thousands of years and adapting them to its own uses. It then modifies and combines those techniques with modern technology to create a wholly new art form. It is the only one of the major art forms that has developed almost totally within this century, and until the advent and subsequent phenomenal growth of television it was the mass art form, usurping the primacy of theatre. And just as film is not theatre, neither is it television. Old movies are *run* on television, and films *for* television are constantly being produced, but the two are separate media, with separate audiences, at least in part, and the viewing conditions are quite different.

The Early Period

In its earliest period, film was less an art form than a curiosity, and its early history is a complex one that includes a number of projection devices. One of the most interesting of those early methods for making pictures move was the Mutoscope, in which photographs printed on cardboard could be put into a viewing machine and flipped over rapidly to simulate motion. Such "peep show" machines continued to be a major aspect of Americana, remaining a feature of penny arcades and amusement parks all over the country until the middle of this century. Serious film, however, required more sophisticated techniques, and it was the Vitascope that started film on its way from curiosity to big business and, almost accidentally one sometimes suspects, from big business to art.

The last half of the 1890s and the first few years of the 1900s saw the development of short films that were rarely more than a few minutes long, although technicians were determinedly seeking methods of increasing the length of film that could be presented. Early film exhibitions featured such exciting (and they truly were, then) short films as *Umbrella Dance*; *Venice, Showing Gondolas*; *Kaiser Wilhelm, Reviewing his Troops*; *Butterfly Dance*; and *Burlesque Boxing*. This last was especially important because of its popularity. As techniques for filming and presenting longer films were developed, they were often devoted to the filming of such epic battles as the Corbett and Fitzsimmons championship bout and the Jeffries and Sharkey fight.

Film Becomes an Art Form

Most American films remained at one reel or less until 1909, with the release of a faked version of the *Oberammergau Passion Play*, shot on a New York rooftop. The hoax was soon exposed, but perhaps in part because of the attendant publicity the film did well enough at the box office to encourage even longer efforts. Those early films, including *The Great Train Robbery*, the original and one of the best of the action-film genre, were first and foremost highly commercial. As a result of some early artistic stirrings, however, the film soon developed a social conscience. Such films as Edwin S. Porter's *The Ex-Convict* and most of D. W. Griffith's films, from *A Corner in Wheat* (1909) to *Intolerance* (1916) championed the poor and savagely attacked the privileges of the wealthy.

Such films not only displayed a growing social consciousness but also turned the curiosity into an artistic force. The day of the *Butterfly Dance* was over, and audiences would no longer pay an admission price merely to watch water pouring over Niagara Falls or gondolas gliding jerkily through the canals of Venice. Films had become "moving fiction," and the emotional impact that a feature-length film could exert on an audience was recognized and combined with the excitement of phsyical action.

The Move to Hollywood

During that period, filming moved to California, and Hollywood became the center of this major industry. Southern California was perfect for the film producers. The weather was generally clear and sunny, and the variety of geographical possibilities was great in that the deserts, the high and the low mountains, the temperate forests, the spectacular scenery of Yosemite, and the Pacific Ocean were all close and could be used at no charge.

The Contribution of Chaplin

Even the shortest history of films would be incomplete without at least brief mention of Charles Spencer Chaplin, the genius of silent films throughout the history of the genre. At the time when the growth of feature-length films had almost taken over the industry, Chaplin began his career making short comedies. By the time that such feature films as *Birth of a Nation* had whetted the public appetite for length and spectacle, Chaplin had, grudgingly it almost seemed, advanced to two-reelers. Aside from a brief supporting role in 1914, he avoided the feature-length film until 1921. In 1931, when sound had firmly established itself and Hollywood was totally in the age of the *talkies*, Chaplin, holding adamantly to pantomime, filmed *City Lights*, which many critics still believe to be the best film of his distinguished career.

Into the Twenties

In spite of Chaplin's foot-dragging, the feature-length film had become the entertainment staple not only of the nation but of Europe as well, and by the 1920s Hollywood was indeed what it billed itself to be: the movie capital of the world. The star system, which producers had once flatly refused to support, had become the Hollywood way of life and business. The major studios, in part as a result of the rising cost factors, nurtured their older stars and blithely developed new ones as box-office insurance. And costs other than salaries rose as well. Simple outdoor shooting techniques that used sunlight and painted backdrops swiftly vanished, to be replaced by giant stages lit electrically, and huge back lots containing not just scenery but real buildings and even miniature towns to provide scenic reality.

The films turned out in the early 1920s capitalized on the permissive "new morality" that had followed World War I. Prohibition might exist everywhere else in the United States, but in Hollywood films the drinking scenes became epidemic, the stars became more glittering in costume and behavior, and sex was the "in" topic. Films promoted the idea that in the "smart" twenties affairs were commonplace and infidelity was the pattern for marital living. That did not last long, because, just as in the past few years, during the early 1970s, Hollywood made the rash assumption that the "new morality" that seemed so evident in Southern California was truly a nationwide phenomenon. Such was not the case then or, apparently, now. Large sections of the country did not subscribe to the new morality and, in fact, opposed it.

Hollywood, as a result of its preoccupation with the "fast life," as it was euphemistically called, was viewed by many people across the country with a deep suspicion that seemed to be confirmed when, in late 1922, a series of scandals shook the movie colony. "Fatty" Arbuckle, one of the most popular of the silent stars, was accused in a rape case that left the country in a mood of disgust. The director William Desmond Taylor was murdered, and though the crime was never solved it implicated two of the top stars of the period, Mary Miles Minter and Mabel Normand. Finally, and in a sense acting as the straw that broke the camel's back, Wallace Reid, a handsome and popular leading man, was revealed to be a drug addict.

Public indignation rose to overwhelming proportions and Hollywood, seemingly disconcerted and even amazed that its concept of morality had proved different from the national standard, hurried to protect itself by agreeing to unite in self-censorship before public censorship was imposed. Will H. Hays was chosen to head a self-censorship organization, the Motion Picture Producers and Distributors of America. The Hays Office, as the organization became known, vigorously pursued a policy of placating the public and enforcing a set of moral standards that now seem highly restrictive and, in a strange sense, immoral in that sinfulness was apparently acceptable as subject matter as long as, at the film's end, virtue triumphed and evildoers were punished. Such rules led to some terribly phoney endings, but they worked in the sense that they staved off a very real threat of external censorship under which we might even now be operating had it not been for the Hays Office.

Films Begin to Talk—In Color

Film scripts were largely business as usual in the mid-1920s, except that the heroes always triumphed and the villains always got their just deserts. Even so, the period was highly important because of two major technical innovations. The first and most important was sound, talking movies. Talkies were not, when *The Jazz Singer* was finally premiered before the general public, a brand new phenomenon never seen before. Even before the turn of the century in France, films had been synchronized to phonographs to produce short (usually about one minute) sound films. Those early works, however, had never been more than interesting curiosities. In 1926, Warner Brothers, facing bankruptcy, gambled on sound and invested in a "talking novelty," the Vitaphone. In August of that same year a gala premiere was held to introduce talking pictures to the general public. The feature of the premiere was John Barrymore starring in *Don Juan*, and the public yawned politely. When *The Jazz Singer* finally appeared it was not just sound that made it so important; it was the fact that this was no short novelty or publicity gimmick, or even a curiosity produced for brief display. It was a feature-length film in which the sound, effectively controlled and projected, complemented the performance. Also, the strong personality of Al Jolson himself, as much perhaps as the sound, helped make the movie a resounding success—such a success, in fact, that within three years movie houses all over the country had been wired for sound. Few periods in history end with exactness, but the end of the silent film era came neatly on October 6, 1927, when Warner Brothers presented *The Jazz Singer* on Broadway.

The second technological innovation of the twenties coincided almost exactly with the introduction of sound. It was the development of color film. Again, color was hardly new when it finally gained acceptance. As early as 1908, in England, a three-color process had been developed and used with some success. Earlier experiments had used color painted directly onto the film. Herbert Kalmus concentrated on developing a method for the mass manufacture of color film, and by 1923, he was ready to market an effective two-color process. In the beginning the public was rather apathetic, but after Lon Chaney's use of color in a sequence of *The Phantom of the Opera* (1925), and after Douglas Fairbanks scored a rousing success in *The Black Pirate* (1926), the public began to demand more and more color, especially in spectacles. By the time sound arrived, color was on hand to complement it.

Gangsters and the Thirties

The 1930s, largely as a result of sound and color, saw a strong movement toward realistic films that somewhat paralleled the earlier realistic movement in theatre. Silent films, by the very nature of the medium, had avoided the extremes of realism and naturalism. The stories or scripts

A scene from The Maltese Falcon *starring Humphrey Bogart, Mary Astor, and Peter Lorre.*

might have had realistic or naturalistic overtones, but the production values tended to destroy any attempt to achieve these modes. Because they were working in a silent and therefore basically unrealistic medium, film makers were concerned primarily with finding methods or techniques of direction and performance that would make sound unnecessary. Acting styles were excessive and highly pantomimic, and directing styles promoted this necessary excess. Suddenly, however, sound was not only available but unavoidable, and the styles that were designed to transmit emotion silently while conveying, in a very real sense, a feeling of dialogue, were all at once so extreme as to seem ludicrous. Also, the harsh economic realities of the thirties made the posturing of earlier films seem almost obscene. With employment scarce to nonexistent, and with hungry people standing in bread and soup and clothing lines, only life's realities seemed fit material for serious artistic examination.

There was, of course, in addition to the realistic films, a continuing market for "escape" films, making no pretense of examining anything that mattered. These were, essentially, frothy musical entertainments designed to distract the viewers from their own immediate problems by contemplating nonproblems faced by, for example, the singing royalty of tiny, mythical Ruritania, or unreal disasters threatening Jeanette MacDonald and Maurice Chevalier. Given the fact of sound, such pictures were certain to come. The Broadway musical, an increasingly popular form that had been unavailable to silent films, was now ripe for exploitation, and *The Vagabond King*, *The Desert Song*, and *Rio Rita* proved very popular film fare, perhaps because they saved movie makers and audience alike from the need for thinking about the reality of the Depression outside the theatre.

When the films of the thirties are discussed, the genre that usually (and deservedly) receives the most applause is the gangster film. An American love affair with the gangster movie began with classics such as *Little Caesar* (1930), with Edward G. Robinson, based on the novel by W. R. Burnett; *Public Enemy* (1931), with James Cagney; *Scarface* (1932), with Paul Muni; and the *Maltese Falcon* (1936), with Humphrey Bogart. Most of those films were screen originals, which is to say that they were written directly for the screen and were not in most cases screen adaptations of novels or film versions of existing plays. Thus, they could make excellent use of filmic techniques and so provide a degree of vitality that was too often lost when movie makers merely concentrated on filming the artistic creations of other media. In addition, such films had an immediacy of appeal in that they were based on contemporary events, written, as the Hollywood public-relations groups constantly blared, out of the headlines in the daily newspapers.

Film comedy was also totally revised because of sound. Many silent-film comics, such as Buster Keaton, with comic styles established on the physical necessity of silence, were (surprisingly) unable to make the transition to sound films. The comic mantle was inherited by new comics such as the Marx Brothers, W. C. Fields, Jimmy Durante, and, toward the end of the thirties, Bob Hope. These new performers were masters of comic dialogue, and most had developed a physical style in burlesque or vaudeville to complement their vocal delivery. The Marx Brothers were absolute masters of manic dialogue, punctuated by equally manic bursts of physical activity. Their style and techniques were those that they had practiced earlier on the stage, but they were nonetheless perfect for film. Jimmy Durante was a whirlwind of motion, and W. C. Fields, with his years of training as a circus juggler, was able to fit perfectly timed physical action to his startling vocal technique: generally a howl of indignant outrage, mumbled imprecations, and then a line of astonishing sardonic clarity.

World War II and the Forties

World War II mobilized the movie industry in Hollywood as it mobilized the automobile factories in Detroit and the shipyards on both coasts. Patriotic films, depicting allied victories over the Axis powers, formed the

Scene from A Night at the Opera *(1935), featuring the Marx brothers.*

Paul Muni and Robert Coote star in a scene from Commandos Strike at Dawn.

largest part of film fare between 1941 and 1946. A few of the films were truly memorable. In England the years of experience in making documentary films resulted in some exceptionally fine motion pictures that had the ring of truth. One of the best, appearing in 1942, was the David Lean-Noel Coward production of *In Which We Serve*. In the United States such films as *The Moon is Down*, based on John Steinbeck's short novel about the German invasion of Norway, or even such films as *Commandos Strike at Dawn*, not only fed the patriotic fervor that audiences felt but also provided some fine moments of film artistry.

When the war ended, American films went back to business as usual, turning out overproduced musical trash featuring platoons of dancers (or even swimmers) doing highly synchronized and usually unmemorable numbers. There were several exceptions. Alfred Hitchcock's *Notorious* (1946) was a serious film that displayed exceptional camera technique as the director zeroed in on Ingrid Bergman in her amorous pursuit of Cary Grant. Also in 1946, William Wyler turned out *The Best Years of Our Lives*, which still stands as one of the finest and most sensitive American films.

In England, David Lean was continuing his love affair with the camera, beginning immediately after the war with one of his finest films, *Great Expectations* (1946). Alongside Lean, Sir Carol Reed was turning out such films as *Odd Man Out* (1947) and *The Third Man* (1949), which has already become a classic of the genre. It was in Italy, however, that the first major postwar innovation in film style had its birth. Roberto Rossellini, in two major works, *Open City* (1945) and *Paisan* (1946), set the tone and style for Italian neorealism, capturing the bleakness of spirit and environment that existed in so many areas of war-ravaged Europe.

Into the Fifties and Beyond

The primary interest in American films in the 1950s has to be the film industry's response to the rapidly growing popularity of television. In the early years of the fifties some distinguished films appeared, such as George Stevens' *Shane* (1953), which turned the American western into a modern morality play exploring the choices that cause good and evil, and the consequences that such choices create.

In the late fifties, and continuing through the sixties and seventies, film makers spent a large part of their time and energy in combating the implied (and very real) threat of television. What seems to have been the final solution, a solution that so many of the film-producing companies still seem to believe in, is to have films provide the public with the kind of material that is unavailable on a home television screen inhibited by the necessity to provide family entertainment. Choices made in that area, however, have not always, or even often, been the best. Thus, films have begun to separate their audiences in the same way as theatre did following the incursion of film into the traditional theatre audience. To many people in recent years, film has seemed to prize the kinky and the abnormal to the exclusion of any valid dramatic values. As a result, film audiences have become younger and younger, apparently restrained only by civil laws from retrogresssing to an ultimate audience of curious children.

In the late 1950s the French *new wave* began attracting attention. To call the new wave a unified school or movement would be granting it too much status. Most of the new wave directors, such as François Truffaut, Jean-Luc Godard, Alain Resnais, Agnes Varda, and Claude Chabrol, had styles and techniques that were individual and diverse but, because most of them also wrote film criticism, they managed to popularize their own and their friends' work and give their concepts the legitimacy of being a cinematic movement. In fact, the one element that they had in common was an impatience with the traditional film, the glossy, well-made product of the Hollywood or Paris studios. In films like Truffaut's *Jules and Jim* and Godard's *Breathless* they created works in which the action was not carefully tailored to build to a major climax, and in which the audience comes to know the film's characters only in terms of what they do, and not in terms of what the director says about them or even what the characters say about themselves. Probably the main effect of the new wave was to expand the potential of film in dealing with narration and characterization and to give impetus to the *cinema verite* style, which is still a major force in film production.

The other primary movement in film during the fifties and sixties has been the breakup of the old studio system. In part that also is a result of the competition from television, combined with rising production costs and the new mobile equipment. In the late fifties the practice of location shooting proved to be so efficient that runaway productions became the rule rather than the exception. New miniaturization processes provided the capability of creating highly efficient mobile units to shoot and even process film on location, suddenly outmoding the major studios and their enormous sound stages and vast lots. Why own and maintain a miniature false front of Buckingham Palace when a location team could shoot scenes against the real palace for less money? This, plus declining profits, ended the giant studios, probably for all time.

D'Artagnan (Michael York) is temporarily inconvenienced by Richelieu's swordsmen in The Three Musketeers.

Along the way, through all of these upheavals, some excellent films have been produced, such as Fred Zinnemann's *High Noon*, Hecht-Lancaster's *Marty*, Sam Peckinpah's *Straw Dogs*, and Elaine May's brilliant and underrated *A New Leaf*. Where the films are headed is anybody's guess. Currently such films as *The Three Musketeers*, *Love Story*, *Jaws*, and *Star Wars* would seem to imply a return to the values that once made film *the* mass media, the darling of people of all ages and economic-social-educational levels. However, when the popularity of such individual films is compared to the multiplicity of porno films, X-rated efforts, and tasteless works designed for public consumption, very few conclusions about the future of film can be drawn. Only hindsight may allow us someday to single out certain films of today as augurs of the future.

Film Techniques

Of the technical opportunities that film offers, some are so obvious, or have become so much a part of common knowledge, that they require little comment. They must be noted, however, just because they are so familiar that many people forget the vast potential these techniques have for telling a story on film and evoking a dramatic response. We all know, for example, and possibly make common use of such terms as *close-up, fade, zoom, cut, camera focus*, etc. Those terms are more, however, than mere film industry jargon or fan magazine attempts at verisimilitude. They identify some of the technical possibilities that film possesses. And these are all possibilities that the stage does not possess. On stage, actors remain always at approximately the same distance from their audience, limited by the depth of the set and by the necessity to project voice and movement. A film camera, using a zoom lens and the above techniques, can characterize and create atmosphere largely through technical means.

Picture a long shot of a native village in a clearing between a jungle and a wide river. The camera pans across the village from medium distance and focuses on a chapel. Then you see a long shot of the interior of the chapel, past the congregation, focusing on the minister at the pulpit and his sister, Rose, at the organ. The camera moves in to a medium shot of the minister, then to a close shot of Rose, who is pumping the pedals of the organ vigorously. Up to this point there has been no dialogue, only indistinct voice sounds and the sound of a hymn, "Guide me O Thou Great Jehovah," but the camera, in its variety of shots, has managed to tell much about the setting while capturing a special mood that sets the tone of the picture. The material just described is the opening sequence from scriptwriter James Agee's *The African Queen* (1951), and it illustrates how even the most conventional camera shots can be utilized to make a particular point or to create a particular atmosphere. Also, close-up can be used to tell at least part of a story without the theatrical necessity of resorting to dialogue. A close-up of a tear-stained face, carefully handled, can say as much about grief as a page of dialogue.

Katharine Hepburn and Humphrey Bogart in a scene from The African Queen.

Settings for film are almost as unlimited as the director cares to make them. Cameras can be transported to almost any location in any climate. If a script calls for the actors to be seen playing before Buckingham Palace, then this can be accomplished realistically by the simple if expensive expedient of going to London and shooting the scene. Less expensive techniques, such as filming the actors before a stock shot of the Palace, also give highly realistic results.

Also, the set can easily be changed many times in many different ways. The most obvious, of course, is the camera's ability to cut from scene to scene, from equatorial Africa to the north pole, without drawing a curtain or resetting the stage. Also, for film, the set is always what the camera frames. Thus, an opening shot of a film might show a man far away, standing alone in the midst of a grass-covered prairie, with the set being the vast prairie itself, dwarfing the lone human figure. The camera zooms in to a medium close shot of the man, and the set has changed. Now the man dominates and the small bit of prairie that still can be seen only *represents* the earlier set. Next the camera moves in for a close-up of the man's face, at the same time changing angle so that it is shooting slightly up. Again the set has changed. All that can be seen now is the man's face, backed by sky, and the prairie is only an audience memory. On stage, no matter how carefully the director blocks the action, and no matter how hard the actors work, the set can never become so plastic. Lights may be cut to a tight spot that illuminates the actor on a darkened set, but the total set remains dimly visible in the peripheral view of the audience.

Out of possibilities such as these have grown the techniques generally known as *filmic*, which provide the motion picture with the opportunity to use some very special images to tell its story. For example, near the beginning of Alfred Hitchcock's *The Birds* a short scene inside a pet shop features a close-shot of a parrot squawking horribly, and behind the parrot the audience can see a man. The image of angry bird and docile man is very effective in setting the scene for a film based on the idea of an aroused and united bird population attacking humankind. Achieving such a scene onstage would be difficult if not impossible. The whole pet shop would always be visible, making almost impossible the tight focus on the angry bird and the innocent man in the background. Also, almost certainly, the parrot would not squawk on cue. The camera, of course, needs only to capture one perfect "squawk" and then the parrot will sound off on cue forever after. Other examples of such filmic techniques are *Moulin Rouge*, which captured the quality of Toulouse Lautrec's paintings of Paris, both the exteriors and the smoky atmosphere of the nightclubs, through the imaginative use of color filters. Even John Ford's early westerns made use of such purely filmic images as the lone rider, seen from a distance against the vastness of the American West, romantic in his isolation and his oneness with nature.

This immense variety of possibilities makes film a director's medium in a way that the live theatre can never be. Directors in both media can rehearse their players to perfection, but onstage, once the actors go before an audience, the director's control is diminished. In film, however, once the perfection is achieved it is captured permanently and the performers give exactly the same performance, night after night and year after year, in movie houses all over the world.

In addition to the variety of filmic techniques at the disposal of the film director is the use of editing to achieve spectacular results that go far beyond the specific efforts of the actors and even beyond the original conception of the individual shots. Perhaps the most spectacular example of this was an experiment performed by the Russian directors Kuleshov and Pudovkin. They took a short piece of film showing a man's face completely devoid of expression, and combined it with shots showing first a bowl of soup, second a dead woman in a casket, and third a child playing with a toy bear. When these three separate sequences were shown to the public there were raves over the acting of the expressionless man. He was called "pensive" over his forgotten bowl of soup, "deeply sorrowful" as he looked at the dead woman, and "lightly happy" as he watched the girl playing with her funny stuffed toy. In other words, the public, shown the shot of the man in conjunction with specific scenes, projected its own emotional reactions to the adjoining scenes onto the blank face of the man,

Super con artist Henry Gondorff (Paul Newman) lectures apprentice con man Johnny Hooker (Robert Redford) on the art of big-time con games in The Sting.

and because these were their own emotions they were delighted with what they saw. By making use of such techniques (totally unavailable to the theatre director), which do not, necessarily, even depend upon fallible actors but on a purely technical process, the film director has made himself the absolute master of his medium.

Film and Theatre

There is, generally, a tendency to think of film and theatre as interchangeable entities, with film a late-blooming younger sibling of theatre. There is some justification for that belief. After all, many actors and directors manage to operate quite successfully in both media, and film did arrive recently to do many of the works on screen that theatre had traditionally done live. And there are other strong resemblances. Both film and theatre operate from a script that calls for certain words to be spoken, certain actions to be performed, and certain specific scenes and effects to be achieved. Both media, as their end product, present to an audience a group of actors portraying specific people who are caught up in dramatic situations. Those end products are, in both cases, supervised (interpreted, rehearsed, and polished) by a director, and are supported by a number of design artists and technical personnel. In addition, many of the products of either medium are capable of being translated, with varying degrees of success, to the other medium. Thus, such stage plays as *Who's Afraid of Virginia Woolf?* and *The Odd Couple* made highly successful films, and such films as *Lilli*, retitled *Carnival*, and *Gone With the Wind* (from the novel by way of the film) have had substantial successes as stage vehicles.

After such obvious and major similarities are enumerated, however, it must be pointed out that the basic differences are even greater than the similarities and that film is not merely an adjunct of the stage. It is its own medium with its own unique potential, its own specific set of demands, and its own special art.

The first, most obvious, and certainly most significant difference between theatre and film is that theatre always consists of the live actor performing before and making emotional and spiritual contact with an audience. Film, in contrast, can never be live, and its contact with an audience depends upon its ability to persuade viewers that the figures moving about and speaking from the screen are in fact live people and not merely pictures of people. In theatre the audiences are willing to accept certain departures from reality (such as accepting that the "aside" cannot be heard by anyone onstage with the actor delivering it), and so it is with the film audience. For the time that they are in the movie house, the viewers are willing to accept the pictures as reality. And if the film is good enough, so that the illusion is strong, movie audiences may even clap and cheer at the movie's end, though they know full well that the players and director are not there to respond to their applause.

It is in the technical area especially that film departs from live theatre. Any number of serious works—books, articles, and essays—have been written to instruct on the basic differences between film and theatre in philosophical approach and understanding, but it is notable that for film much of this philosophy, in the final analysis, grows directly out of the film's technical capacity. These special qualities, generally referred to as filmic techniques, are qualities that are related directly to the technical possibilities inherent in film, aiming at making optimum use of film potential.

Such are the differences between film and live theatre, and in sum they are great indeed. Closely enough related that artists can move comfortably between the two, the media remain quite different art forms, each possessing its own special possibilities, techniques, and demands, and each making its own individual contribution to theatrical art.

twelve

Dance
in
America

Dance is, clearly, an international art form, and in many countries it has a much larger audience than it does in the United States. However, because a study of dance throughout the world would take several volumes rather than several pages, a concentration on dance in America, with a brief look at the history of the form itself, seems the best way to approach the subject.

Dance in America, for the first time, is emerging as big box-office entertainment. One of the reasons for this emergence is that dance has become more than an esoteric art form for an elite audience. It has become a popular, readily understandable form of entertainment. The general availability of dance is partially a result of the fusing together of dance forms. Modern dance has been assimilating ballet technique for years, and in return ballet has developed a new "modern ballet" form which is to some extent performed by every ballet company. Everywhere dancers are more adaptable, showing more technical excellence than they have in the past. Most have no trouble switching from one style to another, so that for the first time modern dance companies are doing repertory. This versatility has caused a blurring of the differences between dance styles.

In the 1930s, when modern dance was developing, choreographers had to train dancers to do their movements before the dances could be learned. There was little time for dancers to absorb the subtler points of dynamics and finer details of technique. Companies, especially those working in what was called "modern dance," tended to concentrate on one style and perform the works of one choreographer, so that they became specialists. There was no necessity to separate the various forms from each other, because the dancers did it themselves. Modern dance was done in bare feet, emphasizing the ground rather than the air, and using more movement in the torso than was true of the classical form.

Today's loosening up of dance styles has come about partially as a matter of aesthetic survival. The second generation of modern dancers broke away from the forms of the thirties in order to dance the way that individual performers wished. Currently, there is very little restriction on dancers. With so many styles accepted, a dancer does not have to break away from ballet to do jazz movements or to dance without shoes.

Because of this freedom, box-office success plays an ever larger role in determining what kind of dances will be performed. Almost no dance company is self-supporting. Ever since the early 1970s, subsidy has played an enormous part in keeping companies alive and allowing them to tour areas traditionally not exposed to live dance. However, the money available for such subsidies is limited, and in order to bring dance to as many people as possible, most subsidies go to the companies which reach the greatest number of people. In short, even with subsidies box-office success is still important.

It is difficult at this point to predict the future of dance in America. Dance evolves rapidly because it can never be repeated exactly. Also, because a dancer's performing life averages only about ten years, almost anything claimed about dance has to be qualified by the time it is uttered. New distinctive dance styles are constantly emerging, and choreographers are regularly creating fresh, crisp, distinctive works. Whatever happens, however, it is easier to appreciate this art when one sees it in perspective.

Dance in the Early Periods

Until the end of the Middle Ages the history of dance parallels that of theatre, and in most cases the two modes are one in the same. The primitive imitation of animal movements as a means of control and assured success in the hunt is as much a case of dance as it is of theatre. The Cretan *pyrrhic* or war dance, for example, was used by the Spartans to develop skill in fighting, but like many primitive dances, it was outwardly mimetic —that is, theatrical. The *emmeleia* was the general classification of dance associated with Greek tragedy. Many forms of dance were lumped under this heading. The entire movement of the Chorus, for instance, was just as

Sixth-century vase painting showing Greek ritual dancers in bird costumes.

much dance as it was drama. In fact, Aristotle describes Thespis as a dancer. The dance characteristic of Greek Old Comedy was the *kordax*. A more obscene version, the *sikinnis*, was done in conjunction with the satyr plays; it probably involved much vigorous leaping, horseplay, and lewd pantomime. The *kouretes*, a dance-drama founded on Crete at an even earlier period than the Greek tragedy, was basically a sword dance.

Existing forms of dance and mime were, by the Medieval period, absorbed into the stock in trade of the traveling jongleur, while the early sword dances, such as the kouretes, were absorbed into the mummings and folk plays. Even the courtly disguisings (where the nobility at court dressed in rich disguises) characteristically concluded with a dance. The late Middle Ages, the eleventh and twelfth centuries, brought increasing instances of ecstatic dance. For example, although the Church attempted to suppress it, men and women began to dance in churchyards, on holy ground, in order to communicate with the dead. This *dance macabre* was similar to both the plague-related St. Vitus dance and the *Tarantella*. The Tarantella, believed to have evolved from the Roman *saltarello*, attempts to show the death frenzy of someone who has been bitten by a tarantula. More and more such dances came into being, many actually interrupting church services. In one instance, as legend has it, a dancer refused to stop when asked to do so by a priest and was thereupon sentenced by the priest to dance for a year. A sympathetic archbishop overruled this judgment, but the tradition is said to be the origin of one of Andersen's fairy tales.

Gradually the *intermezzi*, the short, spectacular shows put on by the Italian courts, became more colorful and complex, and they featured several forms of dance. As reports of these events spread from court to court there developed a kind of informal competition between them. Wandering mimes and jugglers became dance teachers, and the lively "Morris" and other folk dances became more slow and sedate so that they could be performed in the costumes of the court displays.

Catherine de Medici, who had moved from Italy to France on the occasion of her marriage, enlisted the help of one of her valets, who had received training as a musician and dancing master, to stage the *Ballet Comique de la Reine* in the Louvre Palace on October 15, 1581. This was a most important early effort at creating an extended choreographic spectacle. The event is generally considered to be the first faint glimmering of ballet, in spite of the fact that the "dancing" part of the *Ballet Comique* consisted primarily of ordered movements in geometrical figures. During this period there was no essential difference between social and theatrical dance. The dances, which included the *pavane, galliard, courante,* and the *sarabande,* are described in a dance manual called *Orchesographie,* written in 1588. Although women could perform ballroom dances, men usually played all roles in the spectacles.

By the end of the sixteenth century, dancing was in vogue at every European court. Louis XIII appeared in court ballets, especially the ballet *à entrée,* which was essentially a series of short scenes vaguely linked. French court ballet reached its height under Louis XIV, who was called the Sun King because of a ballet role which he played as a young man. When Louis became too old and portly to dance, members of the French court also stopped dancing. So the ballet, which had been moved out of the ballroom and onto the proscenium stage, was now done by professional dancers rather than members of the court.

Theatrical productions of this period were often hybrids. One of the better combinations was the *comedia-ballet* developed by the composer and comic dancer Jean Baptiste Lully and the comic playwright, Moliere. *Le Bourgeois Gentilhomme,* one of the best examples of this genre, is now thought of as a play, but when first performed it contained as much dance as it did drama.

In 1661, Louis XIV established the *Academie Royale de Danse* and, in 1669, the *Academie Royale de Musique* which, under the guidance of Lully, codified the professional ballet and helped turn dance into an art form performed by both sexes. Gradually the teaching of dance became more and more dogmatic. By the early eighteenth century the opera ballet consisted largely of pastoral and bucolic scenes, with dramatic action minimized, and almost completely lacking in structure and content. This was the ballet that Jean-Georges Noverre (1727–1810) protested against in his famous *Lettres sur la Danse et sur les Ballets* (1759). In spite of such protests, ballet did not change overnight.

In 1832, Marie Taglioni danced *La Sylphide* on the points of her toes and ushered in the era of the ballerina as a romantic ideal. Male dancers, who previously had dominated the ballet, were soon reduced to roles as partners. All of the great artists in romantic ballet are women: Marie Taglioni, Fanny Elssler, and Carlotta Grisi. It was during this same period that Carlo Blasis categorized and codified the existing movement material in ballet.

Marius Petipa arrived in Russia in 1847. There he served as ballet master under four czars for a period which spanned almost six decades. He created more than sixty ballets, and as an instructor in the Imperial School he raised the standards of dance technique in Russia; his efforts helped to make Russia the leading country in ballet for over half a century. However, by the end of Petipa's life classical ballet had already deteriorated into a stereotype which relied totally on technique and virtuosity.

It was Diaghilev with his *Ballets Russes* who established the nucleus of people who not only exported the Russian classical tradition, but who returned to the Aristotlian conception of dance as the representation of passions, actions, and manners. Diaghilev combined the work of Fokine, Ravel, Debussy, Satie, Costeau, Proust, Bakst, Benois, Rouault, Picasso, Nijinsky, Massine, Balanchine, and Stravinsky. All of these men influenced ballet in America, but the last two had a major part in creating it.

Twentieth-Century Dance in America

It was at this point, the beginning of the twentieth century, that artistic dance in America began in earnest. Diaghilev and Pavlova both toured the United States, so in spite of the lack of adequate teachers and companies, ballet became a recognized discipline. The only other form of theatre-dance recognized in America at this time was show or vaudeville dance consisting of backbends, cartwheels, splits, and slow kicks.

Loie Fuller was the first of the early American dancers to attempt something which she called "dance," but which did not fit into existing categories. In the early 1890s, she performed solo numbers in which she manipulated gauzy fabrics not only with her body but also with sticks concealed under her draperies. The most astounding of her effects were wrought by using light to augment the shapes that she produced from her fabrics. Fuller toured with a group of electricians who did all of her lighting and who were sworn to secrecy about her techniques. Not until Alwin Nikolais did any other American dancer make such extensive use of lighting.

Isadora Duncan, an American dancer, reacted against the mechanical quality of ballet. Examining her own movements, she decided that they originated in her solar plexus and flowed outward. These were "natural" movements and thus were circular in form, like the motion of trees and waves. She also introduced the idea of dancing to serious or symphonic music, rather than to something which was merely created to accompany dance. Duncan danced in a Greek tunic, without corsets or shoes, against a backdrop of blue drapes. Because the American theatre of the early 1900s had no place for what Duncan did, she earned a living dancing at the salons of wealthy ladies. Finally, tiring of this precarious mode of existence, she went to Europe where she was received as a serious artist. Since Duncan's art was so dependent on the expression of her own emotions, she was unable to found a lasting school of dance. She was, however, able

Robin Edward Johnson and Phyllis Haskell of the Pirie-Woodbury Dance Company in Obliquities. *Music by John Cage; choreography by Ann Brunswick.*

to show that dance could be raised to an art without adhering to the structured forms of ballet. Surprisingly enough, Duncan's greatest impact on her own time was as a woman rather than a dancer. Her costumes and her disregard for convention in her private life made her the social revolutionary figure of her time.

Duncan's contemporary, Ruth St. Denis, made just the opposite impression. Born Ruth Dennis in 1880, she was given her stage name by David Belasco. It was while St. Denis was on tour with Belasco's company that she was attracted to a cigarette poster featuring the Egyptian goddess, Isis. The dance concepts which this poster triggered in her evolved into a series of solo pieces which she performed in 1906. The movements used by Ruth St. Denis were expressive and theatrical, owing much to Eastern dances, which she utilized to create pictures and to evoke moods.

In 1914, St. Denis formed a company, the core of which would be a couple dancing in the manner of Vernon and Irene Castle, who had become great commercial successes. As a partner, she picked Ted Shawn, whom she subsequently married. Shawn's organizing ability and the school they built together made Ruth St. Denis unique among the first generation of American modern dancers. She was able to found a line of succession, a *coterie* of students who built upon her work. Because of this she is often called the first lady of modern dance.

Shawn, a divinity student who had taken up dancing as therapy after an illness, joined St. Denis both because he admired her dancing and because he believed in her attempt to show spiritual truth through dance. "Denishawn," a combination of their two names, became a touring company and school of dance which lasted from 1915 to 1931. This school was the most important organization in the history of American modern dance. Although its main function was to prepare dancers to join the Denishawn Company, it gave students a wide exposure to different dance styles. Out of it came three of the four dancers who are considered the first true examples of American modern dance: Martha Graham, Doris Humphrey, and Charles Weidman.

Denishawn was dissolved in 1931. Ruth St. Denis kept on dancing, but she no longer had direct influence on American modern dance. Shawn, on the other hand, continued to be influential. He felt that there were masculine movements and feminine ones and, from 1931 to 1938, Shawn concentrated on movement for the male dancer. Due to the chronic unemployment of the Depression, he was able to recruit unemployed men to live on his farm, dancing and performing physical labor. "Kinetic Molpoi," which he choreographed in 1933, used movements derived from work and games and made the point that men could dance and still remain masculine. After 1938, when his dance company split up because of the developing World War II, Shawn used his farm to produce "Jacob's Pillow," a famous summer dance festival which enabled American audiences to see many types of dance.

Martha Graham, who broke away from Denishawn in 1923, was neither physically nor temperamentally suited to romantic dance. St. Denis

Merce Cunningham in solo.

Dance in America

had inspired her to dance, but her work had primarily been with Shawn. For Graham, dance existed to uplift, to instruct, and even to distrub. She wanted to express, in universal terms, the passions and problems of her time. She could not make use of Eastern dance movements, as did St. Denis, because she could only express in dance those things she understood. Also, she felt that her concerns could not be expressed within the existing framework of movement. She required dynamically intense, percussive movement, so she created a technique to suit her purposes. Her dance was motivated from within, based on the contraction and release of the body while breathing, because breathing is the essence of life. As Graham's ideas were not romantic, she used percussive, angular, even geometric movement on the floor.

Martha Graham was probably the most controversial dancer of the thirties, and today her name is synonymous with modern dance. She has created an enormous body of works, some of which are still in repertory, and a movement technique that has affected almost every American dancer.

The team of Doris Humphrey and Charles Weidman left Denishawn within five years of Martha Graham and were successful in New York their

Guignol *as performed by the Nikolais Dance Theatre.*

first season. Humphrey, who was the more theoretically inclined of the pair, developed a movement vocabulary in the manner of Graham. However, rather than concentrating on some unique aspect of the body, Humphrey saw the dancer in relation to the physical surroundings. Her technique was based primarily on the fall and recovery of the body in relation to gravity—a concept which was sustained longer than Graham's, was more dangerous, and hence, more exciting. Weidman complemented Humphrey's architectural use of space, creating dances that were grounded in mime and which expressed a real flair for the comic. "And Daddy was a Fireman" and "Flickers" (1936) were followed, in 1948, by a series of Thurber sketches in "Fables of our Time." After the Humphrey-Weidman Company ceased to exist in 1945, Doris Humphrey continued to influence dance as artistic director in the company of José Limon, one of the former members of the Humphrey-Weidman Company.

Perhaps the primary factor behind the spread of modern dance technique was the establishment of academic dance. In 1926, Margaret H'Doubler offered the first dance major in the United States at the University of Wisconsin. Martha Hill, a student in this program who had also danced with Graham from 1930 to 1931, became head of the Bennington School of Dance at Bennington College in the summer of 1934. Hill created a summer program enabling students to work not only with Graham, Humphrey, and Weidman, but also with Hanya Holm, the German modern dancer who had trained with Mary Wigman. Holm originally came to America to teach Wigman's concepts but soon became part of the American dance movement. These four—Graham, Humphrey, Weidman, and Holm—form a generation of modern dance.

Many of the next generation of modern dancers emerged from the Bennington program, and their techniques and philosophies were spread by students across the United States. From Graham and her technique came dancers Merce Cunningham, Erick Hawkins, Paul Taylor, and Anna Sokolow. From the Humphrey-Weidman Company came José Limon, who in turn fostered Ruth Currier and Betty Jones. Alwin Nikolais acquired his primary dance background from Hanya Holm, and out of his company came Murray Louis.

Martha Graham was so personally expressive and domineering as a dancer that it was hard for those who worked with her to remain individuals unless they reacted against her style. Merce Cunningham exemplifies such reaction. First he reacted against the expressionistic elements of her dance, using the choreographic method that he developed for "Suite by Chance" (1953). He prepared a series of charts of dance movements, determining their sequence by tossing a coin. Cunningham developed this method so that dance movements could develop in their own right and not as vehicles for narrative sequence. Like Graham he made use of a musical director and composer, but there the similarity ends. The composer, John Cage, is no more interested in melodic line than Cunningham is in narrative development. Often the dancers, and Cunningham, hear the music for the first time during a performance.

Like Cunningham, Erick Hawkins has also removed the narrative element from his dances, concentrating not on storytelling but on pure movement. He stretches out time to encompass a series of *tableux* in a way which is closer to Eastern dance than to Western.

Another Graham student, Paul Taylor, gave a program of "Seven New Works" in 1957. He had departed so far from Graham's conception of dance that critic Louis Horst gave him a quarter of a column of blank space as a review in *Dance Observer*. Taylor's style of dance makes him one of the most interesting modern choreographers; though he espouses no revolutionary theories about dance he has managed equally to outrage the most radical and the most conservative dance critics.

Neither Doris Humphrey nor Charles Weidman pursued their philosophies of movement with the intensity of Graham, so the reaction against them was not as stringent. José Limon, in sympathy with the narrative ideas of Doris Humphrey, accepted her assistance as artistic director of his company. On his own, in such works as "The Moor's Pavane," "There Is a Time," and "Missa Brevis," the strength of his choreography for the male dancer followed in a different tradition, the one set by Ted Shawn. Limon's choreography was always dramatic in nature, putting real people into larger-than-life situations. However, the drama of his works is inherent in

Nikolais Dance Theatre performs Temple.

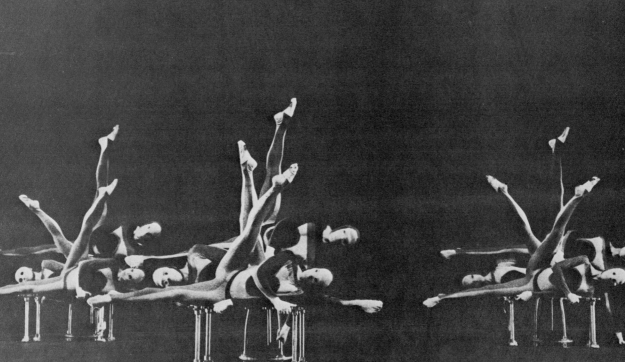

the steps and balance between the parts and not in any "acting" on the part of the dancers.

Alwin Nikolais uses the technical resources of theatre more than any other dancer: "I look upon this polygamy of motion, shape, color, and sound as the basic art of the theatre. To me, the art of drama is one thing; the art of theatre is another. In the latter, a magical panorama of things, sounds, colors, shapes, lights, illusions, and events happen before your eyes and your ears. I find my needs cannot be wholly satisfied by one art. I like to mix my magics." Along with studying at the Bennington Summer School of Dance and with Hanya Holm at Colorado College, Nikolais also played piano accompaniment for silent movies, ran a marionette theatre, and did the lighting designs for a yearly ballet recital. From each of these experiences he gained valuable technical experience in the areas of lighting, costuming, props, and stage scenery. He uses all of this knowledge in his productions.

The multimedia concept is such an integral part of Nikolais' works that many people object to calling his works dance. This does not bother him, however; as long as he can do it, he is not concerned with what it is called. Probably the aspect of his work that has been most criticized is what the critics call his "de-humanization" of the performer. This comes from Nikolais' use of props as an extension of the dancer. He has affixed discs to his dancer's feet, added extentions to their arms, given them costumes that make them look like chess pieces, and even put them in sacks. The purpose of this is to explore movement. As long as the audience sees the dancer as a human form, it may attach human motivations to the dancer's actions. By distorting the form, Nikolais hopes that the audience will be free to see the movement.

In 1948, Nikolais became director of the Henry Street Playhouse in New York, which later became the home for his school and the base for his touring company of dancers. One of his dancers, Murray Louis, wanted to start a company of his own and Nikolais encouraged him in this endeavor. Now both companies are housed in the same building. Louis has kept in his own creations some of Nikolais' abstraction, but he is more directly concerned with the recognizable, unadorned human form.

Robert Dunn, a composer who between 1960 and 1964 gave a series of dance courses at the Merce Cunningham school, found that many of the students were dissatisfied with the structured nature of composition courses. Dunn, his wife Judith, and two young choreographers named Yvonne Rainer and Steve Paxton, requested and received space in the Judson Memorial Church to give a dance concert. As a result, Judson Memorial Church rapidly became a focus for experimental work, and the workshops given there were attended by many choreographers who had not originally been students of Dunn. Among the dancers at Judson were several who had become dissatisfied with dance technique because it was imposing too many limits on their choreography. Among the solutions advanced to solve this problem were everyday movements designed to tone down dance technique, and using nondancers and dancers of various levels of skill.

Merce Cunningham and Dance Company in Sounddance, *featuring Charles Moulton, Chris Komar, Susana Hayman-Chaffey, and Brynar Mehl.*

At this point the most well-known of the choreographers who came out of the Judson workshops is Twyla Tharp, who choreographs for her own company, and who has also created such works as "Deuce Coup" and "As Time Goes By" for the City Center Joffrey Ballet, and "Push Comes to Shove" for the American Ballet Theatre. She is one of the modern choreographers who has a style so much her own that it is recognizable whenever it appears. Even when she uses the movement vocabulary of classical ballet, Tharp twists it until it has as much of her character as the works which she choreographs for her own company. One of the more unusual facets about Tharp is that she considers almost any space to be suitable for dance. After using the nonproscenium space at Judson Church, she choreographed "Medley" in an open field and "Generation" in a gymnasium. "Dancing in the Streets of London and Paris, Continued in Stockholm and Sometimes Madrid" was first seen on two levels of the Wadsworth Atheneum in Hartford, and was later done, among other places, at the Metropolitan Museum in New York.

Meredith Monk studied Merce Cunningham's technique at Sarah Lawrence College, but Monk insists that she is not exclusively a dancer. She claims that her works are of the composite theatre type that could only have been arrived at by a dancer. She has been compared with Robert Wilson and the poet Allen Ginsburg in that she reaches beyond the limits of her discipline. However, dance and music such as that of Satie and Bartok form the basis for Monk's work.

Steve Paxton was a member of Merce Cunningham's company from 1961 to 1965 and was deeply influenced by Cunningham's "chance" choreography. However, because the flip of a coin restricts the random choice in each case to only two possibilities, Paxton began looking for a mechanism that would allow random selection from a wider number of possibilities. Paxton's first "chance machine" was a rubber ball marked with movement directions which he would roll on the floor and stop with a piece of glass. He also used pictures which he had taken of dancers, arranged in random fashion, as the movements for a dance. One of Paxton's most interesting dance forms has been the lecture demonstration. The most successful of these is "Lecture on Performance," a trio of himself, his dog, and a stool. His other experiments include "Jag Ville Gorna Telephonera," a movement score for facial muscles. But most of all, Paxton, along with the other modern dancers who are constantly re-evaluating what they are doing, is presenting new movement that says something about itself and the way that it can be perceived.

Like jazz, modern dance is such a completely American form that one tends to stress its development in America at the expense of classical forms. However, during the same period of time that modern dance was developing, ballet was taking root, and today there are not only American ballet companies, there are also styles of ballet which are distinct as American forms.

Although it was not the first ballet company to be established in America, the New York City Ballet has made New York a focal point of ballet activity. In 1933, Lincoln Kirstein had gone to Paris, asking George Balanchine to come and create an American ballet. Balanchine agreed, but insisted on having a school in conjunction with the company. This foresight is probably one of the main reasons why the New York City Ballet has been able to develop into what it is today.

Balanchine's style is classical, in the sense that it can be expressive without being entirely representational, and his dancers are remarkably fast and accurate. In fact, the "Balanchine dancer" has become a trademark in ballet. His specialty is the ballet with no story, but he is such an amazingly prolific choreographer that he has ranged over many styles. He claims that his ballets are plotless but not abstract, because the music and movements are very concrete. The basic vocabulary of movement used by Balanchine is that of the classical tradition. Music plays an enormous part

Nancy Davis and Charles Flemmer of the Los Angeles Ballet perform Pavanne. *Choreography by John Clifford.*

in Balanchine's choreography. Since the dancer has such a short breath phrase, Balanchine feels that the matter of rhythm should be left to the music. Although the range of music used by Balanchine is wide, his greatest collaboration has been with Stravinsky.

American Ballet Theatre, founded in 1939 as Ballet Theatre, is the country's next most important ballet company. This company, unlike the New York City Ballet, is not the creation of one man alone. Richard Pleasant, American Ballet Theatre's first director, envisioned a company that could preserve and exhibit the dances of many styles and periods. The company has maintained this philosophy. Another way in which American Ballet Theatre differs from the New York City Ballet is that the dancers in the latter have mainly come from the New York company's school, but the American absorbs dancers from all over the world and is never without several guest artists.

The City Center Joffrey Ballet, a smaller company than the two major groups, has always concentrated on appealing to contemporary taste. However, the company has recently added reconstructed works such as "The Green Table" by Jooss and "Parade" by Massine to their repertoire, and they are now billing themselves as a company with a sense of history. The Joffrey's other most significant difference is the prominence of its male dancers; it is probably the only major company with a larger number of men than women. Works choreographed for its repertoire, such as

The Alvin Ailey City Center Dance Theatre Company performs Revelations.

Arpino's "Trinity," have stronger parts for males than most works, as do both "The Green Table" and "Parade."

Ballet activity in America has been much broader than the activity of America's major ballet companies. Adolph Bolm toured the United States for the first time in 1916 as a member of the *Ballets Russes*. He later choreographed for the Chicago Civic Opera, and as ballet master of the San Francisco Opera he founded what is today the San Francisco Ballet. William Christensen took over the San Francisco Ballet in 1937, and when Lew Christensen succeeded William as director, William went to Salt Lake City and established Ballet West.

Agnes De Mille, having received her ballet training in England, came back to an America lacking enough native ballet dancers to support the work of a choreographer without a company. However, she felt that she had something to offer, especially the concept that there was a fund of ordinary American gestures which could be incorporated into ballet. She proved her point with the pieces she choreographed for Ballet Theatre and musical comedy hits such as *Oklahoma*, *Bloomer Girl*, and *Brigadoon*.

The list of significant American choreograhers grows more extensive every day, and regional ballet companies burgeon. There are also companies such as Alvin Ailey's, which do Black dance, and professional companies outside New York, such as the Boston Ballet, the Cincinnati Ballet, and the Pennsylvania Ballet of Philadelphia. Ballet in America is multiplying and moving down to the grass-roots level.

There are several important dancers who have not been mentioned here, people like Jerome Robbins and Lester Horton. But dance is springing up all over the United States, and it is almost impossible to cover every person of importance to American dance. In fact, perhaps the only sure statement that can be made about American dance is that it is healthy and growing. More and more, dancers are being trained in both ballet and modern dance styles, and this ability to draw from both forms allows choreographers to continue to explore the art of dance.

thirteen

The Theatrical Job Market

According to the most recent census figures, nearly 850,000 persons in the United States are employed in some area of the entertainment industry. Hold your resounding cheers, though. This figure includes nearly all aspects of live theatre, film, television, and even nightclub entertainment; that is, not only directors, actors, designers, and writers but also stand-up comics, singers, musical groups, variety acts, exotic dancers, and the myriad technical and business people so necessary for the day-to-day work of production.

If anything can surely be said at this time about the profession of theatre, it is that the outlook for the beginner is far from rosy. The industry, including film and television, has, for more than ten years, been deeply involved in almost total revision of traditional production patterns. In live theatre the preeminence of the New York stage—once meaning Broadway but now including both off-Broadway and off-off Broadway—is continuing to undergo serious challenge from major regional theatres, located primarily in the other highly urbanized areas of the country. Such theatres as the Guthrie, in Minneapolis, and the Mark Taper Forum, in Los Angeles, regularly draw large houses for productions that are in every way equal to the best of the New York stage. In terms of television, Hollywood is still the primary center, but more and more shows are being produced in New York and in such other cities as Miami, Phoenix, and San Francisco. In film, the breakup of the old studio system into independent small production units has tended to scatter the industry, and the move toward economical location shooting has intensified this trend.

What all this means for the theatre student is that although there are more jobs than ever before, finding roles or other theatrical employment is growing more and more difficult. That is true in part because, while the number of jobs has increased, the percentage of increase has not kept pace with the population growth, especially with the growth of schools that provide training for theatre. Thus, there are more applicants for every available position. Jobs are also more difficult to find because the opportunities are so spread out geographically. Where before the budding professional automatically went to New York or Hollywood to find employment, there is now no single specific place representing the very heart of the industry.

PROFESSIONAL THEATRE

Design

Because the field of design—which includes scenic design, scenic art, lighting design, and costume design—tends to divide itself neatly into two parts, with New York on one side and the rest of the country on the other, and because opportunities in film and television design are quite different from those in live theatre, it becomes necessary to treat all of these aspects separately.

New York

The first major step in becoming a professional designer in New York is seeking and gaining acceptance by the United Scenic Artists Union, one of the most exclusive and powerful unions in the theatre arts. There are four branches to the Scenic Artists Union in New York: *scenic designers*, who must qualify in all four branches; *scenic artists*, who specialize in scene painting and who may not design; *lighting designers*, who design only with lights; and *costume designers*, who may only design costumes.

Gaining admission to this union is no simple matter. First, applicants must pay a substantial nonrefundable examination fee. Next, they must pass a demanding in-depth interview, followed by a highly difficult examination that lasts for two full days. In addition, on the day that the testing begins, applicants must present a completed pre-exam project, which was assigned six weeks prior to the examination date. At present, nearly 95 percent fail the examination.

For those who do pass and become members of the union (after paying a substantial initiation fee) there is no guarantee of employment; finding and keeping a job is still the responsibility of the individual designer. Because New York is essentially a closed shop, however, and because the union membership is so restricted, the chances are good that the member will find employment. This beginning job is likely to be as an assistant to one of the better-known designers. In this capacity, the young designer will be required to perform such diverse tasks as doing working drawings from the supervisor's sketches, shopping for special prop, set, or costume items, and whatever else the head designer may specify.

Even for the union member, the employment outlook in New York is getting bleaker. During the past several years the entire Broadway season has provided employment to an average of fewer than forty scenic designers per season. Add to this number another forty assistant designers, plus fifty more to take care of all the off-Broadway productions, and you have a reasonably accurate figure for the number of scenic designers employed in New York during an average season. For lighting and costume designers, the situation is even more severe because in some instances the scenic designer also does costumes and lights.

Outside New York

Outside New York the picture changes radically. Becoming a union member has not necessarily been one of the first steps that a young designer takes. The primary order of business, in most cases, has been seeking out nonunion jobs in which beginning designers can spend several years practicing their art and craft. Certainly, joining a scenic union can open some opportunities, even outside New York, but it can also be a limiting factor by setting up certain situations in which a union member may not work (i.e., a union member may not work on a production with nonunion personnel).

If there has been a trend or movement in design employment in recent years, it has been away from New York and into the smaller, more adventuresome regional theatres with summer, winter, or year-round operations. The pay in any of these is rarely more than minimal, even in the oldest and best-established operations. Salary increases only in terms of knowledge, ability, and years of proved service. The traditional idea of *working your way up* may not be popular currently, but it is still operative in the field of design. Basically, it comes down to ability coupled with perseverance; seizing the opportunities and learning from them. This provides a solid personal background of knowledge and credits. It is an old cliché, though still true in design, that "It's not the person who does it well, but the person who does it well *and on time.*"

In terms of the working conditions that the young designer can expect, a designer usually has some kind of assistant, a master carpenter, technical director, cutter, electrician, etc. An assistant designer, however, is still rather unusual. Rarely does a professional designer, even with the smaller regional theatres, find situations wherein sets, costumes, and lights all must be designed. Such situations are usually made by special arrangement.

Film and Television

Opportunities for the young designer are perhaps even more remote in television and film than they are on Broadway. Unemployment in the major production centers, as evidenced by the reports of the film craft unions, has been incredibly high for a number of years, and much of this unemployed film labor force has moved into television, causing an equivalent situation in that industry. A beginning designer might have a slim chance of gaining employment as a scene painter in a television studio, but such work would be limited to touch-up or drudge base coating. Old-time journeyman painters do any of the "artistic" work, and the apprentices are usually released the moment that the pressure slacks off. In both television and film employment, work is literally on a day-to-day basis, with long periods of no work at all.

Assistant designers in television are often paid out of the head designer's personal salary, so they are a rare breed unless the head designer has enough commissions to need and pay for the help. Such assistants occasionally stick with the television scene long enough to make it on their own, but this, again, is an extremely chancy matter, requiring direct involvement in the business for several years running.

Acting

The fact is that available positions in the area of theatre, film, or television acting are really very few. There are probably more actors employed now than ever before, but in terms of the total percentage of the United States population that this field encompasses, and when compared with employment in the other professions, acting constitutes only a very small portion of the spectrum of American employment. Statistically, as a beginning actor, the chances of becoming a success as a professional (that is, making enough money acting to live on) are fewer than one in a hundred. As an example, for the approximately 31,522 members of the Screen Actors Guild, the most recent figures show that only 1,809 earned as much as $3,500 in 1975. From that gross figure must be deducted taxes, agents' commissions, and the expenses of commuting to interviews and working sessions. Unemployment among professional, unionized screen actors runs between 75 and 85 percent annually. And the situation has not improved appreciably since those figures were compiled.

If all that sounds frightening, it is. It was intended to be. Every year universities, colleges, and professional schools turn out thousands of aspiring young actors and actresses ready to enter a profession that literally has no room for them. And each year that the schools turn out an oversupply of actors, the unemployment in the field increases proportionately.

Even so, acting is such a satisfyingly personal art form, and the rewards are so great for those few who "make it," that very few young people will allow themselves to be dissuaded by cold, hard facts or statistics. For all those hardy ones, who insist on "giving it a try," the following may be of some help.

New York and Hollywood

One of the early hurdles to be surmounted by the fledgling actor is the union situation. That is not nearly as serious as it might seem at first. It can be overcome, though it does present an extra obstacle in a profession seemingly replete with difficulties. To secure a union job, and most professional acting is unionized, it is necessary to belong to either the Screen Actors Guild (SAG), which handles all filmed acting; the Actors' Equity Association (AEA), which handles live theatre acting; or the American Federation of Television and Radio Artists (AFTRA), which handles live and videotaped acting, both for programs and for commercials. These three unions, together with three others in the entertainment field, are all joined together as the Associated Actors and Artists of America.

At first try, the union situation may seem very difficult because an actor cannot join the union without a union job, and it is difficult to get a union job without belonging to the union. Admittedly, that seems like a perfect circle of exclusion, which is exactly what is intended. With persistence, however, the circle can be broken by way of talent, or connections, or usually a bit of both, and the way will be cleared for beginning actors to act; that is, if they can continue to get cast.

The beginner with no desire to start out at a regional or resident theatre will immediately head for New York if determined to carve a career in live professional theatre. Most live theatre is still cast in New York; summer stock companies and directors from the regional theatres usually do at least a part of their casting there, and even such major theatrical centers as Los Angeles and San Francisco, which have large pools of local talent on which they might draw, do enough of their casting in New York to exasperate resident actors.

To paint a rosy picture of the employment situation in New York would be a disservice, both to the aspiring actor and to the profession. Unemployment among New York actors is currently running at about 80 percent, and has been known to rise as high as 85 percent. Even if one is employed (that is, cast in a New York show) the salary usually paid to a beginning actor, at least in terms of the New York economy, will hardly be enough to provide even minimal support. And the demands of rehearsals and performance effectively preclude part-time work. The young actor who is cast in an off-Broadway or an off-off Broadway play will, in most cases, be paid the minimum wage set by the Actors' Equity Association, which means that for the run of the show he will probably be living on something less than a subsistence-level wage.

The performer who has decided that live theatre is not his medium, and who really wants to work in film or videotape, will automatically strike out for Hollywood, where most film features, filmed television, and live television is done or, at least, originated and cast. Again the odds are stacked against success. The percentage of unemployment in the Hollywood membership of SAG has already been mentioned, but in spite of such severe problems Hollywood looks, on the surface at least, to be better off than New York. Currently the pay begins at $138 per day for filmed television, with a minimum of $438 for a full week's work. The only problem with such eyebrow-raising salaries is the occasional nature of film. In New York the performer signs on for the run of the play, long or short, but in Hollywood television, unless you are the one in a thousand who is cast in a recurring role in a continuing series, being cast means a week's work at most, and then the whole process of job-seeking begins again.

League of Resident Theatres

If an actor decides to give live theatre a try but has no desire to enter the New York competition without more experience, the League of Resident Theatres (LORT) circuit provides some excellent possibilities. LORT is composed of major resident or regional theatres in various cities: Atlanta, Houston, San Francisco, Seattle, etc. These theatres regularly do excellent drama and are reviewed not only locally but also in the trade papers and journals.

Another positive aspect of the LORT theatres is that they have refined their casting processes to provide a real opportunity for the college-trained beginning performer. Any performer who is a college senior or recent graduate and who can secure the recommendation of a theatre department chairman can take part in auditions sponsored by the Theatre Communications Group (TCG). Unless, however, actors are objectively sure of their talent and training and a theatre department chairman is equally sure, they are not advised to audition. The primary plague of the most recent TCG auditions has been the number of student performers who fall far below the expected level of talent and training.

The earliest TCG auditions take place in January and are conducted in major regional centers. From those regional auditions approximately eighty actors are selected to attend final auditions in Chicago. The artistic directors of nearly all LORT companies attend these final auditions, and nearly half of those who audition are offered employment. That is all very good and very promising, but the fledgling actor should not be misled into thinking of the LORT circuit as an easy place to find employment. The students who get to the final TCG auditions and who are offered employment represent the best 40 students out of the nearly 800 who begin the process in the regionals. And the original 800 represent the best of the year's crop of graduating seniors, which means that the final 40 make up a very small percentage indeed of the total group of senior acting students. Thus, the average actor will probably find it easier to get cast in a film for television than to get signed to a LORT contract.

For the actor who does find employment with LORT, a final advantage is that employment is usually an Equity contract for one year, not merely for the run, long or short, of an individual production. Thus, the actor can look forward to the challenge and learning experience of working in several roles, in various types and styles of plays, under several directors.

Playwriting

Unlike acting, playwriting is a solitary art to some degree, and for the most part can be practiced in the time the artist has available and is willing to allot to it. That allows the possibility of writing and holding down a full-time job concurrently. Like acting, however, writing is also a full-time occupation, and to give it only part-time attention and dedication is a first major step on the pathway to failure as an artist.

The potential for part-time application makes an assessment of the existing competition in playwriting extremely difficult. The number of individuals, both trained and untrained, who sit patiently night after night turning out potential scripts for their favorite television series or their best-loved movie star is impossible to know or count. All that can be surely said is that the competition is fierce, and that at least in the beginning, the rewards are slim.

The first major hurdle that the budding playwright should leap—and a very difficult hurdle it is, occasioning innumerable falls—is the task of obtaining a reputable agent. More and more, every year, producing companies are refusing to look at any beginner's work, accepting submissions only from agents. In film and television this practice is most pervasive. It is a very rare producer who will read unsolicited manuscripts. Scripts for the legitimate stage fare somewhat better in this regard. A number of small theatre groups and a few of the major ones actually attempt to seek out original plays directly from the authors. Also, a number of playwriting contests, usually sponsored by regional theatres or educational theatres, provide a minimal financial return and, importantly, an opportunity for the writer to get a play produced.

Securing an agent, even a mediocre one, can be a very difficult proposition. For the writer's agent, as for the actor's, taking on a client is a financial investment made in the hope that the commissions for selling the client's plays will fully compensate for the time spent in trying to sell the works. Therefore, the old vicious circle comes into effect once more; the established agent is not interested in handling an author unless that author has a proved sales record, and it is nearly impossible to build a sales record without an agent. To help remedy this situation the Writers Guild of America, both Western and Eastern branches, regularly publishes a list of agents who are currently representing Guild members. This list is highly reputable and not only indicates the agents who are active in the field but also marks those willing to look at the work of beginning writers. This list is available from the Guild offices upon request.

Almost all playwriting, and especially film and television writing, is unionized. And the union setup is exclusive, in this case as in most others. Even so, perhaps because it is run by wiser heads than most other unions, the Writers Guild does provide a reasonable means of entrée for the young writer. A producer may buy without penalty the rights to a first play by a nonunion writer, and that purchase then allows the new author to join the Guild. If he does not join the Guild after his first sale, then sanctions may be imposed to keep him from further sales.

There are a number of works, both good and bad, on the art and craft of playwriting. For the beginner determined to make a success in the field, however, the best advice is perhaps the simplest: know your medium, observe, and *write*. And keep on writing.

Theatre Management

Economics has become an overriding factor in most entertainment production today, professional or amateur. Spiraling costs in these handcrafted art forms are weighed against potential income. Commercialism has become the byword of most such ventures, primarily because survival demands it. Indeed, the present motion picture industry is a prime example of big business versus the creative artist, as large impersonal corporations assume control of a once highly individualistic (or at least paternalistic) medium.

Theatrical production has certainly not been immune to this financial problem. It has become difficult to mount a new major musical production on Broadway for less than a million dollars. As material and labor costs rise faster than income sources for theatres, the squeeze naturally passes to the budgets that can be made available for productions in those theatres. Even the schools, universities, and community theatres are feeling the economic pinch.

Of course, this is a complex problem, so some oversimplification is not only tempting but necessary. Creative artists *never* seem to have enough money or space or time but still manage to practice their particular craft, often with exceptional results, as they have done for centuries. The major concern today has come in securing the maximum result from the limited resource available, and here management has been able to assist the artist. All of this is preface to the fact that perhaps the most open door and broadest range of career opportunities in all of theatre today is in management.

Paralleling the stage manager, who handles the production behind the proscenium, most theatres today have a house manager who is responsible for handling the audience attending that production. His staff includes parking-lot attendants, doormen, ticket takers, security personnel, ushers, washroom attendants, and perhaps various concessionaires who serve refreshments, check coats, rent opera glasses, or sell programs and souvenirs. The staff, of course, varies in size and scope with the nature of the theatrical operation.

The front-of-the-house management responsibilities also include building maintenance and publicity for the theatre's productions. Again, the size, budget, and staff in publicity varies with each theatre, but major tasks are generally divided into writing (news stories, etc.), graphics (designing posters, handbills, etc.), photography (advertising and production records, etc.) and promotion (special events, direct mailing, displays, etc.). Publicity work in theatre is not unlike that in any other organization that seeks to sell a product.

Some theatres have strong public-relations departments to develop new audiences in schools or community groups, to give special attention to season subscribers, and to expand the theatre's influence and importance in the community. Public relations can also raise operating money for the theatre through grants and fund drives, and organize a volunteer theatre auxiliary that can become a free source of labor and, at the same time, a people-to-people support group for the theatre.

Perhaps the most important aspect of theatre management, indeed the heart of most operations, is the box office, through which flow the dollars that keep the theatre functioning. No matter how high the artistic merit of a given production, without sufficient income few theatre operations continue for very long.

Skilled box-office managers are essential for a theatre. They must have the patience of Job and a solid knowledge of public relations in dealing with the thousands of theatre patrons and their ticket requests. They must also have a practical background in theatre to make valuable and accurate estimates on the salability of given shows. Of course they must know accounting or at least have some experience in bookkeeping, since accurate records are mandatory. They, or a member of their staff, may also be involved in special discount-group ticket sales for the theatre. Handling tickets as an usher can lead to a cashier's job in selling tickets, either directly at the box-office window or via telephone reservations, or processing mail orders.

The functions of a general accountant and a lawyer are needed in professional theatre management because the manager must deal with such complex problems as artist contract negotiations, plant management, insurance, and the day-to-day processing and disbursement of funds to purchase the thousands of items needed to keep the theatre running.

Long a neglected area of theatre study (artists have traditionally not wanted to recognize or become directly involved in the realistic and practical necessities of their craft), theatre management has begun to gain attention in the contemporary world and is being made a part of the curriculum of many major universities. Some have developed elaborate training programs covering the total interrelated arts spectrum, from theatre to museums to symphony-orchestra management. Internship and apprentice programs are available for on-the-job training experience, which is still the best way of translating classroom theory into practical skill. The young person who chooses theatre management as a career would be wise while in school to become equipped not only in theatre but also in some of the other particular skills mentioned earlier. The performer in today's theatre may be called upon to sing, dance, fence, or tumble as well as act. Likewise, the theatre manager should supplement specific skills with versatility.

Educational Theatre

Elementary School

Although legitimate (or at least traditional) drama is nearly nonexistent in elementary schools, a number of dedicated theatre people have found themselves teaching youngsters and loving it. Some form of dramatic activity exists in almost every aspect of the elementary classroom, and working with a class in producing a children's play can be exciting for anyone who enjoys working with elementary school children. In large part, this excitement stems from the fact that the elementary school teacher reaches the human being before all the strictures of acceptable social behavior, and the resulting layers of inhibitions, have smothered the natural mimetic instinct. Thus, in the early grades the teacher is privileged to participate in doing theatre for children *by children*.

In most states an elementary credential is required for teaching in grades kindergarten through sixth, which means either taking a degree in education or a subject-matter degree, and also completing a prescribed series of classes in elementary education, including student teaching. Even where the undergraduate major in education is required, an elementary teaching minor in theatre is usually available. Courses in children's theatre, creative dramatics, and dramatic activities for children form the core of such programs, and should be required courses for anyone planning to teach in elementary school.

Secondary School

Teaching theatre in secondary schools is, at present, perhaps the most exciting, challenging, and rewarding area of theatre professionalism. Part of this excitement grows out of the fact that here the job opportunities are greater—limited, certainly, in recent years by a leveling off of the birthrate and by the number of colleges turning out high school teachers—but greater nonetheless, and growing every year. Also, at least a portion of what makes secondary school teaching so challenging and rewarding is the opportunity to help a struggling young area of the performing arts reach maturity in the public-school system.

At present, 63.9 percent of American secondary schools offer no program in theatre arts.[1] As for the 36.1 percent that do, many of the courses in theatre, are, in fact, dramatic-literature courses offered by English departments. There are a number of reasons for this scarcity of courses, ranging from lack of funds, to lack of teachers, to basic distrust of the medium of theatre on the part of some regional school boards who have been horrified by recent, sexually explicit plays. Even so, theatre classes, especially theatre production classes, are growing in number, and the opportunity to help advance the cause is one of the most challenging aspects of contemporary educational theatre.

While few schools have even a minimum theatre curriculum, over 90 percent of American secondary schools put on at least one play per school year. In most cases these plays are directed by teachers from the areas of English or speech, with little or no training in theatre production although they may have had some work in dramatic literature, dramatic criticism, or theatre history. The plays are very likely to be presented in combination gymnasium-auditoriums or in large multipurpose rooms. The lighting and the sets will probably be minimal, and the costumes will usually come from the wardrobes of the student performers.

Teaching in most secondary schools requires the possession of a valid teaching credential. To achieve this state certification means completing a credential program at one of that state's colleges or universities, or, in some cases, presenting evidence directly to the state accrediting body that the requirements for the credential have been completed outside a recognized program.

Beyond the credential, and perhaps even more important, secondary school teaching also requires the basic desire to teach at that level. Teaching at *any* level is not a career to be undertaken as a supplement to professional theatre work, something for the failed or out-of-work actor to fall back on for job security. Such people usually make bad teachers, and are types that school administrators avoid. Teaching is, in fact, one of the most rewarding and demanding careers in the area of theatre, but it demands absolute dedication both to the ideal of theatre and to the education of young people.

College and University

The United States has no national theatre such as exists in most Western countries, and it still has only a relatively weak and struggling regional theatre. It does have, however, an extraordinary network of college and university theatres whose programs depend not on box-office receipts but on public subsidy. Though not generally professional (some campuses do have resident professional troupes), these college and university theatres each year provide their audiences with some of the most exciting live theatre in the country.

[1] Joseph L. Peluso, *A Survey of the Status of Theatre in United States High Schools* (U.S. Department of Health, Education, and Welfare, November, 1970), p. 25.

To a large degree this excitement is generated by the relative freedom of educational theatre in choosing its material. Unlike professional theatre, tied so closely to the box office for support, educational theatre has the freedom to do those older classics that need to be done but cannot attract large audiences, as well as new experimental plays that may be too *avant-garde* to provide a brisk business at the box office. Also, the student actors in the plays add to the excitement with their determination and boundless energy, which can go far in making up for lack of complete training.

An appointment to teach in a college or university theatre department usually requires, or provides professors with the opportunity, to work in their own field or areas of theatrical interest or competence. That is, a director will usually direct at least one major show in each school year; a designer will design; and an actor will act, or at least coach student actors. In addition, each faculty member teaches courses in one specialized area of emphasis and also in such varied areas as dramatic literature, theatre history, dramatic theory, and criticism.

The basic requirement for entry into college or university teaching is an advanced academic degree, preferably a Doctor of Philosophy (Ph.D.). In recent years the Master of Fine Arts (M.F.A.), a production-oriented degree, has achieved some degree of recognition as a terminal degree in the areas of acting and design. All the same, as student enrollments level off and the supply of advanced degrees increases, the Ph.D. is more and more the basic requirement. Thus, the prospective teacher possessing only the M.F.A., or even the Doctor of Fine Arts (D.F.A.), is likely to find it difficult to secure a position.

As a final, cautionary word, it must be pointed out that educational theatre, even on the college and university level, is *not* professional theatre. Thus, a person with a specialty in acting, for example, who finds a position at a college, becomes a teacher of acting and not, primarily, an actor. The same holds true for all the other areas of theatrical specialization. To assure happiness, let alone success, in the academic profession, the potential professor must have a driving desire to teach and to pursue the other aspects of college and university teaching, the search for truth and the need to disseminate knowledge by way of the written page.

As with secondary school teaching, college and university teaching is not a profession at which the actor can earn a living while performing in the professional theatre. It requires full time and more to be a good teacher. Also, earning the necessary credentials, the Ph.D., D.F.A., and M.F.A., is at least as difficult as becoming a success in professional theatre, so the teaching profession is not to be considered a second choice.

Theatre as an Avocation

Having discussed the professional prospects for theatre graduates, and having noted that a large percentage of those graduates will not end up as theatre professionals, it becomes necessary to say a few words to those who will find themselves earning their living outside the theatre. First, it must be remembered that, just as not all English majors intend to become novelists or poets, and just as not all history majors plan to become historians, or science majors feel a necessity to become scientists, neither should all theatre majors expect to become professionals. There is no reason they should. That is especially true for the student who attends a college or university instead of a professional conservatory. The idea that the basic liberal arts degree must be professinally oriented is one of the educational problems of our time, leading a number of students to painful first brushes with cold, harsh reality. In fact, if a student's college or university did its job properly, the bachelor's degree, in addition to basic professional training, will have provided the student with a good, broad, liberal arts education that not only will help make his career a success but will help him live a full, rich, and satisfying life.

If the liberal arts goal of education for life as well as for a profession is accepted, then working at a job other than theatre will not seem to be a "fate worse than death," and such work will not necessarily mean severing all relations with the theatre. Many graduates of theatre programs, while not working professionally in their areas, are highly active in semiprofessional or amateur theatres.

Semiprofessional Theatre

For the student who has real dedication to theatre but is unable to make the breakthrough into the professional world, the semiprofessional theatre is an interesting, demanding, and often highly rewarding choice. The term "semiprofessional," though rarely applied to theatre, is quite accurate. It means a theatre that has a regular season, that rehearses nearly full time and on a regular basis, that has its own "house," and that depends on private donations or selling tickets to the general public to support itself. There are a number of such theatres throughout the country, and they are usually composed of dedicated people who earn their livings by holding jobs outside the theatre but spend nearly every evening and weekend rehearsing and playing.

Such theatres often concentrate on *avant-garde* works or original plays, although at least one such theatre concentrates on lesser-known and seldom-produced classics. In consequence the box-office receipts are usually too small to support fully a professional troupe. The learning opportunities these theatres provide are great, however, the productions are often of high quality, and the shows are usually professionally reviewed. Thus they can provide the performer with a showcase for entrée into fully professional work.

Amateur Theatre

Of real value for those who are unable to work in either the professional or the semiprofessional theatre are the community-theatre amateur groups, usually supported financially by a city recreation department. The productions put on by such groups usually display a wide range of aesthetic and technical accomplishment from very good to terribly bad, but in nearly all cases the enthusiasm of cast and crew is great and the reception is usually warm. This type of theatre is particularly valuable to the graduate trained in theatre, for it not only allows the exercise of those talents developed in hours of study and training but also provides the opportunity to pass on the crafts of the profession to eager beginners.

RADIO AND TELEVISION BROADCASTING

For the budding actor or director who is not already committed to either theatre or film, radio and/or television broadcasting has much to offer. A broadcaster, to succeed, must be multitalented. Knowledge, ability, and skills are required in many diverse areas, for broadcasting as an artistic and technical medium deals with such varied disciplines as performing (including acting, dancing, etc.), musicology, political science, sociology, psychology, business administration, and engineering. Naturally, no single individual can be an expert in all of those highly specialized areas; however, it is important to have at least some knowledge in all, and a specialty in at least one.

Highly recommended for the person interested in television as an art form is serious study in such broad areas as theatre, music, psychology, philosophy, and art. Absolute essentials are courses such as musical form, art appreciation, and philosophy, and such theatre courses as beginning, intermediate, and advanced acting, directing, audio, lighting, makeup, and costuming.

It should be noted here that, in terms of liberal arts institutions, there are several different degrees within the broad area of radio-television. Typical college and university departments offering broadcasting degrees are communications, speech, radio-television, radio-television-film, speech and drama, journalism, and instructional media. Many of these degrees emphasize production, failing to deal with radio-television as art forms. A typical emphasis, unfortunately, is the "point-and-shoot" approach; that is, a very simple journalistic or documentary approach.

It is sometimes difficult to decide in which of the many possible broadcasting areas to specialize. That decision cannot be made easily because, as a preliminary step, it is necessary to determine whether to become a technician (engineer, etc.) or artist. In most television stations, simply by tradition (and strong union demands), those who operate the cameras are engineers first and artists second. As the craft of operating the camera is learned, however, one hopes the people involved will begin to think more seriously in terms of artistic pictorial composition. This tradition of training camera operators to be engineers first and artists second, when examined historically, seems somewhat illogical, but it does exist, fostered by years of somewhat strained relationships between radio and television stations and such engineering unions as the International Brotherhood of Electrical Workers, the National Association of Broadcast Employees and Technicians, and the International Alliance of Theatrical Stage Employees.

If performing and directing are primary interests, it is logical to consider closed-circuit television as a possible career. This is not to say that a novice won't be able to compete successfully in open-circuit broadcasting. At present, however, the closed-circuit area offers a marvelous training ground and is, in fact, doing far more work artistically than the open-circuit networks. The growing power of closed-circuit television can be illustrated by the fact that in 1973 approximately half of the television equipment sold in the United States was sold to closed-circuit installations. Additionally, many businesses are creating programs designed especially for internal informational and educational uses. These closed-circuit possibilities, combined with general open-circuit broadcasting, provide a broad range of employment possibilities for creative, artistic, and determined students.

Generally, individuals who choose broadcasting as a career, whether as performer, engineer, or in any other specific job area, are quite happy with their chosen field. A recent survey taken by the National Association of Broadcasters and the Association for Professional Broadcast Education indicated that 94 percent of the people working in the field are happy with their careers.

To make broadcasting a career, however, it is necessary to get that initial job. One method of finding employment is acquiring some experience in either radio or television while in college. Many schools have educational FM stations, or even closed-circuit radio and television stations to dormitories on campus. Even if a college simply has a television studio for classroom instruction, that may be enough to gain valuable practical experience.

The next step is making up a résumé and sending it to a list of small stations. Such a list can be obtained, along with the address, including the manager's name, by consulting a current edition of *Broadcasting Yearbook*, which is updated annually and lists every radio and television station in the United States.

Beyond the performing positions, for those interested in technical jobs, there are two approaches. The first is studying electronics and becoming knowledgeable in the fields of radio and television engineering. The second is acquiring a first class license. It is important to understand that getting a first class license is definitely necessary if one wishes to work in any engineering-related area of broadcasting. Some stations pay very well for personnel who have a first class license but are not necessarily engineers. Such individuals are responsible for running a camera or an audio control but do not maintain technical equipment. For those who wish to follow the second approach and get their license without the formal (and enormously valuable) preliminary study, there are the so-called "cram schools," which offer courses designed to enable a student to obtain a first class license in as little as three weeks.

Finally, for the person who is not performance-oriented and has no desire to become a technician, there is sales and management. Many possibilities exist here, including saleswork and various administrative positions such as financial comptroller. Sales and management can be challenging, creative, and rewarding. Most management personnel typically begin their careers in sales and eventually graduate to management. It is not uncommon, however, for some managers to have been program directors or even engineers.

Jobs in the radio-television field, especially the highly rated positions (in spite of a great deal of suspicion on the part of the general public), are based on ability. Even when luck may have played a part in obtaining the job, a broadcaster will ultimately be required to demonstrate proficiency on the job, and that proficiency can come only through obtaining the proper training.

Reading
a
Play

Only in the twentieth century could a chapter on how to read a play be considered a necessity. As Robert F. Whitman has so ably pointed out, in any age but this one such a chapter "would have been viewed with amazement, much as a pamphlet called 'How to Listen to Popular Music,' or 'How to Watch Television' would today."[1] For at least the past twenty-five hundred years, and likely for a great deal longer, plays have provided as common and natural and meaningful a form of entertainment as do movies and television in our own age. Plays have been the most immediate of all art forms, even appealing to audiences that other forms of literature have failed to reach. Today, however, for reasons that are primarily economic, there are some otherwise well-educated persons who have never seen a live play, or who have seen only a very few in their lifetime. For this group, for the film-television generation, some suggestions on play-reading may be necessary and valuable.

[1]Robert F. Whitman, *The Play-Reader's Handbook* (Indianapolis, 1966), p. vii.

As a beginning, two basic steps may be pointed out that, if carefully followed, can be of real value to the beginning play-reader. First, the play should be read straight through, with as few stops as possible to consult glosses, indices, or even to reread specific major scenes within the play. Instead the reader should seek, in this first read-through, to get a "feel" for the action, the sweep, and the characters. Second, after this first reading has been completed, the play should be read again, somewhat more slowly, this time with an emphasis on those elements that were ignored in the first read-through. Finally, during this second reading, it is necessary to keep asking one basic question: "Why?" Why did Calderone choose to set his play, *Life is a Dream*, in Medieval Poland? Why did Shakespeare include the minor characters of Rosencrantz and Guildenstern in his *Hamlet*? Why does Edward Albee, in the opening of *Who's Afraid of Virginia Woolf?* have George and Martha playing a game that involves lines from an old Bette Davis movie? If such questions are asked, and answers are sought, it will help lead the reader to the heart of the play. Along the way such questioning will raise other questions that will aid greatly in gaining a complete understanding of the work.

Essentially, the play-reader makes use of some of the techniques for examining plays that have already been discussed in the chapter dealing with the director; these are, "finding the controlling idea," "determining the mood," and "examining the formal structure of the play." In addition to these, the play-reader can make excellent use of several valuable techniques that tend to be more often used by literary critics than by directors working to put productions on stage before audiences.

Explicating the Script

Almost every literary critic has his own method of explicating dramatic literature, based on his own personal principles, beliefs, and biases. Certainly there is no one way to approach a dramatic work. However, certain general steps in the process can be determined and even listed on some scale of order. One of the first of these steps is determining the play's meaning in a capsule sense. Lajos Egri refers to this process, to formulating a simplified statement of a work's meaning, as finding its "premise." For example, Egri finds the premise of *King Lear* to be "blind trust leads to destruction," and for *Romeo and Juliet* he finds the premise to be "great love defies even death."[2] In many ways this is an unfortunate example of a belief, popular not too many years ago, that any individual work of art could be summed up neatly in one topic sentence. This belief, now generally out of favor, was succeeded by the equally unfortunate concept that great works of art are always mysterious and inexplicable, beyond the ken of even the most sensitive critic.

[2]Lajos Egri, *The Art of Dramatic Writing* (New York, 1946), p. 3.

Somewhere between these two extremes there is a middle ground that can be achieved and that has real value. On one hand, *Romeo and Juliet* is not nearly as simplistic as Egri would have us believe, but on the other hand it is not inexplicable. Several interlocking premises regarding the play can be derived from the script, and these can legitimately be called the play's *meaning*. For example, on one level Egri is right and this is one more play in a whole tradition of literary works celebrating the belief that great love does defy even death. On another level it is Shakespeare's statement that human-wrought divisions in a country are harmful and can only be healed by the shedding of blood. On a third level the play makes an ironic statement on the blind fate that seems to rule the affairs of humankind. On still another level it is a play illustrating the age-old conflict between youth and age, in which age learns through the sacrifice of youth. At still another level the play may be understood, in terms of the deaths of Tybalt, Mercutio, Romeo, and Juliet, as a statement on the evil of violence as a solution to man's problems. Each of these meanings or premises—inseparable, intertwined by the plot and so necessarily to be taken together—provide the complexity that makes this a truly great play.

"Hearing" How the Lines Work

The reader should make himself aware of all the many auditory possibilities inherent in the play he is reading. This means that he must *hear* the line and not just read it to himself coldly and without inflection or emphasis. To achieve this, the reader must discover how a line *works* in order to understand the *effect* that the author presumably desired. While especially common to poetry, there are a number of devices that are commonly used in prose to accent or heighten a passage. Recognition of such devices and their purpose will help the reader determine proper line readings, which will be of immeasurable help in understanding the whole play. Reasonably complete studies of poetic and rhetorical devices are generally available in nearly any good handbook on poetic techniques. Such reading is highly recommended for anyone who wants to get the most out of play reading.

Reading the Stage Directions

Beginning play-readers are sometimes tempted to skip over stage directions, especially long ones. What difference, they wonder, does it make where the actor is standing or sitting? Why should I care whether the coffee table is covered with magazines or newspapers? The answer, of course, is that it makes a great deal of difference. The stage directions, describing some aspect of the set and indicating how that set is to be used, are of great help in visualizing the action; and in a play what is *done* is often at least as important as what is *said*. Often, in fact, it is not so much what is done, but the *manner in which it is done*, that is important, and a reading of the directions will help the play-reader to visualize this.

The older plays, the Greek Classical, Renaissance, and even those of the eighteenth century, have few obvious stage directions about which the reader must worry. Because these plays were designed to be performed on simpler stages, without the many contemporary staging techniques, the stage directions were "sunk" into the dialogue to help the audience visualize a physical scene that could not be represented onstage. Thus, in Marlowe's *Edward the Second*, physical action, and even the stage setting, is usually implicit in the lines, with no stage directions present or necessary:

EDWARD: What? Are you moved that Gaveston sits here?
It is our pleasure; we will have it so.

LANCASTER: Your Grace doth well to place him by your side,
For nowhere else the new earl is so safe.[3]

In these four lines, without any help from stage directions, we learn that Gaveston is on stage, that he is sitting, where he is sitting, why he is sitting, and the attitudes of both Edward and Lancaster toward him. The inclusion of such material in the dialogue serves not only to advance the action, but also aids the reader's understanding in the same way that it helped a Renaissance audience to visualize the action.

Contemporary plays, however, often make extensive use of stage directions and set descriptions to aid them in making their statement, and to ignore them is to miss a great deal of the play's significant action. In Eugene O'Neill's *Long Day's Journey Into Night*, for example, the directions to the actors often far exceed the dialogue which they complement. At one point in the action, when the two sons have not yet discovered that their mother is again taking drugs, the stage directions for physical action are far more important than the lines the mother speaks. She is speaking to her younger son, Edmund, telling him that he mustn't keep on coughing as it is bad for his throat. This tells the audience very little. On the other hand the stage direction that accompanies this short passage of dialogue, while too long to be quoted directly, lets the audience know that the older son, Jamie, sees the bland, withdrawn expression on his mother's face and knows that she is again on drugs. Edmund, we are shown, is still unaware of his mother's return to drug addiction because he is seated in a chair, with his mother seated on the chair's arm, above and behind him, where he cannot see her face.

---

[3]Christopher Marlowe, *Edward the Second*, ed. by W. Moelwyn Merchant (New York: Hill and Wang, 1967), p. 19.

Allowing the Intelligence Free Rein

Finally, the play-reader must allow his intelligence free rein. It is not enough to stick tightly to the facts and actions of the play under consideration. Instead, it is necessary to consider each play in terms of the total literary experience, to compare and contrast it not only to other plays but to other works of literature as well, and even to film and television scripts. For example, the play-reader coming upon *Hamlet* for the first time, may be struck by some similarities between Shakespeare's play and the film *On the Waterfront*. Or, the play-reader considering the script for the musical show *Cabaret* may compare it with the stage play on which it was based: *I Am a Camera*. Or, it may be compared with the film versions of both the musical and the stage play, or even with the original "Berlin" stories of Christopher Isherwood, which began the sequence and on which all of the later stage and film works are based. Such considerations, placing the work of dramatic literature in a context of other literary and even social material, will aid the reader's perceptions not only of the play being considered, but will also expand his understanding of the works to which it is being compared.

Play reading is one of the most demanding of all critical tasks, for the play demands more of the reader than, say, the novel, where the author is free to give the reader insight into almost any aspect of any character. The play, because it was meant to be acted, depends on the actors to give the characters depth and dimension, to put flesh on the bare bones of dialogue. For the reader to fulfill this function imaginatively is very demanding indeed, and this is exactly what makes it so satisfying.

Plot Summaries of Works Discussed in the Text

The Adding Machine (1923), Elmer Rice.   This play, one of the very few fully expressionistic works by an American author, creates a horrible vision of our future society: a mechanized world tended by shabby, dehumanized little people. Mr. Zero, a nonentity, is the epitome of the new man. He is an office clerk who has spent twenty-five years adding up figures, only to be replaced by an adding machine. Driven to desperation he kills the boss, is tried, and executed. After his death he goes to Elysian Fields, an idyllic place without the confining walls of convention, but Mr. Zero does not like this new freedom. A celestial repair shop is more acceptable to him, and he is allowed to work on an adding machine for what he hopes will be eternity. However, an illusory blonde named Hope leads him back to earth where his slave nature finds fulfillment operating an adding machine with his big toe.

Agamemnon (458 B.C.), Aeschylus.   A tragedy that begins with a watchman in the Kingdom of Argos looking for the light from a distant signal fire that is to announce the fall of Troy. From the watchman's monologue it becomes clear that Argos is unhappy and that Clytemnestra, the Queen, has been unfaithful to her absent husband, King Agamemnon. The light appears and shortly thereafter Agememnon arrives. He has with him a captive princess, Cassandra. Agamemnon is welcomed home by Clytemnestra, and his arrogant manner following his victory shows him to be excessively proud. Clytemnestra shows Agamemnon into his house. Cassandra, who follows him and who has the gift of prophecy (and the curse that no one will believe her), foresees death for him and for herself. Cries are then heard from inside the house and Clytemnestra appears to display the dead bodies of Agamemnon and Cassandra. They have been stabbed to death by the Queen and her lover, Aegisthus. The people start to protest the murder of their King, but Aegisthus enters with an armed guard and the play ends with Clytemnestra seemingly triumphant. This play is, however, the first in the *Oresteia* trilogy, and in the second play Clytemnestra will herself be murdered by her vengeful son.

Ah, Wilderness! (1933), Eugene O'Neill.   O'Neill's only happy comedy, this play deals with the Millers, a typical American middle-class family with those problems that seem momentous at the time but that always can be resolved. Nat, the father, is a happy, humorous man, in love with his wife and understanding of his children. Essie is his loyal, loving wife. The scant plot of the play revolves about Richard Miller, age sixteen, one of the four Miller children. Richard's love poems, written to Muriel McComber, have fallen into the hands of her humorless and puritanical father, who is greatly angered. Misunderstood by an insensitive world, Richard seeks "vice and depravity" in the arms of a "college tart." However, he only succeeds in getting sick and alarming his family. The following day Richard's father gently straightens his son out regarding the facts of life. This event, plus the fact that he is also reconciled with the fair Muriel, makes Richard happy once more, and Nat and Essie watch with affection the spring awakening in their son. However, in many ways the tender love that exists and endures between Nat and Essie becomes far more important than Richard's coming of age.

All for Love (1667), John Dryden.   A tragedy that is substantially the same as Shakespeare's *Antony and Cleopatra* in plot but rewritten to suit Restoration ideals. Action is restricted to a single location and time is telescoped to a single day. For summary see *Antony and Cleopatra*.

All My Sons (1947), Arthur Miller.   A work based on the fact that during World War II a shipment of defective cylinder heads caused the death of over twenty pilots in combat. Joe Keller, one of the manufacturers, has been cleared of wrongdoing but his partner has been found guilty and imprisoned. Keller is the father of two sons—Chris, just returned from the war, and Larry, a pilot missing in action for more than three years. Chris and Ann (who is Larry's former fiancee and the daughter of Keller's jailed partner) plan to marry in spite of the opposition of Chris' mother, who still believes that Larry is alive. She believes this because of the guilt she experiences over her husband's negligence. She refuses to admit that he could be responsible for the deaths of over twenty young men, perhaps including their own son. Chris tries desperately to believe in his father's innocence, but eventually can no longer delude himself and in a dramatic confrontation he forces his father to confess. Faced with his son's scorn, Joe kills himself because of his guilt in placing his own financial well-being before the welfare of society.

Anatol (1893), Arthur Schnitzler.   A comedy in seven vignettes, each of which includes Anatol and all but two of which include his friend Max. Each, however, features a different woman. The vignettes, which could be presented as one-acts, show Anatol playing the games of love which eventually leads to his impending marriage. However, the love-games have incapacitated Anatol who cannot feel real love. The humor is light and gay, in the tradition of Vienna just before the turn of the century, and the romantic fencing between Anatol and the women remains as fresh and meaningful now as it originally proved to be more than eighty years ago.

Androcles and the Lion (1915), George Bernard Shaw. Based on the fable about Daniel and the lion. Androcles is a meek little tailor with a shrewish wife. He loves animals, and when he makes friends with a wounded lion his bad-tempered wife leaves him. Later Androcles is arrested by the Romans and, with a group of Christians, is sentenced to be thrown to the lions. Among the potential martyrs is a young Roman noblewoman accused of bewitching a soldier, a wrestler who has difficulty containing his temper, a coward, and a number of lesser characters. Upon facing death in the arena these martyrs laugh and sing. They are saved by the skillful performance of the wrestler. One of them, however, must be fed to the lions, and Androcles is chosen. The lion released from the cage turns out to be the one which Androcles befriended in the forest and the two waltz around the arena. This turn of events wins Androcles his freedom.

Annie Get Your Gun (1946), Book by Herbert and Dorothy Fields; lyrics and music by Irving Berlin. Annie Oakley, a sharpshooting star of Buffalo Bill's Wild West Show, is living in a summer hotel on the outskirts of Cincinnati. A girl without "learnin'" who always acts naturally, she meets handsome Frank Butler, a performer in the Pawnee Bill Show, a rival of Buffalo Bill's group. Unfortunately, Frank likes demure, well-bred girls, and even Annie knows that "you can't get a man with a gun." In spite of these differences, Annie and Frank fall in love. However, one obstacle still stands in the way of their happiness: they work for rival shows. Just when all seems lost the rival productions merge and all is well, though Annie and Frank are now competitors in the same show.

Antony and Cleopatra (c. 1606), William Shakespeare. A tragedy in which Antony, the "triple pillar" of the Roman Empire, is seduced by the charm and beauty of Cleopatra, Queen of Egypt. When he receives news of his wife's death and a growing rebellion in Rome, Antony decides to leave Cleopatra. He returns to Rome, makes a shaky peace with Lepidus and Octavius Caesar by marrying Caesar's sister, Octavia. However, this marriage cannot keep him away from Cleopatra, and he returns to Egypt. Octavius, enraged at the dishonor done his sister, sends his fleet after Antony, who mistakenly decides to fight Caesar at sea and is severely beaten. His true defeat, however, is not military but rather his moral disintegration. He loses his generalship and his ability to lead troops. He is deserted both by his men and Cleopatra. His suicide becomes an extended agony. Cleopatra also kills herself rather than be shamed by being led captive through the streets of Rome.

Arden of Feversham (1592), Anonymous but often ascribed to Thomas Kyd. Based on an actual murder case in 1551, this play is the earliest extant example of domestic tragedy. The action concerns the repeated attempts of Mistress Alice Arden and her lover, Mosbie, to murder Alice's husband. They are finally successful but are soon caught, brought to justice, and executed. The play is generally of low quality, but the character of Alice Arden is one of the strongest in Elizabethan drama. This work is the first to make use of middle- and even lower-class characters as central figures.

The Birds (414 B.C.), Aristophanes. A comedy. Two down-at-the-heels Athenian adventurers, Pisthetaurus and Euelpides, decide to escape the bill collectors of Athens by emigrating to the land of the birds. Upon arrival they persuade Epops, the King of Birds, to set up a city called Cloud Cuckooland that will exist in the air, midway between the world of humans and the ethereal realm of the gods. Both men and gods will then have to pay tribute to the birds before they will allow the incense smoke of prayers to pass through Cloud Cuckooland to the gods. However, like all utopias, Cloud Cuckooland is soon invaded by all the evils the two adventurers had left behind in Athens. Eventually the gods give in, unable to stand a life in which they receive no prayers. As surety of their submission they let Pisthetaurus marry the goddess Iris. However, the beautiful utopia of Cloud Cuckooland has been destroyed and is now no better than earth.

The Black Crook (1866), Book by Charles M. Barras; music mostly adaptations of current popular songs, with some original numbers by Guiseppe Operti. Often called the first true example of musical theatre. A slight story merely serves as an excuse to present a series of dances and spectacles. Herzog, the Black Crook, makes a pact with the devil to deliver up a human soul each year, before midnight on New Year's Eve. In return, Herzog is given supernatural powers. For one of his victims Herzog selects Rudolph, a painter imprisoned by Count Wolfenstein. Herzog gets Rudolph released and then leads him away in a false search for hidden gold, during which Rudolph saves the life of a dove that is really a fairy queen. The fairy queen reveals Herzog's evil plan and Rudolph is saved. Herzog, unable to keep his bargain, is taken away by the devil. Rudolph, thus freed, is reunited with his beloved Amina.

Bloomer Girl (1944), Book by Sig Herzig and Fred Saidy; lyrics by E. Y. Harburg; music by Harold Arlen. Set in Cicero, New York, in 1861, *Bloomer Girl* is based on the adventures of Dolly Bloomer (actually Amelia Bloomer), an ardent feminist who passionately espouses temperance, women's rights, and the practicality of women wearing bloomers instead of hoop skirts. The bloomer issue becomes significant when Dolly's brother-in-law, Horatio Applegate, a wealthy manufacturer of hoop skirts, maneuvers five of his six daughters into accepting his values by getting them married to hoop skirt salesmen. His sixth daughter Evelina, however, rebels and becomes an ally of Dolly. She even persuades her southern boyfriend, Jeff, into arranging the escape of his own slave. As a subterfuge, Evelina consents to model hoop skirts for her father at a garden party, but shocks everyone when she removes her skirt to prove that she is wearing bloomers. Jeff's brother, meanwhile, has caught his escaped slave and has brought legal action against Dolly. Dolly, Evelina, and the slave are put in jail, but are freed to put on *Uncle Tom's Cabin* at the opera house. Jeff, in retaliation, joins the Confederate Army, and Evelina gives him up. However, all is resolved when the governor takes over the Applegate factory to manufacture army uniforms—and bloomers—and puts Dolly in charge. Evelina and Jeff are reconciled, and the musical ends happily, with Dolly and Evelina triumphant.

Brigadoon (1947), Book and lyrics by Alan Jay Lerner; music by Frederick Loewe. A musical fantasy about a small Scottish town which disappeared in 1747 and then comes back to life for one day in each century. Two American tourists, Tommy Albright and Jeff Douglas, are wandering in the Scottish Highlands when they hear the strains of a song. Suddenly the village of Brigadoon appears before them.

There, at a fair, they meet Fiona MacLaren and her sister Jean, who is about to be married to Charlie Dalrymple. Tommy is immediately enchanted with Fiona. At the MacLaren home Tommy and Jeff discover in a newspaper that Jean and Charlie were to have been married exactly one-hundred years earlier. Only after the village schoolmaster, Mr. Lundie, explains the history of the village, can they understand what has happened. After the wedding of Jean and Charlie, Tommy tells Fiona that he loves her and intends to remain in Brigadoon forever. Jeff, more realistic, tells Tommy that a person cannot live forever in a dream. They must both return to New York, where Tommy's fiancee is waiting. But in New York Tommy cannot forget Brigadoon and Fiona. He returns to Scotland in search of his dream world. Mr. Lundie appears out of a Highland mist to lead Tommy to Brigadoon, a miracle that can happen because of the love between Tommy and Fiona.

The Cherry Orchard (1903), Anton Chekhov.   Concerns the futile attempt of the Ranevskaya family to hold on to aristocratic ways in a Russia becoming steadily more bourgeois. At the time the play was written Russia was only two years away from the revolution of 1905. The Ranevskaya family finances are in such bad shape that a part of the estate, a large cherry orchard, must be sold or else the entire estate will be lost. However, while each member of the family understands the importance of selling the orchard, no one can bear the idea. The orchard represents some aspect of past happiness for each individual. To Madame Ranevskaya it represents an innocent and secure youth; to Gayeff, her brother, it represents a time of wealth, freedom, and the leisure to concentrate on billiards rather than economic affairs; to Lopahin, a freed serf, the orchard symbolizes a childhood in which the people in the manor house were like kindly, beautiful gods—but the orchard also signifies Lopahin's own growing wealth and power, for he will be the one who buys it. The members of the family, a faded and incompetent aristocracy, retreat into fantasy or nostalgia whenever reality becomes threatening. At the end of the play when the entire estate is sold, the family, pursuing their vanished dream, departs to the accompanying sound of an ax as the new owner begins to chop the orchard down.

Cabaret (1966), Book by Joe Masteroff; lyrics by Fred Ebb; music by John Kander. This musical begins in the Kit Kat Club in Berlin, in 1929–1930, the years when Nazism was on the rise. The club's clients (and the theatre audience) are welcomed by the Master of Ceremonies, who says that here life is carefree. The plot concerns a young American writer and teacher, Clifford Bradshaw, who has come to Berlin to write. He helps a young German, Ernst Ludwig, through customs. In gratitude Ernst finds Cliff a place to live in a boarding house run by Fräulein Schneider. There, Cliff meets Herr Schultz, Fräulein Schneider's lover, and Sally Bowles, who performs at the Kit Kat Club. Sally and Cliff become lovers and live in his room. Sally seems contented in her life with Cliff, eventually telling him that she is pregnant. Cliff is delighted. Determined to get enough money to support a child, he accepts an offer by Ernst to make a trip to Paris on an unspecified mission. Sally promises to quit working at the Kit Kat Club. In the meantime, Fräulein Schneider and Herr Schultz are considering marriage, but Ernst warns against it, reminding Fräulein Schneider that Herr Schultz is a Jew and in the new Germany this kind of marriage would be dangerous. Cliff, back from Paris where he has been an unwitting messenger for the Nazi party, tries to convince Ernst that the author of *Mein Kampf* is a madman. Fräulein Schneider decides not to marry Herr Schultz as she would lose her property if the Nazis come to power. Cliff decides to return to

America. Sally, once more performing at the Kit Kat Club, confesses that she has had an abortion and tells Cliff goodbye. Cliff gets on the train to Paris. As he tries to write about his experiences, his German friends appear once more, but there is an ominous quality about them now, and the play ends with the Master of Ceremonies assuring everyone that life in the cabaret is carefree and gay.

Carnival (1961), Book by Michael Stewart; lyrics and music by Bob Merrill. Based on the film *Lili*, which was in turn derived from a Paul Gallico short story, *Carnival* tells of the initiation into adulthood of a young, innocent girl named Lili. The show opens onto a scene of roustabouts setting up a traveling carnival, and the story commences when Lili appears. She is a thin, gawky waif in an ill-fitting suit and black, heavy stockings, and carrying a worn suitcase. The carnival becomes, for her, a place of magic and enchantment, and its magician, Marco the Magnificent, is the major enchanter. She immediately develops a case of puppy love for the magician. However, the puppets in the show become her best friends and, through them, she begins to understand the puppeteer, Paul Berthalet, a lame, surly, antisocial man who reveals the warm, decent aspect of his nature only when speaking through the puppets. Slowly, Lili begins to realize her love for Paul, and recognizes that her feelings for Marco were only those of a little girl. The closing scene depicts the roustabouts disassembling the carnival.

Camille (1852), Alexandre Dumas *fils*. Dumas' play tells the story of Marguerite Gautier, a beautiful young courtesan who has legions of lovers and the beginnings of tuberculosis. This woman of legendary beauty falls in love with an admirer, the shy and honorable Armand Duval. When Armand's father learns of their liaison, and their plan to marry, he begs Marguerite to break off the engagement for the sake of the family honor and Armand's reputation. Because she loves Armand she does as his father asks, but never tells Armand why she has left him. He does not understand and, believing that she has left him for other men, he treats her cruelly. When he finally learns the truth it is too late. Marguerite's disease has become terminal and she dies in his arms.

The Cenci (1819), Percy Bysshe Shelley. Never truly successful on the stage but important because it exemplifies Shelley's theory of tragedy. Takes place in the late sixteenth century in Italy. Count Cenci, a cruel, depraved monster who delights in the suffering of everyone around him, including his children, has sent his two sons to Salamanca in the hope that they will starve. His daughter, Beatrice, has, earlier on, fallen in love with Count Orsino, a scoundrel who has become a priest for purposes of monetary advancement. Beatrice sends Orsino a letter telling of her father's many cruelties and begging for papal intervention. Orsino, however, decides not to show the Pope the letter as he may then have no chance of winning Beatrice outside of marriage. Cenci gives a banquet to celebrate the accidental death of his two sons, an event which he considers just punishment for their rebellion and disobedience. Beatrice tells the guests of her father's cruelty and begs for their protection, but Cenci passes her off as insane. Beatrice then confesses to her stepmother that Cenci has raped her. Orsino arranges to have Cenci murdered, and when the two assassins are unable to kill the old man in his sleep, Beatrice, now brutalized by life's cruelties and disappointments, drives them to complete their mission. A papal legate arrives with an order for Cenci's execution, but, discovering that he has been murdered, they soon arrest the murderers along with Beatrice and her stepmother. The assassins die on the rack without telling who

Plot Summaries of Works Discussed in the Text

hired them, and at the end of the play Beatrice and her stepmother are led out to their own execution.

A Chorus Line (1975), Book by James Kirkwood and Nicholas Dante; music by Marvin Hamlish; lyrics by Edward Kleban; conceived, choreographed, and directed by Michael Bennett. A musical with very little story and none of the traditional show-stopping songs. Basically, this work is a dancer's musical with songs existing mostly as a means of imparting information to the audience. The slight story involves a choreographer-director auditioning a group of dancers from which he will eventually select eight, four men and four women, to become the chorus line of his new show. He puts the dancers through their paces and encourages them to step forward and say a few words about themselves. Eventually he makes his selection and then each of the eight dancers fill in the sketchy information they provided earlier with long monologues about their life and how it has affected their art. The show ends with all the dancers returning in a slickly costumed, carefully rehearsed chorus number which represents the ultimate of the chorus dancer's artistic creation.

Le Cid (1636), Pierre Corneille. Plot revolves around the conflicts of love, honor, and duty. Don Rodrique, soon to win the title of Le Cid for his deeds in battle against the Moors, loves Chimene, who loves him. However, when her father insults his own far more elderly father, Don Rodrique challenges Chimene's father to a duel and kills him. Before Rodrique can be brought to justice—the king has ordered that dueling among his nobles be ended—he leads the Spanish forces to victory over the Moors attacking Seville. He is then forced to duel with Don Sanchez, who is also in love with Chimene and whom Chimene has incited to the duel to gain revenge on Rodrique for killing her father. To do this she has promised to marry the winner of the duel, but when Rodrique wins she will renege. The king decides the outcome. Chimene must spend a year in a nunnery and Rodrique a year leading the Spanish troops. At the end of the year they must marry.

Company (1970), Book by George Furth; lyrics and music by Stephen Sondheim. The story opens on Robert, a New York bachelor who is celebrating his thirty-fifth birthday. Robert has a number of friends who, with the best of intentions, keep trying to find him a wife, unable to recognize that Robert does not lack for female companionship or sexual fulfillment, being involved with a trio of young ladies. The play covers several years, during which Robert visits a number of his "happily married" friends, finding in each case something lacking or disappointing in the marital relationship. One couple drown their problems in smoking pot; another features an alcoholic husband fighting off the need for drink while his overweight wife (and karate expert) suffers on a perpetual diet; a third couple play contemporary "head games," with the wife agonizing over whether marriage will cost them their identities. These vignettes have an imponderable effect on Robert. The final curtain finds him still unmarried but half convinced that there is something wrong with this status.

Cyrano de Bergerac (1897), Edmond Rostand. Cyrano, the greatest poet and swordsman in France, loves his cousin Roxane but will not tell her because he is ashamed of his long, grotesque nose. She, in turn, begins to develop a romantic interest in Christian, a young and handsome guardsman in Cyrano's company. Because Christian is a good man, and to assure Roxane's happiness, the poet-swordsman decides to help Christian attain her love by writing the poems and dialogue that the good but rather dull young man needs to woo her. The endeavor is successful, but Christian is killed in battle. Cyrano vows never to tell Roxane that he is the one who composed all the beautiful words she fell in love with, and in her sorrow she becomes a nun. Cyrano continues to visit her and at last, ambushed by his enemies, he comes to her wounded and dying. The truth comes out, that he was the heart and soul of the man she loved, and then he dies, still fighting in his imagination the enemies who have killed him.

Death of a Salesman (1949), Arthur Miller.   Willy Loman, a traveling salesman, has always believed that "being well liked" is the secret of success in business and life. However, when the play opens he is sixty-three, and no longer able to sell. In a series of episodes that take place in the past and the present, we see how Willy's world fell apart. His two sons, Biff and Happy, fall victim to Willy's mistaken approach to life, believing that athletic success and social popularity are more important than education and hard work. Willy makes himself the model for his children, so when Biff catches his father in a hotel room with another woman, the boy's life is shattered. Eventually Biff leaves home for the west where he serves time in jail for theft, and Hap becomes a miniature version of Willy. Fired by his young, impersonal boss and forced by Biff to realize that they are both failures, Willy comes to the end of his rope. He goes to the garage to start the car, planning to kill himself in a highway accident. Linda, his wife, foresees what is going to happen, but though she loves him for what he is and not how much he can earn, she is powerless to prevent his suicide.

Desire Under the Elms (1924), Eugene O'Neill.   A tragedy based on the Greek legend of Theseus-Phaedra-Hippolytus. Ephraim Cabot, a stern, tyrannical New England patriarch, has already married and buried two wives. His sons—Simon, Peter, and Eben—hate him and Simon and Peter both leave home to join the Gold Rush in California. Eben, the youngest son, remains at home because he considers his father to be responsible for his mother's death and, thus, he believes himself to be the rightful heir to the hard, stony farm that huddles beneath giant, brooding elm trees. Ephraim takes a third wife, Abbie Putnam, a sensuous but strong young woman who also hopes to inherit the farm. Abbie seduces Eben, hoping that if she bears a child her husband will believe it is his own and thus leave her his property. Abbie becomes pregnant and a child is born; however, the plan backfires when Abbie and Eben are caught up in their passion. To prove that she now loves him alone and is no longer concerned with inheriting the farm, Abbie smothers her child. Eben is at first furious at her and reports her to the sheriff, but then he relents and claims a share in her crime and the two face their doom together.

A Dream Play (1901), August Strindberg.   An expressionistic drama attempting to present a complete view of life. The plot, such as there is, begins with the daughter of the god Indra coming to earth to learn firsthand about the problems of human-kind. When she arrives she undergoes a kind of journey on which she meets three men, an officer, a poet, and a lawyer, whom she marries. Through these experiences Indra's daughter sees all of humanity's problems: the love that turns to hate; the claustrophobia of marriage; the death of romance. But also, along the way, the daughter learns about the beauty of the human race, which Strindberg symbolizes in a flower. Like the flower, human beings grow up out of the mud, bloom briefly and beautifully, and then fall back again. At the end of the play, after all the

Plot Summaries of Works Discussed in the Text

characters have passed before her to burn their illusions in a cleansing fire, Indra's daughter ascends to heaven to present what she has learned of humankind to her father.

Dubarry (1901), David Belasco.   This plot is fully recounted on pages 7 and 8.

Edward the Second (1591), Christopher Marlowe.   A complex Elizabethan tragedy in which a lengthy series of short, swift scenes is held together by the underlying metaphor of fortune's turning wheel. Edward, through his growing concentration on satisfying his own appetites, his supercilious humiliation of his own nobles, and his elevation of such depraved court favorites as Gaveston, provokes the Mortimers into open rebellion. Queen Isabella joins the rebels and Edward is finally killed. However, because rebellion against the crown was believed by most Elizabethan dramatists to be a major evil, the rebels are at last defeated upon the ascent of the Child King, Edward III, to the throne.

Emilia Galotti (1772), Gotthold Ephraim Lessing.   Written by Lessing to display his ideal of dramatic form; that is, Aristotelian form and German content. The German content was disguised by setting the scene in Italy, but the moral implications of the plot were directed at German audiences. The basic plot of this play is summarized on page 81.

The Emperor Jones (1920), Eugene O'Neill.   Makes use of many of the techniques of expressionism. The story involves the last days of Brutus Jones, a black ex-Pullman car porter and escaped convict who, using tricks he learned from white businessmen, has made himself emperor of an island in the West Indies. He has greedily exploited his primitive subjects, expressing contempt for them in the term "bush niggers." When the play begins Jones' palace is deserted. Native tom-toms in the wilds are beating with the rhythm of a human heart. Jones knows his time is up, but he is unconcerned. As he explains to the white trader, Smithers, he has planned his escape carefully. During the night he will cross the forest and sail to Europe where the money he has gouged from his subjects is deposited. However, when he at last enters the forest a number of dreamlike happenings take place, leading Jones back through his own history and prehistory. As this happens, and Jones' fear increases, the beat of the ever-present tom-toms increases in corresponding tempo. Crazed by his experience, Jones at last staggers out of the jungle at the same place he entered. He has run in a circle, and his victims, who had mystically known this would happen, are waiting. They shoot him.

Endgame (1957), Samuel Beckett.   The plot of *Endgame* is fully summarized on pages 9 and 10.

The Eumenides (458 B.C.), Aeschylus.   The third play in Aeschylus' trilogy, *The Oresteia*, which ends the story of Orestes, who has killed his mother Clytemnestra in revenge for her murder of his father, Agamemnon. The play begins with Orestes at the altar of the temple of Apollo in Delphi. Surrounding him are the Furies, sleeping, waiting to torment him if he leaves the sanctuary of Apollo's altar. The ghost of Clytemnestra appears and urges the Furies to seize Orestes, but they are restrained by the intervention of Apollo. The Furies claim that Apollo has no right to keep them from Orestes, who is their rightful prey because he has acknowledged committing matricide. After some debate all parties agree to refer the case to the judgment of Athena. Athena hears arguments that relate mostly to male or female superiority, and then the case is referred to the jury. The vote is six for Orestes and six against, and Athena breaks the tie by voting for Orestes, thus absolving him of blame for his act. The Furies, outraged at the decision, are calmed by Athena and finally agree to give up their role of avengers and become the Eumenides, the friends and protectors of humankind.

The Farce of Master Pierre Pathelin (late fifteenth century), Anonymous.   The greatest of the extant Medieval farces. This work contains outstanding dialogue to complement its potential for physical farce, and also provides a sharp, biting satire on the legal profession and the merchant class. In it a sharp, shyster lawyer (Pierre Pathelin) has lost his clients since his last trickery was exposed and he was sentenced to be publicly pilloried. Flat broke because he is no longer getting legal fees, he cheats a greedy merchant out of a bolt of cloth so that his wife can make them new clothes. As soon as the episode with the merchant is over a shepherd, who also works for the greedy merchant, appears at Pathelin's door and asks Pathelin to represent him. (The merchant is suing the shepherd for killing and eating his sheep.) Pathelin agrees and, in the ensuing court scene before a stupid, insensitive judge, he manages to reverse justice and get the shepherd freed by reason of insanity. The shepherd, who is sharper than Pathelin had guessed, then uses his established insanity and refuses to pay Pathelin's fee. The play ends with Pathelin, the shyster, recognizing that he has been cheated by an even greater trickster, the wily shepherd.

The Father (1887), August Strindberg.   This naturalistic tragedy features a wife (Laura), who, in her struggle to control totally the upbringing of her daughter, destroys her husband, a cavalry captain. Laura promotes in her husband's mind the belief that he is not the child's father, and then provokes him into a series of statements and actions designed to make him appear insane. Eventually, having convinced their doctor of her husband's madness, Laura has the husband's faithful and trusted nurse truss him up in a straightjacket, a betrayal that causes him to have a stroke. The play ends with the mother victorious and the father destroyed.

Faust (1808), Johann Wolfgang von Goethe.   We deal here only with Part 1 of Goethe's tragedy, as Part 2 is almost never produced on the stage. Part 1 is based on the popular Medieval legend of Faust, the man who sold his soul to the devil in exchange for supernatural powers. In some versions of the legend Faust loses his soul and, in the end, is carried away to hell (as in Marlowe's play on the same subject). In most versions, however, Faust is ultimately saved, as is the case in Goethe's work. This salvation takes place in Part 2 and must be kept in mind when considering Part 1 as a work standing by itself. The play begins with Faust, the prideful scholar, ever-searching for knowledge. He makes his bargain with Mephistopheles, who then attempts to corrupt Faust by urging him to use his new powers in the service of drink and gluttony. Failing in this first attempt, Mephistopheles is much more successful in corrupting Faust with lust. Faust seduces, impregnates, and then deserts the innocent, pure Margaret, who as a result is driven to child-murder and madness. Margaret's tragedy ends Part 1, with Margaret the recipient of Divine Grace because of her suffering, and Faust seemingly on his way (with Mephistopheles) to damnation.

Finian's Rainbow (1947), Book by E. Y. Harburg and Fred Saidy; lyrics by E. Y. Harburg; music by Burton Lane.   A musical fantasy set in southeastern America, in the State of Missitucky. The plot is provoked by the arrival in Rainbow Valley of Finian McLonergan and his daughter Sharon, both fresh from Ireland. Finian has stolen a crock of gold from the leprechauns and he wants to bury it in American soil where it will multiply—for, after all, the United States has buried its own gold in nearby Fort Knox. Finian buys a small plot of land from a group of sharecroppers, mostly black. One of the white sharecroppers, Woody Mahoney, is always in danger of losing his farm because he cannot pay the mortgage. He is presently trying to recoup by experimenting with a process for growing mentholated tobacco. Meanwhile, Senator Billboard Rawkins, a black-hating schemer, has discovered gold in this particular area (actually Finian's gold) and begins plotting to defraud Woody and the black farmers out of their land. Finian saves Woody's farm by giving him the money to pay the mortgage. But Finian's crock of gold is magical, able to provide three wishes. It transforms the senator into a black evangelist, it restores to Woody's deaf-mute sister Susan the ability to hear and speak, and it assures happiness to Sharon and Woody, the man she has come to love.

Fiddler on the Roof (1964), Book by Joseph Stein; lyrics by Sheldon Harnick; music by Jerry Bock.   Loosely based on the short stories of Sholom Aleichem, *Fiddler* tells the story of Tevye, an Eastern European Jew, and his family—Golde, his wife, and his five daughters. The play proceeds on two levels. On the first, is the essentially romantic tale that tells how each of the five daughters find men to love, and how Tevye and Golde, married by arrangement as was common for their generation, discover that they do love each other. On the second level the story shows us the disintegration of the Jewish community. First the traditions change. The daughters insist on picking their own husbands rather than having them selected by the parents. Indeed, Chava even elects to marry a Russian Christian, thus breaking tradition in a way that not even the good-natured and liberal Tevye can accept. The disintegration in the community is physicalized in the destruction of their village, Anatevka. The Russian constable announces that all Jews must leave the village and the age-old forced migration of the Jews begins once more. Tevye and Golde, with their meager household belongings, leave to join Uncle Abram in Chicago, and their family is scattered across the face of Europe. Perhaps the most touching moment in the play is Golde's last minute insistence on sweeping the floor of their house, since she does not wish to leave behind a dirty home. The villagers bow to each other and depart, and only the fiddler on the roof is left, playing a tune.

Flower Drum Song (1958), Book by Oscar Hammerstein II and Joseph Fields; lyrics by Hammerstein, music by Richard Rodgers.   Concentrates on a familiar problem faced by many Americans—the gap that grows between immigrant parents who try to hold on to their old world culture and their children who want to become part of the American way of life. In this case the setting is San Francisco's Chinatown. Sammy Fong, an Americanized Chinese, is trying to arrange a marriage between his friend Wang Ta and Mei Li, a young girl from the old country. Wang Ta's father is delighted because Mei Li is old country, but Mei Li's father insists that she must honor an earlier marriage contract and marry Sammy Fong. Wang Ta is pleased because he wishes to marry Linda Low, an Americanized Chinese woman who runs the Thunderbird Club. To keep Wang from marrying Linda, Sammy invites Wang's parents to come to the Thunderbird Club, where Linda does a strip-tease act. There are a number of complicated misunderstandings, during which Mei and Wang fall in love, as do Sammy and Linda, but the Three Family Association decide that Sammy must honor the first contract and marry Mei. There is a ceremonial wedding procession in which the heavily veiled bride is carried on a sedan chair down Grant Avenue to Sammy, but when the veil is lifted the bride turns out to be Linda. Mei Li now announces that since she entered the country illegally, all previous contracts are null and void, leaving her free to marry Wang.

Forty-five Minutes from Broadway (1906), Book, lyrics and music by George M. Cohan. Cohan's second successful musical is set in the New York suburb of New Rochelle. A local miser and millionaire has just died, but no will can be found. Everyone had assumed that the money would be left to the faithful housekeeper, Mary Jane Jenkins, but in the absence of a will so stipulating, the money will go to the miser's only living relative, Tom Bennett. Tom arrives in New Rochelle to claim his inheritance, along with his showgirl sweetheart, Flora Dora Dean, her nagging mother, and his secretary, Kid Burns, a former horseplayer and ne'er-do-well. Kid Burns provokes a fight between Tom and Flora Dora, and himself falls in love with the housekeeper, Mary Jane. He then discovers the will making Mary Jane the heiress, but when he manfully refuses to marry a rich woman, Mary Jane destroys the will.

Ghosts (1881), Henrik Ibsen. One of Ibsen's attempts at domestic tragedy. Deals with a woman's inability to escape the ghosts of her past, especially the ghost of her dead, profligate husband and, more importantly, the ghosts of outmoded social conventions. Much of the play is exposition, a recounting of past action. The woman had married Captain Alving not out of love but because he was socially acceptable, and after she discovered him to be completely dissolute the social conventions prevented her from leaving him. After a son is born she sends him away so that he will not be corrupted by his father. After the Captain dies she uses all of his money to build an orphanage in his name, an ironic gesture given the number of illegitimate children the Captain has certainly sired, and a gallant gesture in the sense that it gets rid of all the Captain's money, so that their son will inherit nothing from him. As the play begins, Mrs. Alving believes that all the ghosts of the past have been laid to rest, but Oswald, the son, returns from Paris for the dedication of the orphanage and immediately stirs up the past by playfully beginning an affair with the housemaid, who turns out to be one of the Captain's illegitimate children and his own half-sister. Then Oswald tells his mother that he is fatally ill; he has inherited syphilis from his dead father. Mrs. Alving tells Oswald the truth about his father and this emotional strain, in combination with the debilitating effects of the disease, drive Oswald to the madness he has feared. While still rational, and knowing that he will eventually go mad, he asks his mother to give him a lethal dose of morphine when the time comes. The time has now come and the play ends with the mother unable to act in this final visitation of the ghosts.

Gorboduc (1561), Thomas Norton and Thomas Sackville. Subtitled ''or, Ferrex and Porrex,'' this play is usually considered to be the first English tragedy in blank verse. Written by the law students of the Inner Temple, one of the Elizabethan Inns of Court, its popular reception provoked a vogue for Senecan-style drama that continued throughout the sixteenth and early seventeenth centuries. The plot is concerned with the disastrous consequences that come about when Gorboduc, the elderly King of Britain, decides to divide his kingdom between his two sons, Ferrex and Porrex. After the division is completed the two brothers, misled by evil counselors and prey to their own ambitions, begin a civil war, each seeking to conquer the other. The result of this conflict is that Porrex kills Ferrex, his older brother. In revenge for this murder of her first-born, Queen Videna kills her younger son, Porrex. The deaths of the two young kings, and the miseries of the civil war they caused, bring on anarchy and the populace rises in revolt, slaying both Queen Videna and King Gorboduc. The debilitated kingdom may now fall prey to the evil nobleman, Fergus, and on that gloomy note the play ends.

The Great God Brown (1925), Eugene O'Neill.   In this complex play O'Neill used masks to make apparent the lack of direct communication between people, and to emphasize how we all put on different masks to face the world. Dion Anthony is, as far as the world can see, full of high spirits, creative, and sensual. This representation is the Dion that his wife Margaret knows, but it is merely the Dion of the mask. Without the mask Dion is a haunted, sad, spiritually empty man, and a lonely artist. When Margaret at last sees him without the mask she is frightened and unable to understand. Only the prostitute Cybel understands the man beneath the mask. Dion's friend, William Brown, understands the power of Dion's mask and, while seeming to help Dion, seeks to possess this aspect of him. Dion wills himself to Brown and dies, and Brown immediately puts on Dion's mask and takes his place in his friend's family, gaining Margaret whom he has desired since their youth. However, to become his friend completely, William learns that he must destroy the Brown beneath the mask. He does so and dies in the arms of Cybel who, when asked to identify the body replies, "Man!" Margaret, surrounded by her family, takes comfort in the knowledge that love does not die and Dion lives on in her heart.

The Guardsman (1910), Ferenc Molnar.   Based on what seems to be little more than a frivolous, comic anecdote, this play tells the story of an actor who, in order to test his wife's fidelity, attempts to seduce her while disguised as a Russian officer of the guard. The actor thus tests not only his wife but his whole life and profession in the sense that his success or failure both depend on his success as an actor. It also touches a poignant string in that the actor believes himself to be a failure. He believes himself unable to keep his wife based on what he is, and so he must resort to being what he is not, to being what he thinks his wife truly desires. The resolution of the plot is frustrated when the wife's expected betrayal of the husband with the husband-in-disguise cannot take place because of the actor's self-revelation. The whole pretense becomes meaningless with the wife's subsequent pretense that she saw through the husband's disguise.

Guys and Dolls (1950), Book by Jo Swerling and Abe Burrows; lyrics and music by Frank Loesser.   This musical fable opens with a scene of almost frantic activity, punctuated by the frenzied efforts of some horseplayers to pick a winner. Sky Masterson, one of the gamblers, meets Sarah Brown, a virtuous Salvation Army member from the nearby Save-A-Soul Mission. Sky shows interest in Sarah, but she dismisses him. The scene then shifts to the Hot Spot nightclub where Adelaide, the star performer, is suffering from a psychosomatic cold because she has been engaged to Nathan Detroit for fourteen years and he keeps putting the marriage off. Nathan, meanwhile, is looking for a place to hold a floating crap game and cannot understand how Adelaide can be so hung up on marriage. Sky, still determined to capture Sarah's love, mentions his feelings to his gambler friends, who tell him that winning Sarah is impossible. However, convinced of his own powers, Sky bets one of the friends that he will get Sarah to go to Havana with him. Sarah does agree to go, not for the romance but because her Mission is in financial trouble and Sky has promised to find a way to save it. However, when she gets to Havana she discovers that she is really interested in Sky, and Sky discovers that he truly loves Sarah. When Sarah learns that Sky took her to Havana to win a bet she decides never to see him again, but soon realizes that she needs Sky's help to save the Mission. Their romance now takes a serious turn and even Nathan Detroit decides it is time to marry Adelaide.

Hair (1968), Book and lyrics by Gerome Ragni and James Rado; music by Galt MacDermot. There are really two versions of *Hair*—the one that became the opening production of Joseph Papp's New York Shakespeare Festival Public Theatre, and the one that finally moved uptown to the Biltmore Theatre. Both, however, have no plot, no recognizable sequence of events, and no ongoing theme except, perhaps, protest. The musical opens with the proclamation that a new age is coming, the age of Aquarius, when peace will rule the planets and love will guide the stars. It then goes on, in a haphazard manner, to condemn all that is wrong with the establishment and promote everything that is right with the antiestablishment. The characters all wear the antiestablishment uniform of the sixties, or wear nothing at all, and speak mostly in obscenities about the quality of life in the establishment. Highly popular in its own day because of its topicality, *Hair* is rarely revived.

Hamlet, Prince of Denmark (c. 1600), William Shakespeare. In this greatest of Elizabethan tragedies, Hamlet has the misfortune to be Prince of Denmark when "the times are out of joint" and the court has become corrupt. Hamlet's uncle, Claudius, has secretly murdered Hamlet's father and married Gertrude, Hamlet's mother. Sworn to take vengeance by his father's ghost, Hamlet must first ascertain certainly that Claudius is guilty. He does so by using a group of players to put on a short play wherein the murder is re-enacted. Claudius betrays himself and so Hamlet begins his revenge. He feigns madness to discover the extent of the possible conspiracy, becoming suspicious of the Lord Chamberlain, Polonius, and even suspecting Polonius' daughter, Ophelia, whose only crime is loving Hamlet. Inadvertently he kills Polonius, which brings him exile and Ophelia madness. Laertes, Polonius' son, vows vengeance and challenges Hamlet to a duel, with the approval of Claudius who himself has prepared a cup of poison for Hamlet. However, events go wrong for the plotters. Gertrude accidentally dies of the poison prepared for Hamlet, and Hamlet kills Claudius. Laertes kills Hamlet, and is in turn killed by a poisoned rapier.

Hedda Gabler (1890), Henrik Ibsen. Hedda, a strong personality frustrated by the social conventions that restrict women, is capable only of destroying others. She marries a meek, mild professor to attain security, not because she loves him. When she becomes pregnant she refuses to admit her condition. She even tries to regain her erstwhile influence over Eilert Lovborg, once a brilliant young scholar whom she had led to drink and destruction. Unable to find meaning in her own life, she plots the suicide of Lovborg. Her plan succeeds, but Hedda does not get the thrill she had expected—the suicide is not glorious, as Lovborg shoots himself in the stomach by accident. A lecherous judge, discovering that Lovborg killed himself with one of Hedda's dueling pistols, threatens to reveal the sordid situation unless Hedda agrees to have an affair with him. Sickened, afraid of the scandal, and equally frightened of the affair, she uses the other dueling pistol to kill herself.

Hellzapoppin' (1938), Book primarily by Olsen and Johnson; lyrics by Irving Kahal, Charles Tobias, and others; music primarily by Sammy Fain. This musical revue began life as a one-hour burlesque farce, but by the time it arrived on Broadway it ran a full two hours. It contained skits about English detectives, cabinet meetings, Wall Street, and maternity wards; songs; and satire on popular radio programs and such personalities as Walter Winchell, Kate Smith, and Rudy Vallee. What made the show unusual, and outstanding, was a series of outrageous farcical intrusions —a short film of Hitler speaking with a Yiddish accent, a woman running up and down the isles shouting for Oscar, a ticket scalper trying to sell audience members tickets for a competing show, a lady leaving her seat and announcing loudly that she is going to the bathroom, and even a male Godiva who rides a horse in the balcony. The show contained no plot or theme, but it was a great deal of fun and ran for over a thousand performances.

Henry IV, Part 1 (c. 1597), William Shakespeare. Henry's throne, usurped from Richard II, is being threatened. In the north Henry Percy (Hotspur), son of the Earl of Northumberland, has refused to surrender his Scottish prisoners to the King. To the west the superstitious Owen Glendower is raiding the Marches. Perhaps most disappointing of all to Henry is that his son, the future Henry V, is carousing about with the "fat old knight," Sir John Falstaff, and some other doubtful companions. Finally, Hotspur and Glendower join forces to usurp Henry. This causes Henry's son, Prince Hal, to give up his playboy role and join the battle against the rebels. At the battle of Shrewsbury he engages Hotspur in single combat, kills him, and leads the King's forces to victory.

Hernani (1830), Victor Hugo. Takes place in early sixteenth-century Spain. Hernani is a young nobleman in rebellion against King Charles of Spain, who was responsible for the death of Hernani's father. Hernani is in love with Doña Sol, who has been unwillingly betrothed to her uncle, Don Ruy. This beautiful woman has also won the love of the King, and it is in her room that these two adversaries first meet. The confrontation is inconclusive, and they part after agreeing to try to kill each other. The plot becomes lengthy and complex, but later Hernani spares the King, and Don Ruy, practicing the outmoded principles of personal honor toward a guest in his house, saves Hernani. Eventually all the conspirators are captured and spared by the King, who has just been elected as Emperor of the Holy Roman Empire. Hernani will be allowed to marry Doña Sol. Then Don Ruy shows up and demands that Hernani kill himself as he had promised earlier to do if Don Ruy should demand it. Hernani keeps his promise; then Doña Sol kills herself and the play ends on the premise that the two are united in death.

H.M.S. Pinafore (1878), W. S. Gilbert and Sir Arthur Sullivan. This comic operetta begins when Sir Joseph Porter, First Lord of the Admiralty, announces his intention to inspect the ship *Pinafore*. On the *Pinafore* a lowly seaman, Ralph, is miserable because he is in love with Josephine, the captain's daughter. She repulses his advances and rejects his love because of his low rank. Then, Little Buttercup comes aboard to sell notions and, in a conversation with the captain, she hints that appearances are often deceiving. The captain notes that Little Buttercup is very attractive. Sir Joseph arrives, inspects the crew, and tells them the secret of his own success—polishing door handles, sticking close to his desk, and never going to sea. Then he comes to the real point of his visit and asks Josephine to marry him. Josephine, who realizes that she really does love Ralph, excuses herself from marrying Sir Joseph because he is the Lord Admiral and she is only a captain's daughter. Sir Joseph tells her that rank should be no barrier. Ralph, in the meantime, is about to kill himself because he cannot have Josephine, but she rushes in and stops him, proclaiming her love for him and maintaining that rank is no longer a barrier. They plan to steal ashore and get married, but are caught. Then Little Buttercup again appears, announces that she was once a baby farmer (someone who "farms out" or adopts babies), and had two infants in her care, one of lowly birth and the other of high birth. Because she was especially fond of one of them she switched them around and the captain is the one of low birth while Ralph is of high birth. The captain and Ralph then switch places, so that Ralph becomes captain and the captain becomes a seaman. Josephine then marries Ralph, the captain marries Little Buttercup, and Sir Joseph has no one to marry except a well-born cousin.

The House of Bernarda Alba (1936), Federico Garcia Lorca.   A modern tragedy that begins with the burial of Bernarda's second husband. In his honor, she decides that she and her five daughters will go into cloistered mourning for eight years. Bernarda, who rules her household in stern, matriarchal fashion, pays great attention to personal honor, making it central to her life. She has lost her own sensuality and now seems determined to surpress sensuality in her daughters also. The youngest, Adela, is in love with one of the village youths, and refuses to live by Bernarda's restrictions. She sneaks out to meet her lover, but the affair is revealed to Bernarda by another daughter, the hunchbacked Martirio, who is in love with the same youth. Bernarda gets a gun, goes to the window, and shoots at the youth who is waiting for Adela in the courtyard. She misses, but tells Adela that she has killed him. Adela kills herself, but as the play ends Bernarda proclaims proudly that Adela died a virgin and that she and the rest of the daughters will "drown in a sea of mourning."

The Importance of Being Earnest (1895), Oscar Wilde.   A light, witty, and totally delightful comedy in which two young men, John Worthing and Algernon Moncrieff, seek to marry two young ladies, Gwendolen Fairfax and Cecily Cardew. However, certain social obstacles bar both unions. John has no real social or family status, having been found in a handbag in Waterloo Station and Algernon has lived a do-nothing life of idleness for so long that he cannot summon up the necessary energy to fall in love. An additional obstacle exists for both men: their chosen young ladies can only love a man named Earnest. John and Algernon thus plan a baptism to overcome this obstacle, and the other obstacles are resolved by a "revelation scene" in the last act of the play. The delight of this work is in the wit, style, and characterizations that Wilde used for this satiric portrait of Victorian hypocrisy and self-deception. Lady Bracknell, for example, does not approve of anything that "tampers with natural ignorance." She is also certain that "to be born, or at any rate bred in a handbag, whether it had handles or not, seems . . . to display a contempt for the ordinary decencies of family life that remind one of the worst excesses of the French Revolution." Algernon insists that divorces are made in heaven. When Cecily, who claims to be fond of straight speaking, insists that when she sees a spade she always calls it a spade, Gwendolen replies that she has *never* seen a spade and that "it is obvious that our social spheres have been widely different."

Johnny Johnson (1936), Paul Green.   In this work about the horrors of war, Green tried to intermingle comedy, tragedy, and satire, and punctuate the resulting complexity with songs, ballads, marches, and hymns by Kurt Weill. The result is not completely successful, but as with *Lysistrata* it manages to stand as one of the few effective antiwar plays. Johnny Johnson, an honest, open young man volunteers to fight in the "war to end all wars." In a series of scenes, we see him at the peace monument as President Wilson declares war; with his girlfriend Minnie Belle, who is in love with soldierly heroism; at the Statue of Liberty, speaking to it; at the front, making a separate peace with a young German soldier; in the hospital, dosing the allied commanders with laughing gas to achieve a temporary halt to hostilities; in an asylum where he is discovered to be suffering from a St. Francis complex; and, at the end, selling toys on the street, a vocation at which he is unsuccessful because he does not sell tin soldiers.

Julius Caesar (1598), William Shakespeare.   Because the common people of Rome are pleased with Caesar's triumph over Pompey, and thus support him so strongly that he cannot be easily curbed, the patricians of Rome grow fearful that he may become too ambitious and eventually gain absolute power even over them. Thus, led by Cassius, they plot against him. With the aid of Casca and Cinna they gain the support of the noble Brutus in their plan to assassinate Caesar. The plot is successful and when Caesar arrives in the capitol he is stabbed to death by Brutus. Marc Antony, faithful to Caesar and hoping to stir up the populace against the assassins, pretends to accept the reasoning of the conspirators, and delivers a public oration on Caesar's death which begins the tragic consequences. He then aligns himself with the forces of Octavius Caesar and Lepidus. Their armies are triumphant and Cassius and Brutus fall.

King Lear (c. 1605), William Shakespeare.   Lear is an arrogant, headstrong, and in a sense foolish old man who decides to divide up his kingdom among his three daughters, with the largest share going to the one who loves him the most. Two of the daughters, who love him not at all, make extravagant claims for their love, while Cordelia, the youngest and his favorite, merely says that she loves him as a daughter should love a father, just as when she marries she will love her husband. Lear is unable to differentiate between honest love and flattery, so he banishes Cordelia and divides his kingdom between Goneril and Regan. Once these two schemers have power, they strip their father of the rest of his possessions, not even leaving him his pride and dignity, and no longer pretend to love him. Lear, unable to comprehend such treachery, goes mad. Like Lear, Gloucester is also unable to perceive evil in his own offspring, specifically in his illegitimate son, Edmund. Later, blinded physically and saved from suicide by his legitimate son, Edgar, who is disguised as a madman, Gloucester gains spiritual insight. Adversity does its utmost to both Lear and Gloucester, but it leaves in its wake a true spiritual regeneration.

Kismet (1953), Book by Charles Lederer and Luther Davis; lyrics by Robert Wright and George "Chet" Forrest; music adapted by Wright and Forrest.   In this musical, with its story adapted from a play of the same name by Edward Knoblock and its music adapted from the hauntingly beautiful works of Alexander Borodin, Broadway was treated to a musical extravaganza. The plot is extremely simple, with the public poet of ancient Bagdad, Hajj, bringing to town his beautiful daughter, Marsinah. Hajj plans to marry the girl to the handsome young Caliph. After some mistaken identity problems he accomplishes his aim and he himself elopes to an oasis with the beautiful widow of the police wazir. There, he competes successfully in poetry writing with his major adversary, Omar the Tentmaker.

Kiss Me, Kate (1948), Book by Bella and Samuel Spervack; lyrics and music by Cole Porter. This musical concerns a touring theatrical company about to present Shakespeare's *The Taming of the Shrew.* As the show opens the company is in Baltimore. The four principals are Fred Graham; Lilli, his former wife; Bill Calhoun; and Lois Lane, a girl in whom Bill is deeply interested. Fred and Lilli, though divorced, are still in love with each other, but pretend indifference. Bill is a hopeless gambler who is facing the problem of redeeming a $10,000 I.O.U. from some professional gamblers. The opening scene of *Shrew* sets forth the problems faced by Shakespeare's characters. Bianca cannot marry until her older sister, Katherine, has found a man. Then a candidate for Katherine's unwilling hand is found when Petruchio arrives in Padua to seek a rich wife. Katherine rejects him, and Petruchio is not convinced he really wants her, but he is willing to go through with the marriage for the sake of the money. The scene then shifts back to the present. Lilli is furious with Fred because of a mixup over some flowers, and the gamblers have arrived to collect the $10,000 from Bill. The action then cuts back to *Shrew*, with Katherine now Petruchio's wife and making his life miserable. While this is going on "onstage," backstage Bill is angry at Lois for flirting with other men. In *Shrew* Petruchio solves his problem by taming his shrewish wife. In the company, Bill is relieved of paying off his I.O.U. by a shakeup in the criminal world, and he is then reconciled with Lois. Fred and Lilli finally admit the basic truth: that they cannot live without each other.

Knickerbocker Holiday (1938), Book and lyrics by Maxwell Anderson; music by Kurt Weill. Begins in New Amsterdam in 1647, with the town council discussing the coming arrival of the new Governor, Peter Stuyvesant. Then the audience is introduced to the romantic hero of the play, Brom Broeck, a knife sharpener who loves Tina, the daughter of the head of the town council. It happens that this is hanging day, and as they have no one handy the council elects to hang Brom because he forgot to obtain a business permit to sharpen knives. Brom responds that everyone on the council should hang as they have all sold brandy and firearms to the Indians. Brom is saved from hanging by the arrival of Stuyvesant, who places the entire community under strict discipline and issues a number of new, restrictive laws. Tina's father, a practical man, decides to marry his daughter to the Governor, which pleases Stuyvesant but throws Tina into a panic. Brom confronts Stuyvesant, objecting to his despotism. This activity merely gets Brom imprisoned. Some of the councilmen also object, but the muskets of the governor's guard soon change their minds. Stuyvesant now plans to go to war, since he believes that a nation at peace grows stagnant. He also revises the economy to get rid of free enterprise. This proves unnecessary when Indians attack. Brom escapes from jail and becomes a hero fighting off the Indians, but when the battle is over he accuses Stuyvesant of illicit dealings with the Indians. Stuyvesant orders him hanged, but Washington Irving steps in to tell Stuyvesant that if he wishes to be remembered well by history he must relax his despotic ways. Stuyvesant is convinced and even allows Brom to marry Tina.

The Libation Bearers (458 B.C.), Aeschylus. This middle play in Aeschylus' trilogy, *The Oresteia*, tells how Orestes, son of Agamemnon who was murdered by his wife, returns home from the exile imposed on him by Clytemnestra. He meets his sister, Electra, and tells her he has come home to seek revenge for his father. Orestes and a friend disguise themselves and go to the palace where they ask for Clytemnestra, saying they bring news of the death of her exiled son. Clytemnestra is stricken by the news and sends for her lover, Aegisthus. Orestes lures him into the house and stabs him. He then confronts his mother and, in spite of her pleading, forces her into the house and stabs her beside her dead lover. Orestes then departs for the temple of Apollo at Delphi to seek divine sanction for his crime of matricide. However, even as he leaves he can feel the wrath of the Furies who are gathering to pursue and torment him, and he rushes out madly.

Life is a Dream (1635), Pedro Calderón de la Barca.   When a son, Segismundo, is born to King Basilio of Poland, the portents say that he will bring disaster with him. Therefore, King Basilio has the infant locked up in a tower in the wilderness. When the boy reaches manhood the King decides to test the portents and, after Segismundo is given a sleeping potion, has him brought unconscious to the palace. When the prince awakens and finds himself a ruler he is as cruel as the stars said he would be. The King has him drugged once more and taken back to the prison tower, where he awakens and decides that it was all a dream. Eventually, when rebellious soldiers liberate him, Segismundo rules with generosity and justice, just in case this too is a dream. He does not want it to turn out the way the last dream did.

Little Johnny Jones (1904), Book, lyrics, and music by George M. Cohan.   Set at the turn of the century, this musical tells the story of Johnny Jones, an American jockey who goes to London to ride in the Derby. While there he meets Anthony Anstey, an American gambler, who tries to bribe Johnny to throw the race. He refuses and so Anstey tries to ruin Johnny's reputation, telling people that Johnny is dishonest. As a result, a mob follows the American to Southampton, where he has gone to say goodbye to some friends. Because of the mob Johnny learns about the rumors and decides to stay and clear his name. He engages a detective, who poses as a drunk to gain evidence to clear Johnny. The two have arranged a signal; if the detective finds the necessary evidence he is to set off some fireworks from the ship where he has been sailing with Johnny's friends. As the ship sails away Johnny sees the fireworks and knows that proof of his honesty exists. He then sails for home, where he finds out about Anstey's guilt in damaging his reputation and also uncovers evidence implicating Anstey in criminal activities in Chinatown. At last, his reputation cleared, he is free to marry his girlfriend, Goldie Gates.

The London Merchant (1731), George Lillo.   Probably the best example of domestic tragedy. This play tells the story of George Barnwell, a young apprentice merchant in London, who becomes involved with an evil prostitute named Millwood. Under her spell he robs his employer and kills his uncle. George and Millwood are finally caught and, after Millwood defiantly explains that she practices her evil tricks to get even with men for the miseries they have inflicted upon her, and George displays the proper remorse, they are sentenced to death and exit to mount the scaffold.

Long Day's Journey into Night (1940), Eugene O'Neill.   James Tyrone, a successful actor who gave up serious art for an economically rewarding career as matinee idol, now past his prime but still active, allows the penny-pinching that grew out of his poor Irish childhood to ruin not only his artistic life but also his relationship with his family. He prefers to spend his money acquiring land, rather than "squandering it" on proper medical care for his wife and youngest son. The wife, Mary, has lost a child, spent months in a hospital, and become addicted to drugs as a result of the painkiller given to her. The oldest son, Jamie, has become a cynical alcoholic. The youngest son, Edmund, has returned from the sea where he worked as a deck hand and is suffering from what the family fears is consumption. Mary, who has promised to give up her drugs, has been taking them secretly. Edmund learns that he must go into a sanitorium. Jamie and Tyrone, now both drinking, evoke all the family's old sorrows and misunderstandings. Mary, as the play ends, appears drugged and carrying her wedding gown, seeking somehow to return to the past.

Love for Love (1695), William Congreve.   Valentine, an idler and spendthrift, agrees to give up his inheritance in favor of his brother Ben if his father, Sir Sampson Legend, pays off Valentine's debts. Ben has been brought back from the sea to marry Miss Prue, the daughter of Mr. Foresight, a superstitious and illiterate lout. It is an arranged marriage which Ben does not want; in fact, he has no interest in the fashionable social whirl of London. Valentine, who is in love with Foresight's wealthy niece, Angelica, pretends to be mad to keep his father from disinheriting him. Angelica, who pretends to agree to marry Sir Sampson, in the end marries Valentine when he at last proves his devotion to her.

Love's Labours Lost (c.1595), William Shakespeare.   At the urging of the King of Navarre, two young men agree to give up worldly pleasures, shutting themselves away for three years to live in austerity. They vow to fast, sleep no more than three hours each night, and abstain from seeing or even speaking to a woman. Biron, a merry and wise character, has serious doubts about the value of this cloistered life, but his friends ignore his advice and so he, too, joins in the experiment. The decision is barely arrived at when news comes informing them that the Princess of France has arrived. The King admits that courtly formality must be observed, but the princess must remain outside the gate. However, the King and his lords are all entranced by the beauty of the princess and her three ladies-in-waiting. They each compose a sonnet and secretly try to deliver it to the woman they have chosen, but their plots are uncovered and they all discover that each is, in his heart, a traitor to his vow. They then begin to woo the princess and her ladies. The ladies, however, are not yet interested and tell the men that they must do penance before making offers of love.

The Lower Depths (1902), Maxim Gorki.   A seamy group of misfits and social outcasts is gathered in the cellar of Kostilyoff the landlord. They are like lost souls in hell, and the display of their character and the social injustice that has led them into this situation are the subjects of the play. The group includes Kleshtch, a poor locksmith, and his wife Anna, whom he continues to beat even though she is dying; the Actor, a pompous ham who bores and angers everyone with long tales of imaginary triumphs; the Baron, a depraved nobleman who is reduced to pimping for Nastya, a prostitute; Pepel, a thief who has been carrying on an affair with the landlord's wife and who is now making advances to her sister; and Satine, a gambler and realist who sees life as it is and not as he wishes it to be. Into this group comes Luka, a pilgrim who offers pity, comfort, and understanding. He helps Anna die at peace and prevents a fight between Pepel and the landlord. He convinces the Actor to seek help in a town that has a free hospital for alcoholics. And then he disappears. Satine, Nastya, and the Baron argue about the pilgrim, with Satine the realist deciding that Luka lied to them, out of pity. Then the other lodgers enter and the fighting and bickering begin anew, at last interrupted by the Baron entering to announce that the Actor has hanged himself.

Plot Summaries of Works Discussed in the Text

Lute Song (1946), Sidney Howard and Will Irwin.   Derived from an ancient Chinese classic, this work tells the story of a brilliant young scholar named Tsai-Yong. Following his father's orders, Tsai-Yong seeks fame and fortune at the court of the Son of Heaven, even though he would much prefer to stay with his young wife. Arriving at the court he is forced, by royal decree, to marry Princess Nieou-Chi, the daughter of the evil Imperial Preceptor, who then holds him a virtual prisoner. Back home his young wife maintains her faith, but she waits in vain. Finally, her husband's parents die in a famine and she leaves, dressed as a mendicant nun, to seek her husband, Tsai-Yong. When at last they meet he fails to recognize her, but the princess discovers the truth and, in noble resignation, gives up Tsai-Yong and reunites the couple.

Lysistrata (411 B.C.), Aristophanes.   To put an end to the war between Athens and Sparta, Lysistrata asks all the women in Greece to go on a strike, refusing all sexual contact with men until they agree to stop fighting. The women agree, though with great reluctance. They take over the Acropolis and lock the men out. The men try to smoke the women out, but only get doused with water for their trouble. Several individual men try tricks to get their women to come out and make love, and Lysistrata has a difficult time keeping the women from going. Eventually the men agree to stop making war and the women come out for a celebration.

Macbeth (c.1606), William Shakespeare.   Macbeth hears a prophecy from three witches on the heath that implies his own kingship. Driven by the prophecy, by desire of his wife to be queen, and by his own ambition, Macbeth murders King Duncan while the King is an honored guest in Macbeth's castle. The crown is now his, but Macbeth is haunted by his conscience. A murderer, he now trusts no one and keeps spies in all the noble houses. The murder of Duncan is suspected by Banquo, a general in the Scottish army, and so Macbeth also murders him, only to be unmanned when he is confronted by Banquo's bloody ghost. Guilt and despair drive Lady Macbeth to suicide, but Macbeth will not cave in and plays out his damnation to the bloody end. Macduff, a Scottish lord, together with Malcolm, Duncan's son, join forces to lead the loyal Scots to victory. Macbeth, deserted by his supporters and no longer convinced of his own invulnerability, is killed.

Man of La Mancha (1965), Book by Dale Wasserman; lyrics by Joe Darion; music by Mitch Leigh.   This musical, based in part on the novel *Don Quixote* and in part on an incident in the life of Miguel Cervantes, the novel's author, intends to capture the spirit of the original work. It begins in a dungeon in Seville at the end of the sixteenth century, when Cervantes and his servant are imprisoned because Cervantes, as tax collector, has foreclosed on a church that failed to pay its taxes. Upon entering the dungeon they are put before a kangaroo court of prisoners and Cervantes, if found guilty, must surrender all his possessions. However, all Cervantes owns is the manuscript of *Don Quixote* and some theatrical makeup and props. Speaking in his own behalf, Cervantes tells the prisoners the story of how a country squire aspires to become Don Quixote de la Mancha, a knight errant. Cervantes takes the role of Quixote, his servant becomes Sancho Panza, and they set out on the quest. The poor, mad knight errant mistakes muleteers for fellow knights, an inn for a castle, and a kitchen slut for a lady. Most of the people he meets merely laugh at him, but Aldonza, the woman, is puzzled. Quixote insists that she is his lady Dulcinea and that he wants nothing from her but to serve her, fight his battles against evil in her name, and if necessary to die for her. He tells her that when he looks at her he sees beauty and purity. Taking Don Quixote's belief in the necessity of doing good seriously, Aldonza tries to help the muleteers after they lose a battle to Quixote, but they respond by raping her. She entreats the knight errant to see her as she really is, pointing out that what he is doing to her is more cruel than what the muleteers did. Then the Knight of the Mirrors arrives to challenge Don Quixote to a duel. The Knight of the Mirrors is really Dr. Carrasco, sent by Quixote's niece to cure the squire of his delusions. Carrasco's shield is a mirror in which all men see themselves as they truly are. Don Quixote sees himself as a madman and falls weeping to the ground, his quest seemingly ended. Inside the prison the spokesman for the court tells Cervantes that his time is running out, and Cervantes picks up his tale with the squire, a broken man and near death, being tended at home by Sancho. Aldonza appears, but the squire does not recognize her. She tells him that she is his Dulcinea and reminds him of the quest. Suddenly he recognizes her and briefly revives as Don Quixote, ready once more to go forth and do battle with evil. Then he dies. Sancho announces his death but Aldonza will not believe it. The transformation is now complete and she is no longer Aldonza the slut, but Dulcinea. The story of Don Quixote is at an end and the soldiers of the Inquisition come to drag Cervantes to his trial, but the prisoners have, like Aldonza, been changed by this story of the mad, gallant, good knight, and as Cervantes is taken away the final sound on the stage is of Dulcinea, joined slowly by the other prisoners, singing about the quest.

The Master Builder (1892), Henrik Ibsen. Possibly Ibsen's best tragedy. Deals with the problems faced by Halvard Solness, an aging master builder (or architect-contractor) who has for many years been at the top of his profession. Solness is tortured by guilt, believing that his success was achieved at the cost of his wife's fulfillment as a mother, and at the cost of her traditional roots. He also feels cheated for having had to give up his youthful creativity in order to achieve material success. Additionally, now that he has reached late middle-age, he feels threatened by youth. Solness' firm was built on money derived from insurance when his wife's ancestral home burned. As an indirect result of the fire—his wife's depression—his twin sons also died. Solness' guilt stems from the fact that the fire started in a defective chimney which he had failed to repair. Desperate to regain the vigor and creativity of his youth, Solness turns to Hilde Wangel, a young woman who, as a child, had known Solness when he was still young and creative and built magnificent, soaring church spires instead of nice, safe little houses. Hilde, who in the play seems like a creature out of Nordic myth, and who seems to represent the creative aspect of Solness' personality, convinces him to build the highest tower of his career atop a new home he has just created for himself. Although heights now make him dizzy, at Hilde's urging he climbs the tower to hang on its peak a wreath, symbol of his victory and rejuvenation. However, when he reaches the peak he falls to his death.

Mourning Becomes Electra (1931), Eugene O'Neill. In this long play O'Neill sought an equivalent to the dramatic form of the Greek trilogy; that is, three full-length tragic plays on the same theme, linked together, and designed to be presented in a single showing. As his model he took the only surviving Classical Greek trilogy, Aeschylus' *Oresteia*. The first play of O'Neill's trilogy is *Homecoming*, in which townspeople await the return of General Mannon, who is away at the Civil War. In his absence, Mannon's wife has entered into an affair with Adam Brant, a member of the "disgraced" branch of the Mannon family. Lavinia, Mannon's daughter, hates her mother because she cannot bear to see her father hurt, or, as Christine says, because she would like to replace her mother as the General's wife. The General returns and is poisoned by his wife and her lover. The second play in the trilogy is *The Hunted*, in which Orin, Lavinia's brother, returns home from an army hospital. He loves his mother with an Oedipal intensity, but he also loves Lavinia. Mother and daughter struggle to dominate the young man and Lavinia wins. Orin then kills Brant and drives his mother to suicide. The third play is *The Haunted*, and in it a strange change has overcome Orin and Lavinia. He now resembles the General and she has become tempting and sensual like her mother. She wants to begin a new life by marrying a young neighbor, Peter Niles, and Orin becomes engaged to Peter's sister, Hazel. However, he is obsessed with death. Only in death can he rejoin the mother he still loves. He kills himself and Lavinia tries desperately to leave her morbid surroundings, but she cannot escape. Neither can she marry Peter. The dead are too strong, and she reverts back to her former self.

Murder in the Cathedral (1935), T. S. Eliot.   Thomas à Becket returns to his cathedral in Canterbury after an exile of seven years. He is greeted by a Chorus representing the women of Canterbury, and by the three priests of the cathedral. Becket is then tempted by four knights who offer him several possibilities of action: he may return to the pleasures of the flesh that he knew when he was chancellor to the king; he may again become chancellor; he may seek to become king himself by becoming head of a powerful new third party; or he may seek martyrdom. He rejects each tempter, even the last, knowing that martyrdom may not be sought, it must be bestowed. Becket preaches a Christmas sermon and then the four knights return and murder him, thus giving Becket the martyrdom he had refused to seek. The knights then speak directly to the audience, presenting their reasons for the murder and asking the audience to judge their guilt. The play ends as it began, with the Chorus, but now they are triumphant because of Becket's martyrdom. As long as men are willing to die for it, the Church will remain strong.

My Fair Lady (1956), Book and lyrics by Allan Jay Lerner; music by Frederick Loewe.   Based on the play *Pygmalion* by George Bernard Shaw. This musical follows Shaw's play closely except for the ending. After an opera performance at Covent Garden in 1912, Eliza Doolittle, a cockney flower girl, has her flowers upset by Freddy Eynsford-Hill. She is noticed by a famous phonetician, Professor Henry Higgins, who bets another phonetician, Colonel Pickering, that he can so change Eliza's speech, manner, and dress that she will be mistaken for a duchess. Higgins convinces Eliza to come and live in his house, where he can conduct this experiment. He assigns her a number of exercises that finally result in totally altering her speech and behavior patterns. The first test of the experiment is at Ascot. Freddy Eynsford-Hill sees her and falls in love, and with only a few minor problems Eliza is accepted as a woman of good birth. The decisive test is the embassy ball, where everyone is captivated by Eliza, convinced that she is a Hungarian princess. Higgins has won his bet and Eliza is happy, at first, but realizes that she cannot keep up the "fine lady" life without funds, and that she cannot now go back to being a flower girl. Higgins tells her not to worry as she can find a gentleman to marry. Angry at this suggestion, Eliza moves out of Higgins' home and runs into Freddy, who declares his love. Eliza brushes him aside and returns to Covent Garden, but the flower girls no longer recognize her. Higgins, meanwhile, cannot get Eliza out of his mind, and he is sorely puzzled. At his mother's house he meets Eliza and learns that Freddy has proposed marriage. Higgins voices his objections, but Eliza states that she can marry anyone she chooses. Higgins returns home, saddened, and sprawls in his favorite chair. He is so taken up with his misery that he does not notice at first that Eliza has slipped into the house. When at last he does notice, he feigns indifference and asks her to fetch his slippers, but it is clear that a commitment to love has been made by both.

The Odd Couple (1965), Neil Simon.   Perhaps the most successful comedy of this century. Tells the unlikely story of how two men learn to live together in a parody of all the usual husband and wife situations. Oscar Madison, a sloppy, disorganized sports writer lives alone after his divorce because his wife was unable to cope with his messy habits. His friend, Felix Unger, is the exact opposite of Oscar. Felix is overorganized and excessively neat. As the play opens Felix's wife has just left him, unable to cope with his fussiness. Felix moves in with Oscar in what starts out as a temporary arrangement, and in the beginning they have a terrible time adjusting to each other. Most of the play concerns this adjustment, and the humor grows out of the situations that develop between two men playing husband and wife roles. However, by the time the play ends the arrangement looks permanent and the adjustments, while not completely made, are well along.

Oedipus Rex (c.430 B.C.), Sophocles.   A full plot summary of this play is presented on pages 2 and 3.

Of Thee I Sing (1931), Book by Morrie Ryskind and George S. Kaufman; lyrics by Ira Gershwin; music by George Gershwin.   Takes place in Washington, D.C., in the year 1931, during the second year of the Depression. The main plot is a presidential campaign for the 1932 election carried on by candidate Wintergreen. We see a number of ironic and often satiric scenes, such as a smokefilled room containing Wintergreen, a number of tough politicians, and a meek, timid little man named Throttlebottom. Nobody knows Throttlebottom and he finally admits, rather shy and ashamed, that he is Wintergreen's running mate, the candidate for vice-president. Further, he relates, he must now withdraw from the campaign as he cannot face telling his mother that he is actually running for vice-president. The politicians calm his fears; if he is elected his mother will never know. Since Wintergreen is a bachelor, the campaign is organized around a beauty contest. The winner will be named Miss White House and, after the election, will become the first lady. The contest is held but Wintergreen wants his campaign secretary, Mary Turner, to win because he loves her corn muffins. After the judges taste the muffins, they agree. The campaign is successful and Wintergreen wins by a landslide. The scene after the election is a hodge-podge of almost silly, satirical happenings, with the impeachment of the president staved off only by Mary's pregnancy and Throttlebottom's marriage to the girl who had first been selected by the judges at the Atlantic City beauty contest.

Oklahoma (1943), Book and lyrics by Oscar Hammerstein II; music by Richard Rodgers.   This folk musical takes place in Western "Indian country" just before the turn of the century. Basically the plot is concerned with the romance between Laurey and Curly, but there is a subplot that tells of the romance between Ado Annie and Will Parker. The story begins with Curly inviting Laurey to go to the box social to be held that night. He even promises to take her there in a "surrey with the fringe on the top." Laurey becomes angry with him when she discovers that the surrey was just fiction, and she agrees to go to the social with Jud Fry, a hired hand. However, Laurey is rather piqued when she discovers that Curly is now going to the social with a different girl. Curly and Laurey make up and decide to go to the social after all, but to be polite and discreet so that their neighbors will not get ideas about the seriousness of their relationship. After a dream Laurey has about what it would be like to be married to Curly—a dream in which Jud Fry appears as a sinister, threatening figure—Jud turns up to demand that Laurey keep her promise to go to the social with him. Afraid that her dream is a portent of events to come, and afraid to provoke Jud, Laurey agrees, leaving Curly puzzled by her apparent change of heart. At the box social the men bid on the box lunches the women have prepared, and each winner gets to share the lunch with the woman who made it. The bidding for Laurey's lunch becomes a competition between Jud and Curly, with Curly finally winning. Three weeks after the social Curly and Laurey are married. The festivities are interrupted by Jud, drunk, who tries to kill Curly with a knife. In the struggle Jud falls on his own knife and is killed. A court is swiftly convened to declare Curly innocent of any crime and the couple leave on their honeymoon to a land soon to become known as Oklahoma.

On the Town (1944), Book and lyrics by Betty Comden and Adolph Green; music by Leonard Bernstein.   Written during World War II, this musical tells the story of three sailors on a twenty-four hour shore leave, doing what sailors on shore leave are traditionally supposed to do: looking for girls. In the subway Gabey, the romantic member of the trio, sees a picture of Ivy Smith, that month's "Miss Turnstiles." He becomes determined to find her and have a date with her. His buddies, Chip and Ozzie, agree to help him on this seemingly senseless quest, each going off alone in a separate direction to seek out Ivy. Chip, the serious-minded member of the trio, subsequently meets Claire, a woman cabbie who fascinates him with her enthusiasm and appetite for men. Ozzie, carefree and irresponsible, while at the Museum of Natural History, meets Hildy, a serious anthropology student. In the meantime Gabey ends up at the music studio in Carnegie Hall, where he finds Ivy taking singing lessons.

Our Town (1938), Thornton Wilder.   Set in Grover's Corners, New Hampshire, around the turn of the century. Deals with life, death, and the hereafter as experienced by the people of this small American town. The plot is episodic, held together by a "stage manager" who acts as narrator, and it centers around George, the son of Dr. Gibbs, and Emily, the daughter of the newspaper editor, Mr. Webb. The two youngsters are seen going to high school together, falling in love, getting married, and suffering tragedy when Emily dies during the birth of their second child. In a sad and touching scene they are reunited briefly at the graveside, and Emily learns how painful returning to life can be, because those who have never died take the beauties of life for granted.

Pal Joey (1940), Book by John O'Hara; lyrics by Lorenz Hart; music by Richard Rodgers.   Set in Chicago's south side. Tells the story of a "heel" named Joey Evans who begins as a nightclub entertainer, cons his way up to nightclub operator, and then falls as people discover what he really is like. Joey is a hoofer who never misses a chance to better himself, no matter whom he hurts. Beginning in a small Chicago club he wins the interest of two women—Gladys, a member of the chorus line and Linda, a nice girl who works in a pet shop. Joey convinces Linda that he loves her, but when she comes to the club to see him perform he snubs her to make advances to another member of the audience, Vera Simpson, a rich, pleasure-loving, cynical matron. Joey knows that if he can arouse her interest, Vera will advance his career, and so he tries the unusual tactic of insulting her. She leaves in a huff and the management is ready to fire Joey. However, he insists that she will return. She does, surprised by his public treatment of her, and fascinated by him. An affair begins and Vera buys Joey a nightclub, Chez Joey, which is an immense success. Meanwhile, Linda has overheard a plot to blackmail Vera by exposing her affair with Joey to her husband, and she comes to warn Vera. Vera is amazed that Linda would do this and asks if it is because she still loves Joey. Linda says no and that Vera is welcome to him. When the blackmailers arrive they discover that Vera will not be blackmailed and has called the police. Vera tells Joey that she is tired of his antics and the way he hurts innocent people like Linda and sends him on his way, without his nightclub. The story ends with Joey, everything lost, leaving town to try his luck and charm somewhere else.

Phèdre (1677), Jean Racine. (To clarify characters for English readers, the French spelling of names has been avoided except in the case of the title character, usually rendered in English as Phaedra.) Phèdre, the wife of Theseus, has been cursed by Aphrodite to follow in the footsteps of the women of her line, and love monstrously. As a result of this curse she conceives an incestuous love for her stepson, Hippolytus. Theseus is mistakenly reported dead, killed on his expedition to Hades, and Phèdre's nurse, Oenone, convinces her that now she can declare her love because it is no longer adulterous or incestuous. Phèdre confesses her love and Hippolytus is shocked and disgusted. Then Theseus returns and Phèdre, desperate, allows her nurse to accuse Hippolytus of her own crime. Theseus exiles his son and invokes his own father, Poseidon, to punish his son. Hippolytus is killed and Phèdre takes poison. She dies after confessing her crime.

Pins and Needles (1937), Book by Arthur Arent, Marc Blitzstein, Emanuel Eisenberg and others; lyrics and music by Harold Rome. This work, more revue than musical play, contained songs, sketches, and topical routines. It gave satirical attention to labor problems, domestic politics, the international situation, and most of all to the economic problems of the Depression. Because it was, essentially, an amateur production put on by a labor union, the show maintained a kind of dogmatic liberality and insisted on social significance in terms of everything it turned its eye upon. Capitalism was ridiculed as a failed economic system; the money-based caste system was satirically devastated; and the growing wave of European Fascism was decried. The revue ran for more than a thousand performances and the material was regularly changed to keep it current.

Porgy and Bess (1935), Libretto by DuBose Heyward; lyrics by Dubose Heyward and Ira Gershwin; music by George Gershwin. Set in a black ghetto, Catfish Row, in Charleston, South Carolina. The story begins with a crap game which flares into violence. One of the players, Crown, kills another of the gamblers and must go into hiding, leaving behind him his girlfriend, Bess. Another gambler, Sportin' Life, tries to get Bess to go off to New York with him, but she prefers to remain in the protection of the cripple, Porgy, who truly loves her. Bess gradually becomes contented with the new life she leads with Porgy, and grows to love him. After a lodge picnic she is accosted by Crown who breaks down her resistance and drags her into the woods to share his exile. Several days later Bess returns, sick and feverish. Porgy nurses her gently and they pledge their love. Again Crown appears. He taunts Porgy for being a cripple and Porgy kills him. Porgy is taken to jail for questioning and Sportin' Life again tries to tempt Bess to go to New York. Again she refuses, but he uses a package of "happy dust" to break down her resistance. Porgy is released because no one will testify against him, but when he comes back he learns that Bess has gone to New York with Sportin' Life. The final scene has Porgy climbing into his goat cart to go after Bess.

Pygmalion (1912), George Bernard Shaw.   The basic plot of *Pygmalion* was discussed under the musical *My Fair Lady*, which retained the main structure of Shaw's play, except for the ending. Henry Higgins, a professor of phonetics, coaches Eliza Doolittle, a cockney flower girl, in speech and social graces. Higgins is so successful in this experiment that Eliza is finally accepted by high society as being a Hungarian noblewoman. However, along with language and behavior, Eliza also acquires a new sensitivity and intellectual development. She becomes offended at Higgins' lack of humanity in treating her as an experimental object rather than a human being, and ultimately leaves him to find this appreciation elsewhere.

Richard III (1593), William Shakespeare.   Richard, according to Tudor legend—if not fact—is a deformed monster who is determined to capture the throne from his brother, Edward IV. Subtly he plots to make Edward angry with their brother, the Duke of Clarence. The plot succeeds and Clarence is arrested, whereupon Richard arranges to have him murdered in his cell. He then pays court to Anne, widow of a son of Henry VI (whose death he has caused) in the shadow of her husband's corpse. After the King dies a natural death, Richard has the two young heirs to the throne murdered in the tower. He has removed everyone who stands between him and the crown, but he is finally defeated and killed at the battle of Bosworth Field by the man who will become Henry VII.

The Rivals (1775), Richard Brinsley Sheridan.   A comedy that mocks social pretensions and the excesses of the established sentimental movement. Its heroine, Miss Lydia Languish, is a wealthy and sentimental girl whose fortune is controlled, until her marriage, by her aunt, Mrs. Malaprop. Because of an earlier misunderstanding, Lydia is in love with Ensign Beverly, who is in fact Captain Jack Absolute. Sir Anthony Absolute meets with Mrs. Malaprop in an effort to match his son Jack with Lydia. They come to an agreement, but confusion is spread through the mistake in identity. Further complication is provided by bumbling, cowardly Bob Acres, who is also in love with Lydia; by Sir Lucius O'Trigger, who carries on an amorous but mistaken correspondence with Mrs. Malaprop; and by a second set of lovers, Faulkland and Julia. Eventually the problems are settled and Lydia and Jack become engaged, even though it offends Lydia's silly, sentimental view of life to be engaged to a rich captain rather than an impoverished ensign.

Romeo and Juliet (c. 1595), William Shakespeare.   The plot of this play is fully summarized on pages 5 and 6.

The School for Scandal (1777), Richard Brinsley Sheridan.   Chronicles and satirizes the manners and morals of English society in the late eighteenth century. Lady Sneerwell, the leader of a pack of scandalmongers, sets the social pattern. Joseph Surface, a sly, scheming, underhanded young man, is widely considered to be a model of prudence and virtue because he accepts the false front of social graces and always says the right things, no matter what evil he does. His brother

Charles, on the other hand, who always says what he thinks and has no patience with social pretense, is considered to be a rake and a libertine. Both young men are in love with Maria, the ward of Sir Peter Teazle. Charles loves her for her beauty and inherent goodness; Joseph loves her for her money. Lady Sneerwell, for selfish reasons, is determined to prevent Maria's untimely marriage. Finally the uncle of the Surface brothers, Sir Oliver Surface, arrives and through an intricate plan exposes the true nature of each of his nephews. Charles is rewarded for his honesty with Maria's hand, and the whole Sneerwell plot is unmasked.

The Second Shepherd's Play (mid-fifteenth century), *Anonymous.* From the Townley manuscript, Wakefield Cycle is one of the finest Medieval dramas. The play tells two stories using interchangeable characters. The first story is a comic telling of the virgin birth in which Mak, a sheep stealer, takes a lamb from three shepherds. With the help of his wife, Gill, he hides it in a cradle, while Gill pretends to be suffering the pangs of childbirth. The shepherds search Mak's hut without luck and leave, convinced only that Gill has just given birth to an extremely homely child. After leaving they realize that they did not give the newborn child a birth gift, and returning to perform this good deed they catch Mak unaware and recover their lamb. As punishment for the theft they toss Mak in a blanket. The scene then changes to the hills outside Bethlehem, and the English shepherds become the shepherds before whom the Angel of the Lord appears to announce the birth of Christ. They go to Bethlehem as the Angel directs them and, at the manger, give their gifts to the baby Jesus.

She Stoops to Conquer (1773), Oliver Goldsmith. The best of Goldsmith's two comic dramas. Tells of the romance of young Marlow and Kate Hardcastle. These two young people were matched at birth by their parents, but they have never met. Marlow and his friend Hastings are on their way to Hardcastle Manor to meet Marlow's bride-to-be, and stopping in a local pub they ask to be directed to an inn. They are misdirected by the country wag, Tony Lumpkin, Mrs. Hardcastle's son by an earlier marriage, to Hardcastle Manor. They arrive at the home of Squire Hardcastle, believing it to be an inn, and treat Hardcastle as the landlord and his daughter Kate as a maid. Kate, who soon catches on to the situation, uses it to break down Marlow's extreme fear of "nice" girls. Meanwhile, Marlow's friend Hastings and Mrs. Hardcastle's niece Miss Neville plan an elopement, aided and abetted by Tony because his mother wants him to marry Miss Neville and this seems a fine way to get rid of her. There is a bevy of comic servants, a screen scene, and a wild coachride that ends up going nowhere. In the final scene, the "mistakes of a night" (as the play was subtitled) are corrected and the lovers are united.

Show Boat (1927), Book and lyrics by Oscar Hammerstein II; music by Jerome Kern. Begins in Natchez in the 1880s when the show boat, *Cotton Blossom*, arrives. The boat is under the command of Cap'n Andy, and his show includes the glamorous Julie LaVerne. After the boat arrives and the crowd disperses, the handsome gambler, Gaylord Ravenal, remains behind. He has caught a glimpse of Magnolia, Cap'n Andy's daughter, and is deeply attracted to her. On her part, Magnolia has noticed the handsome gambler and is much impressed. Meanwhile, Julie and her friend Queenie are both upset about their own men. Magnolia tells Julie that she is in love and Julie cautions her to be careful in selecting a man. The sheriff has received information that Julie has Negro blood, and because racial intermarriage is forbidden, Julie and her husband must leave the ship. Replacements are needed for their roles in the show, and Gaylord Ravenal and Magnolia are recruited. With this chance to be together they fall in love, and after their premiere performance Gaylord proposes. Several years go by and a daughter, Kim, is born to Magnolia. The showboat troupe is in Chicago for the 1893 World's Fair, and all is not going well. Gaylord is gambling again and has deserted his family. Magnolia is forced to seek a job at the Trocadero Music Hall, where the star is Julie LaVerne. Learning that Magnolia needs work, Julie resigns and Magnolia gets her job. She becomes a success, but Cap'n Andy convinces her to leave and return to the *Cotton Blossom*. There, a penitant Gaylord is waiting for her. They resume their marriage and Kim becomes the star of the showboat.

Song of Norway (1944), Book by Milton Lazarus; lyrics by Robert Wright and George "Chet" Forrest; music adapted by Wright and Forrest. Supposedly relating a part of the life of composer Edvard Grieg, the musical begins with the town of Bergen getting ready for the Midsummer Eve Festival of St. John. A close friend of Grieg, Rikhard Nordraak, predicts that his friend Edvard will become the voice of Norway, writing music that will represent the land and its people. Grieg, who longs to be a composer, is also in love with Nina Hagerup, a singer. However, a lusty prima donna named Louisa Giovanni lures Grieg away from his beloved Nina and takes him away to Rome. In the beginning it seems an exciting adventure, but before long Grieg is longing for Nina and the northern beauty of his homeland. The unexpected death of his friend, Nordraak, brings him back to his senses and Grieg goes back to Norway to marry Nina and fulfill the destiny that Nordraak predicted for him.

The Sound of Music (1959), Book by Howard Lindsay and Russell Crouse; lyrics by Oscar Hammerstein II; music by Richard Rodgers. Based on the history of the Trapp Family Singers. Takes place in 1938. Maria, a postulant at the Nonnberg Abbey in Austria, seems too deeply committed to the beauty of the world outside the Abbey, and the mother abbess and her assistants feel that she is not ready to take her vows and renounce the world. They therefore decide to send her away to work for awhile as governess to the seven children of a widower, Captain Georg von Trapp. When Maria arrives she finds that the Captain is a stern disciplinarian with inflexible rules, but Maria gives the children love and warmth, and they respond with love. She also teaches them the delights of group singing. The Captain makes a trip to Vienna and brings back his fiancee, Elsa. At a party that Elsa encourages the Captain to give, Maria realizes that she loves him and flees back to the Abbey, but the abbess encourages her to meet life squarely and not run away. Elsa and the Captain quarrel over Germany's growing totalitarianism, with Elsa in favor and the Captain violently anti-Nazi. The romance between Maria and the Captain now begins. They are married, but when they return from their honeymoon the Anschluss has been completed and the Nazis order the Captain back to sea duty. The Captain refuses and, with Brown Shirts pursuing them, the family takes refuge in the garden of the Abbey where the nuns hide them. After the Brown Shirts are gone the Trapp family decides to seek their freedom by climbing over the mountains to Switzerland.

Strange Interlude (1928), Eugene O'Neill. Nina Leeds leaves her home because her father prevented her from marrying the boy she loved, who subsequently was killed in World War I. After her father's death she returns home and marries Sam

Evans, by whom she becomes pregnant. Learning that there is a streak of insanity in Sam's family, Nina takes steps to abort her child. Then, striking a bargain with the local doctor, she becomes pregnant by him and bears his child. Her son at last grows up and marries, and then her husband Sam dies. Nina at last marries Charlie Marsden, an old admirer who is a father image for her.

Summer and Smoke (1948), Tennessee Williams.   Takes place in Glorious Hill, Mississippi, in 1916. On one side of a small park lives Alma, the nervous, straight-laced, puritanical daughter of a local minister and his deranged wife. On the other side lives Dr. John, whose son's "demoniac" unrest has earned him the title of the wildest man in town. When young John returns home from medical school, Alma urges him to give up his wild behavior and act in a manner befitting the dignity of the medical profession. John tries Alma's advice, even attending a meeting of the town intellectuals. However, even one night is more than he can take, and he leaves to enjoy the company of Rosa Gonzales. Later, John takes Alma to Moon Lake Casino and suggests that they take a private room. Alma runs away. John's father, who has been away, comes home to find Rosa and her drunken father living in his house. There is an argument and John's father is killed. Alma admits that she asked the older doctor to come home in the hope that he could make his son reform. Summer passes and winter comes and John takes over his father's practice, doing an outstanding job. Alma becomes ill and goes into seclusion. Finally she comes to John and offers herself, but John says that he has come to share her view that there is more to being human than is contained in an anatomy chart. Nellie, a former piano pupil of Alma's, tells her that she and John are engaged. Alma, in the park, meets a young traveling salesman, and suggests they go to the Casino.

The Taming of the Shrew (c. 1594), William Shakespeare.   The play opens with an Induction which is, in fact, an unfortunate conceit. A drunken tinker, Christopher Sly, is thrown out of a tavern and falls asleep in the street. Finding him thus, a "merry lord" decides to play a prank on Sly and takes him, still unconscious, to a rich apartment, provides him with a "wife" in the person of a disguised page, and tells him that he is a nobleman who has for fifteen years been suffering from amnesia. The play is then performed by a troupe of actors, supposedly to prevent Sly from again losing his memory. Sly is scarcely mentioned again, and the play is in many ways better off when the Induction is omitted. The primary action of the play tells how the madcap, unpredictable Petruchio woos and wins Katherine, the perfect wife except for one failing: she is a terrible shrew. From the moment they meet Petruchio subjects Kate to a series of indignities, both physical and verbal, under the pretext of kindness. The purpose of these indignities is to break down her shrewish ways. The cure works, and despite her resistance she is at last ready to swear that the sun is the moon if Petruchio says so. When the play ends, Kate defends marriage as stoutly as she opposed it when the play began.

Tartuffe (1664), Moliere.   Tartuffe, a confidence man pretending to Christian saintliness, has wormed his way into the trust and affection of Orgon, a rich bourgeois who in his later years has become deeply concerned with his own salvation. Tartuffe is invited into Orgon's home, where he soon becomes the virtual master of the household. Seeking to marry into the family and thus assure his inheritance, he asks for the hand of Orgon's daughter, Marianne, who is herself in love with Valere. Physically, however, Tartuffe is most strongly attracted to Elmire, Orgon's beautiful, young second wife. He makes two attempts to seduce Elmire. After the first she tells Orgon, who refuses to believe that Tartuffe would do such a thing. He cannot refuse to believe the second attempt, however, because Elmire arranges it so that he is hiding under the table in the same room. At last Orgon sees Tartuffe for what he is and attempts to throw him out, but Tartuffe has gained legal control of Orgon's property and for a while it appears that Orgon himself, along with his family, will be ejected. However, the king, who has learned of Tartuffe's plots, intervenes and Tartuffe is taken off to prison.

Thérèse Raquin (1873), Emile Zola.   Thérèse, married to a good but boring husband named Camille, takes Laurent as a lover. At last, desperate to be together all the time, they drown Camille. Thérèse's mother-in-law gives her consent for Thésèse and Laurent to marry, but their guilty secret slips out. The old woman goes into shock and awakes completely paralyzed so that she cannot accuse them. However, there is a world of accusation in her unblinking stare, and under this constant reminder of their guilt Thérèse and Laurent grow to hate each other. Even after she begins to recover, the old woman does not expose the murderers, continuing to torture them with her presence until, unable to stand the pressure, they kill themselves at her feet.

Three-Penny Opera (1928), Book and lyrics by Bertolt Brecht; music by Kurt Weill. Based on *The Beggar's Opera* by John Gay. Tells the story of Mack the Knife, also known as Macheath, a well-known criminal who is never caught at the scene of the crime. However, Macheath makes a mistake when he secretly marries Polly, the daughter of the king of the beggars, Jonathan Jeremiah Peachum. Peachum runs a business, a beggars supply house that rents appropriate outfits to beggars and thieves. While Peachum explains the difficulties of running a business designed to soften people's hearts, Macheath and Polly have their honeymoon in an empty stable, with stolen furniture providing the decor, and with such guests as Tiger Brown, the London police chief, and the Reverend Kimball. The Peachums are upset at their daughter's marriage and try to get rid of their undesirable new son-in-law by telling the police about his crimes. Macheath escapes the resulting manhunt, turning his "business" over to Polly, but is eventually caught, betrayed by his favorite whore, Jenny, while paying his weekly visit to the brothel. In jail, Macheath pays court to another old girlfriend, Lucy, the daughter of Tiger Brown. He promises to give up Polly, and so Lucy helps him escape. However, he is again captured when he visits the brothel. This time, it seems, he is really going to hang, but when he mounts the scaffold Peachum steps forward to say that Macheath will not hang after all because this is an opera and not real life. Then a messenger arrives from the queen giving Macheath a pardon, a title of nobility, a castle, and a pension. The story ends with a hymn asking humankind not to be too severe towards injustice.

The Three Sisters (1901), Anton Chekhov.   A year after the death of their father, commandant of the local army post, the three Prozoroff sisters—Olga, Masha, and Irina—find their lives empty and purposeless, without any meaning. They each seek to find something which will restore the happiness and hope for the future that had been theirs. Olga seeks happiness in teaching, although she really yearns for a home and family. Masha has a home and family but, married to a cold, pedantic schoolmaster, she is miserable and falls into a hopeless affair with a married Colonel. Irina tries to make her life meaningful through the "dignity of work," but her employment in the local telegraph office promises only a dull and undistinguished future. Gradually all three realize that their effort to put meaning into their lives is futile, and their sense of their own importance is further diminished when their brother marries Natasha, a peasant woman. She gradually takes over running the family home, which leaves the sisters without a sense of identity. They talk of moving to Moscow and starting over, but are too overcome by hopelessness to do anything that positive. Finally, when the army post is closed, they are forced out of their retreats and, as the play ends, they again vow to find a sense of purpose in their lives.

Two Gentlemen of Verona (c. 1592), William Shakespeare.   Two close friends, Valentine and Proteus, take leave of each other. Valentine, seeking honor, is off to Milan, and Proteus, deeply in love with Julia, remains in Verona. Proteus' father, however, insists that his son also go to Milan. Proteus vows constancy to Julia before he leaves, but as soon as he arrives in Milan he falls in love with the Duke's daughter, Silvia, who is also loved by his friend, Valentine. Proteus schemes against his friend and gets the Duke to banish Valentine, who is subsequently captured by outlaws in the forest near Mantua. Soon he becomes the leader of the band. Meanwhile, Julia is pining for Proteus and comes to Milan disguised as a boy. She discovers his faithlessness but enters his service. The Duke tells his daughter that he has arranged a marriage between her and the wealthy Thurio, and she runs away to join Valentine. Eventually all the characters meet in the forest and true love is served.

Waiting for Godot (1952), Samuel Beckett.   Early evening on a country road in a landscape that is flat and unending. Estragon and Vladimir are waiting, vaguely and disconsolately, for someone named Godot. They whine about life, play games of repentance, fall asleep and have nightmares, quarrel, make up, and wonder what they can expect of Godot if he does come. Then down the road comes Pozzo, a pompous, dictatorial taskmaster, accompanied by Lucky, who has been driven close to idiocy by near slavery and never-ending obedience. Lucky pours out a jumble of politics and theology and then disappears into the darkness with Pozzo. Vladimir and Estragon trade funny hats, play slave and master games, recite what they consider to be humorous poetry, and argue about anything and everything. Pozzo and Lucky return, the former now blind and the latter dumb. They cannot remember who they are, or were. Godot sends word that he will not be coming today, but will surely come tomorrow. Vladimir and Estragon know that they should move on, but neither can bring himself to stir, and so they just go on waiting.

West Side Story (1957), Book by Arthur Laurents; lyrics by Stephen Sondheim; music by Leonard Bernstein.   Modeled after Shakespeare's *Romeo and Juliet*, this musical concentrates on the tragic love story of Tony and Maria. Shakespeare's Verona becomes contemporary Manhattan, and the feuding Montagues and Capulets become two street gangs, the Jets and the Sharks. The Jets, a gang of American boys, are determined to put an end to the growing flood of Puerto Ricans moving onto their block. The Sharks, a Puerto Rican gang, are determined to establish their superiority in the block. Tony, the story's hero, was the founder and leader of the Jets until he turned his position over to Riff. However, Tony still supports the gang. Both gangs meet at a dance in a neighborhood gym, where Tony meets Maria, a beautiful girl just arrived from Puerto Rico, who is the sister of Bernardo, leader of the Sharks. Tony and Maria fall in love at first sight and plan to meet in the bridal shop where Maria works, where they will improvise a marriage using the dress manequins as attendants. In the meantime the gangs are planning their big rumble. Through Tony's influence they accept a proposal to have just one representative from each gang meet to fight it out on the following day. Bernardo, however, learns of the affair between Tony and Maria and threatens Tony. This causes a fight that turns into a major rumble and Tony's friend Riff is killed. Tony, blinded by anger at the death of his friend, kills Bernardo with Riff's knife. Tony is then killed by Chino, Maria's intended husband, and the tragedy is complete.

Who's Afraid of Virginia Woolf? (1962), Edward Albee. Act 1 of this play, entitled "Fun and Games," introduces a middle-aged history professor and his wife, George and Martha, who have asked another younger married couple, Nick and Honey, to their home following a faculty party. Nick is an assistant professor of biology evidently engaged in a series of experiments that will alter humanity. George and Martha carry on what seems to be a long-running quarrel that slightly embarrasses their guests, but the guests remain, perhaps because Martha is the daughter of the college president. Martha denigrates George for his failures, and there are rather mysterious references to their son. In Act 2, "Walpurgisnacht," some painful incidents, that may or may not have happened, are dredged up from George's past, and it is revealed that Nick married Honey because she underwent a hysterical pregnancy that they both thought was real. Honey gets drunk and Nick and Martha go off to make love. In Act 3, "The Exorcism," they come back without having made love satisfactorily, and George gets even with Martha by announcing the death of their son. The son is imaginary, but he has been a myth both George and Martha shared. Now George has exorcised him, and the play ends with a new phase of the relationship between George and Martha in sight.

A Woman Killed with Kindness (1603), Thomas Heywood. John Frankford, a good and gentle man, marries Anne Acton, and they seem destined forever to enjoy domestic bliss. However, this bliss is destroyed when John's friend, Master Wendell, betrays his trust and seduces Anne. Discovering what has happened, John does not seek violent revenge but sends Anne to live in another manor house. There she dies of contrition and, in the eleventh hour, earns her husband's forgiveness. The play also has a significant subplot in which Anne's brother, Sir Francis Acton, plays the role of a young ruffian and harasses Sir Charles Montford and his virtuous sister, Susan. Slowly Sir Francis grows to love and respect Susan, begins to act nobly, and wins her hand.

appendix c

Glossary
of
Theatre
Terms

Abstract set   An attempt to capture the idea or concept of a setting without resorting to realistic construction. "Sketches" scenes through the use of drapes and set pieces, such as window and door frames.

Absurdism (*Theatre of the Absurd*)   An attempt to break through the boundaries of realistic theatre to show the absurd, illogical, irrational aspects of life. *Endgame* is an example.

Ad lib   On-the-spot improvisations, word or gesture, that were not originally in the script or added during rehearsals.

Anagnorisis   In Classical Greek tragedy, the frequently used plot device of "discovery" or "recognition."

Antagonist   The character who stands in opposition to the leading character (protagonist) of a play.

Apron   The space on stage in front of the curtain line. Sometimes used interchangeably with *forestage*.

Arena stage   A form of center staging in which the audience surrounds the stage. Sometimes called theatre-in-the-round.

Arras setting   A semicircle of unpainted draperies that serve as a formal background for the stage area.

Aside   One of the conventions of theatre in which the audience accepts the idea that the words spoken by an actor, with appropriate side gesture and tone, can be heard by the audience but not by the actors onstage.

Backdrop   Large flat area, usually canvas hanging at the rear of the stage, that can be painted to represent the desired locale. Today the backdrop usually represents the sky and is sometimes called the *skydrop*.

Backing   Flats or drops used to mask the backstage area by limiting the audience view through doors, windows, or archways in the set.

Backstage   The area behind the proscenium arch that, during the production of a play, is not seen by the audience.

Blackout   The sudden extinguishing of the stage (but not house) lights. This is used at the end of an act, or to separate scenes or sketches, or for some special dramatic effect.

Blocking   The movements or locations of actors onstage.

Border   A short curtain often hung above the stage to mask the flies when the set does not contain a ceiling.

Borderlights   A series of lights hung above and toward the front of the stage area to provide general illumination.

Box set   The standard set for contemporary realistic theatre, showing a back wall and two side walls, with the fourth wall understood to be the "transparent one" through which the audience views the play.

Burlesque   A stage exaggeration of a person or object that destroys reality for comic purpose. In terms of entertainment, a format that developed in the United States, featuring comic monologues, skits, and, increasingly, nude women. Little seen since the 1940s.

Catharsis   In Classical Greek tragedy, a "purging" of the audience by arousing pity and fear.

Cheat   In acting, to turn the body slightly out toward the audience while seeming to play in profile.

Chorus   Originally a group of approximately fifty men who performed songs and dances, dithyrambs, at religious celebrations. Out of these choral dithyrambs grew the Classical Greek tragic drama. The Chorus remained as part of the drama but was gradually reduced in size until it became, finally, an onlooker and commentator. The Chorus is used only occasionally today, in such plays as T. S. Eliot's *Murder in the Cathedral*.

Chronicle plays   Dramatic versions of stories from such chronicle historians of England as Raphael Holinshed. Shakespeare's *The Tragedy of King Richard the Second* is an example.

Claque   Audience members who are friends or relatives of performers, or hired especially to applaud and cheer loudly, thereby giving the impression of general enthusiasm for a particular actor or performance.

Classical tragedy Tragic plays written either by Aeschylus, Sophocles, or Euripides. In a limited sense, later plays that follow the model developed by Aristotle. *Oedipus Rex* is an example.

Climax The moment in a play of the highest dramatic or emotional intensity.

Comedy A term generally used to describe plays in which the characters undergo embarrassment or discomfiture, and even severe physical accident, but so handled that pain is not present and the audiences are interested and amused without feeling profound sympathy. The action usually turns out well for the major characters. (See also such specific modes of comedy as romantic, sentimental, high, low, farce, etc.)

Comedy of humors A mode of comedy established by Ben Jonson, which derives from the Medieval concept that the body (and the character) is controlled by four fluids: blood, phlegm, black bile, yellow bile. An oversupply of one or another fluid causes excessive behavior and, thus, comedy. Ben Jonson's *Every Man in His Humour* is an example.

Comedy of manners Plays dealing with the intrigues and counter-intrigues of highly sophisticated ladies and gentlemen living in an artificial, polished society. The comedy grows out of the violations of these artificial social conventions, as well as out of sparkling dialogue and wit. William Wycherley's *The Country Wife* is an example.

Comic relief Humorous speeches or incidents woven into the fabric of tragedy that are sometimes used to enhance and enrich the action but always exist primarily to relieve tragic tension. The drunken porter in *Macbeth* illustrates comic relief.

Commedia dell'arte A form of street theatre that began in Italy near the beginning of the fifteenth century and spread all over Europe. The players worked improvisationally from scenarios. Such characters as Harlequin and Pierrot, still seen today, grew out of the *commedia*.

Constructivism A graphic arts movement that became popular, especially in Russia, in the early part of the twentieth century. It was adapted to theatrical sets by Meyerhold. The essence of constructivism is to display space as a series of planes furnished with distorted objects.

Convention In theatre, a special relation between the audience and the play, in which the audience accepts certain obvious departures from reality such as aside, soliloquy, monologue, etc.

Corpus Christi plays Generic term for the cycle plays of the Middle Ages that were produced on Corpus Christi Day, the Thursday after Trinity Sunday.

Cothurnus A high-soled boot designed to give added dignity to actors in Classical Greek tragedy.

Cue The final words, business, or movement of one character, which signals the next character to begin his own.

Cyclorama (cyc) A large canvas hung in a semicircle that covers the back and part of the sides of the stage. It is often used to represent the sky, though any aspect of the set may be projected onto it.

Denouement From the French, this means "untying the knot," which is to say, the end of the play, when the last problems are resolved or unknotted.

Deus ex machina   Literally "God from the machine." In Classical Greek tragedy a person or dummy suspended from the roof of the stagehouse to represent the god who would resolve all the problems of the play.

Deuteragonist   The "second actor" of Classical Greek tragedy. Often a supporting actor, friend or confidante, to the protagonist.

Dithyramb   In ancient Greece, a choral ode performed by a Chorus of approximately fifty men at festivals honoring Dionysus, the god of wine and the reproductive force of life.

Domestic tragedy   Plays with bourgeois or lower-class heroes and heroines who suffer from commonplace trials and tribulations and are usually defeated to provide audiences with a moral exemplum. *George Barnwell, or the London Merchant* is an example.

Downstage   That part of the stage nearest the audience.

Dramatic action   Simply, everything that happens within the play. What happens to the characters, physically, emotionally, psychologically.

Dressing the set   The placement of furniture and prop items on the raw set to provide mood and a sense of identity.

Dress rehearsal   A rehearsal that simulates the conditions of public performance, with full costume, makeup, props, lights, etc.

Drop   A flat curtain, often painted, that is suspended from the flies.

Eccyclema   In Classical Greek tragedy, a wheeled vehicle or moveable platform upon which were depicted events and actions that took place offstage.

Elizabethan tragedy   Often Senecan in nature, these tragedies depart from the strictures of Aristotle as to unities and character. For example, the protagonist of *Macbeth* is not so much a good man with a tragic flaw as a potentially great man who uses his gifts for evil purposes. *Macbeth* and *Hamlet* exemplify this form of tragedy.

Emotional recall   After Stanislavski, an acting technique in which the player responds to an emotional scene by summoning up similar emotional circumstances in his own life.

Epic drama   A term used by Bertolt Brecht and Piscator. Brecht called all drama preceding his own "Aristotelian," and described his own plays as seeking to arouse the spectator's intelligence by preventing emotional involvement. A didactic narrative drama that usually covers an extended period and makes no pretense of always being in the present.

Exodos   In Classical Greek tragedy, the final exit of the Chorus.

Expressionistic drama   Plays that attempt to show the inner psychological reality of people, often by making use of the *dream vision*. A relative of realistic drama.

Farce   A mode of comedy that usually contains one-dimensional characters who are involved in outlandish situations. The normal laws of probability have no effect in farce, and there is a maximum of boisterous physical action. *The Farce of Master Pierre Pathelin* is an example.

Flat   A piece of scenery built out of wood and muslin or canvas. Used to create walls or to back a set.

Flies   The area above the stage where borders, drops, and scenery are hung.

Floor plan   A plan that shows, from a point of view above the set, the location of walls, doors, windows, and furniture. Often called *ground plan.*

Fly   To raise scenery items off the floor of the stage and out of view of the audience, in most cases, via lines run from the grid.

Forestage   That part of the stage nearest the audience. Sometimes used interchangeably with *apron.*

Fourth wall   The imaginary wall at the proscenium opening, "through" which the audience views the play.

Freeze   In acting, to stand absolutely still for an agreed-upon number of counts, or until curtain or blackout. Used for tableaux.

French classical tragedy   Seventeenth-century neoclassical tragedy that strictly followed the French interpretation of Aristotle. Racine's *Phèdre* is an example.

George Spelvin   An alias often used by an actor for a second role he is playing.

Grand drape   A curtain that hangs from the top of the proscenium arch and that is often drawn back and tied at the sides to decorate the proscenium opening.

Gridiron (grid)   A framework, usually of steel, above the stage area. Used to support flown scenery.

Ground cloth   Waterproof canvas that is used to cover the stage floor.

Groundlings   In Elizabethan theatre, those persons who stood in the yard, or pit.

Ground plan   A plan that shows, from a point of view above the set, the location of walls, doors, windows, and furniture. Often called the *floor plan.*

Hamartia   In Classical Greek theatre, the *tragic flaw* or weakness of character in the protagonist that provoked the tragic action.

Happening   A semidramatic event, often taking place outdoors, that is a planned reality involving the audience in the action.

Heroic drama   Primarily drama of the English Restoration period. Such plays are epic in scope and length, with love and valor as their subject, written in an elevated style, with the fate of empires hanging on the action. *Conquest of Granada* is an example.

High comedy   A term introduced by George Meredith to identify that type of comedy which provokes "intellectual laughter" in an audience that is emotionally detached from the action.

Hubris   In Classical Greek tragedy, the sin of excess that caused pride and arrogance.

Ingenue   The actress who plays the role of an innocent and attractive young woman.

Inner stage   In Elizabethan theatre, the recessed area, or the alcove directly behind the thrust stage.

Juvenile   The male equivalent of the *ingenue.*

Kommos   A responsive lyric between Chorus and actors in Classical Greek tragedy.

Legitimate drama   A term that comes from eighteenth-century England when theatres had to hold a license from the king. Writers and actors sought to avoid the necessity of the license by pretending their plays were operas, which were exempted from the Licensing Act. Thus, legitimate drama was licensed drama that was spoken rather than sung. Today, the term is used to differentiate live stage drama from film and television drama.

Light leak   Light that inadvertently shows through a crack or seam in a set.

Light spill   Light that strikes the proscenium arch or some area of the set and then "spills" off onto the stage.

Low comedy   The opposite of intellectual high comedy; low comedy makes use of violent, boisterous physical action, with a minimum of dialogue, using exaggerated physical and social types. Related to and only slightly more sophisticated than farce. Nicholas Udall's *Ralph Roister Doister* is a low comedy.

Mask   To hide a lighting instrument from the audience, usually by means of scenery.

Masque   An elaborate form of court entertainment combining poetic drama, music, song, dance, elaborate costuming, and spectacle. Especially common to the reigns of Elizabeth, James I, and Charles I.

Melodrama   Plays (originally with music) in which protagonists are totally pure, antagonists totally evil, and both dramatic action and characterization are sacrificed to violent effect. Such plays end with exact demonstrations of poetic justice. *Ten Nights in a Bar-room* is a melodrama.

Mime   A performer who seeks to express the dramatic through body movement, without vocal accompaniment. Unlike dance, the movement is not keyed to music.

Miracle plays   Often difficult if not impossible to distinguish from *mystery plays*, these are Medieval verse dramas that take their plots from Biblical history or the legends of the saints. Some critics insist that this category includes only plays based on the lives of the saints.

Mise-en-scène   The total physical environment of a play, the sets, costumes, movement, etc.

Monologue   Related to the soliloquy, this form of stage address is delivered by a character who is usually, though not always, alone on stage. The material does not represent that character's thoughts, however, but is clearly what the character wishes to communicate, primarily to the audience.

Mood (atmosphere)   The prevailing emotional context of the play.

Morality play   A Medieval play allegorically presenting the Christian way of life by having the characters represent the virtues and vices struggling for the human soul. In later plays, primarily in the Tudor and Renaissance periods, the format of the morality was adapted to teach things other than Christianity. *Everyman* is a representative morality play.

Moscow art theatre   Established by Constantin Stanislavski and Vladimir Nemirovich-Danchenko in 1898, this theatre and its practices, especially those of Stanislavski exerted great influence on the total development of Western theatre practice.

Mystery play   A Medieval style of drama, taking its plots from incidents in the Old and New Testaments. *Noah* and the *Second Shepherd's Play* are examples.

Naturalistic drama   A form of dramatic realism, based primarily on social Darwinism, which shows middle- and lower-class characters being shaped by their environment. Clifford Odets' *Awake and Sing* is a naturalistic drama.

Obligatory scene   A scene that the playwright leads the audience to expect, without which the audience would be disappointed. Sometimes called *scène-à-faire*.

Orchestra   In Classical Greek theatre, the circular dancing place in front of the scene house. In the Hellenistic theatre the circle was cut to a semicircle. Today the term is used to designate the area immediately in front of the stage.

Outer stage   The forestage or thrust stage of the Elizabethan theatre. This is where most of the dramatic action took place.

Pageant wagons   In Medieval England, these were wagons containing a curtained playing area, set, and technical equipment necessary for staging a play. The exact structure is still debated. Apparently similar wagons were used by traveling troupes in Medieval Spain.

Parabasis   In Greek Old Comedy, the coming forward of the Chorus to address the audience and promote the playwright's views.

Papering the house   A term referring to the practice of issuing large quantities of complimentary tickets, or selling large numbers of tickets at reduced prices, in order to secure a large audience.

Parados   In the Classical Greek theatre, a passageway through which the Chorus entered the *orchestra*. Also, the opening choral dance.

Peripetia (peripety)   In Classical Greek tragedy, a reversal of circumstances. Usually, a reversal in the fortunes of the hero of the play.

Plant   An apparently casual insertion of an idea, comment, or prop in the dramatic action, which will become highly important later in resolving the action.

Point of attack   The point at which the playwright arbitrarily chooses to begin his script.

Practical   A term referring to scenery that works; in which doors or windows open or shut. The term developed to differentiate this realistic workable scenery from the more traditional painted scenery.

Project (projection)   Usually referring to the voice, projection means increasing audibility so that the actor can be heard at the rear of the house. Also, though less often, properly applied to stage movement and gesture, which must be enlarged in proportion so that it "projects" visibly to the rear of the house.

Prologue   In Classical Greek theatre, the action before the entry of the Chorus. In later theatre the introduction to the play.

Properties (props)   Articles or pieces of furniture used by the actors.

Proscenium   The wall separating the audience from backstage. In Classical Greek theatre the front wall of the stagehouse.

Proscenium arch   The opening in the proscenium wall through which the audience views the stage.

Protagonist From Classical Greek theatre, the leading character in a play. The character for whom the audience has the most sympathy and in whom they are most interested.

Rake To slant the stage floor up from front to back. Sometimes used to identify an auditorium in which the house floor is slanted up from the first row of seats to the back of the auditorium.

Realistic drama An attempt to transplant to the stage, life as it actually exists. Sometimes called slice-of-life drama in that, to simulate reality, many realistic plays attempt to lift out sections of the life of their protagonist, with little or no discernible attempt to provide a beginning, a middle, or an end. In most cases, however, realistic drama is primarily an attempt to make stage action, dialogue, design, and plot believable in terms of life outside of the theatre. Eugene O'Neill's *Beyond the Horizon* is a realistic drama.

Repertoire (repertory) A selection of plays or roles that a performer or a performing troupe has perfected and is prepared to present.

Repertory company A theatrical company that performs, in some method of rotation, the works in their *repertoire*.

Resolution That point in the play when the conflicts are resolved. Also, the method used to solve the conflicts within the play.

Return A flat used at the right and left wings, which can run offstage behind the *tormentor*. Sometimes the flat, or return, can serve as the tormentor.

Romantic comedy A play in which the central plot concerns a love affair between a beautiful, idealized heroine and a handsome hero. The affair does not run smooth but ends well. *As You Like It* and *Twelfth Night* are romantic comedies.

Satiric comedy Plays that ridicule, for a corrective purpose, violations of moral or social standards. *Lysistrata* and *Volpone* are satiric.

Scenario The written prose plot and description of events for a play or performance. For playwrights, the first step (prose outline) in creating a play. In *commedia*, the material from which the performers worked onstage.

Scène-à-faire The French term for "obligatory scene," which essentially means a scene that the playwright leads the audience to expect, without which the audience would be disappointed.

Senecan tragedy Tragic drama based on the formulas of the Roman tragic dramatist Seneca. These include revenge, adultery, incest, murder, mutilation, torture, and general carnage. Seneca's *Thyestes* and Thomas Kyd's *The Spanish Tragedy* both illustrate Senecan tragedy.

Sentimental comedy A type of comedy in which characters suffer disasters and tribulations, with tears the result as often as laughter. All ends well for the major characters. *The Conscious Lovers* is an example.

Set pieces Scenery that is capable of standing without support, or that has some form of acceptable support built into it, such as door frames, window frames, etc. Often used in nonrealistic productions.

Setting The locale and period in which a drama takes place, or, more practically, the scenery, props, and costumes used in its staging.

Skeleton set   The rudiments or bare essentials of a set that are used to provoke the imagination of the audience. Usually made up of *set pieces*.

Skene   Originally a small hut behind the orchestra of the Classical Greek theatre, used for costume changes. Eventually this became an elaborate building, with its façade used to provide a set. Its popularity in Classical theatre has led to the English term "scene."

Sky-drop   A large fabric drop painted to represent the blue sky and used to mask the backstage area. Sometimes, though not always, the sky-drop is the same as the *cyclorama*.

Soliloquy   A speech delivered by an actor alone onstage, which by convention is understood by the audience to be the character's internal thoughts, not a part of the dialogue.

Stage left   The left side of the stage from the actor's point of view.

Stage right   The right side of the stage from the actor's point of view.

Stasimon   In Classical Greek theatre, a choral ode sung and danced after the Chorus enters the orchestra.

Strophe   A movement or division of the choral ode.

Stock (stock company)   A resident acting company that presents a series of plays for limited runs, but not brought back as in repertory.

Stock characters   Character types that regularly occur in certain types of drama. Greek New Comedy and Roman comedy provided later drama with most of these characters, such as the prostitute, parasite, and miser. The *commedia* provided such characters as Arlecchino, Pantalone, and Zanni. More recent stock characters are the stage Irishman, Englishman, Scotsman, and the down-east Yankee.

Subtext   After Stanislavski the interaction of objectives between characters in a scene.

Superobjective   In scoring a role, the overall objective of any character in a play.

Tableau   Often used in melodrama, the actors "freeze" at certain points where the stage picture has artistic visual values, or where the director wishes to emphasize certain emotional situations. In many cases the tableau comes at the end of an act, on the curtain line, and is held until the curtain falls.

Teaser   A border that is just upstage behind the front curtain. It masks the flies and may be used to adjust the effective height of the proscenium opening.

Theatre-in-the-round   Theatre in which the audience surrounds the action of the play. Often called *arena staging*.

Theatron   In Classical Greek theatre, the place where the audience sat.

Theologeion   In Classical Greek theatre, a high platform from which the gods and heroes spoke.

Thrust stage   A stage with a projected apron or playing area that allows the audience to view the action from three sides.

Thymele   In Classical Greek theatre the altar of Dionysus, which stood in the center of the orchestra.

Tormentors Flats at the right and left wing areas, close to the proscenium opening, that help mask the backstage area.

Tragedy Generally, plays of high seriousness in which the protagonist, in asserting himself and his humanity, meets disaster. See also such special types as *Domestic Tragedy* and *Tragicomedy*. *Oedipus* and *Hamlet* are tragedies.

Tragicomedy A play in which the action is serious and seems to threaten disaster to the protagonist but ends with a happy reversal. Shakespeare's *The Merchant of Venice* is tragicomic.

Trap An opening in the stage floor, usually covered by a trapdoor, that permits entrances and exits from belowstage.

Traveler A slotted track used to hang a draw curtain.

Typecasting Casting an actor or actress on the basis of age, size, physical appearance, personality, and, in some cases, temperament to resemble those of the character portrayed.

Unit set A set consisting of various pieces of scenery designed to fit together in several combinations to shift the scene.

Upstage The back of the stage. For many years, stages were raked; that is, they slanted up toward the back to provide the audience a better view. Thus, when actors moved toward the back of the stage they became elevated.

Vaudeville From the French, *Chanson du vau de vire*, this originally meant a light-weight theatrical work interspersed with songs and dances. Later, the term came to mean a production of several acts, including songs, dances, monologues, etc., which were essentially unrelated but offered a variety of entertainment. Popular in the United States throughout the early 1930s, vaudeville still exists in England under the title of "Music Hall."

Well-made-play Based primarily on the works of Scribe and Sardou, this term refers to a play that follows a certain set pattern in its construction; that is, a three-act structure that emphasizes popular stock scenes and devices and that neatly resolves all plot elements.

Wings The offstage space on the left and right of the playing area. Sometimes this term also is used to refer to wing pieces or flats utilized at the left and right edges of the playing area.

Index

Index

Index

Index